The Animal Liberation Front In Canada: 1986 to 1993 (Animal Liberation Zine Collection)

This compilation first published in 2022 by Warcry.

ISBN 978-1957452050

For information, submission guidelines, bulk requests, or general inquiries, please contact:

peter@peteryoung.me

Also published by Warcry:

Last Words, For War: Statements Of The Symbionese Liberation Army

The A.L.F. Strikes Again: Collected Writings Of The Animal Liberation Front In North America (Animal Liberation Front)

Animal Liberation Front: Complete US Diary Of Actions

Liberate: Stories & Lessons On Animal Liberation Above The Law (Peter Young)

Flaming Arrows: Collected Writings of Animal Liberation Front Activist Rod Coronado (Rod Coronado)

From Dusk 'til Dawn: An Insider's View of the Growth of the Animal Liberation Movement (Keith Mann)

Underground. The Animal Liberation Front in the 1990s (Various)

THE ANIMAL LIBERATION FRONT IN CANADA

1986 to 1993

Bryan Fellwell, owner of Billingsgate Fish Company, and his wife Ziathy survey the fire damage to three of the company's trucks Sunday

Contents

A.L.F. CANADA
issue no. 1
FRONT LINE NEWS

P.O. Box 915, Station F, Toronto, Ont. M4Y 2N9 Canada

Welcome !

Welcome to the first issue of FRONT LINE NEWS! On these pages we hope to bring you news of events and actions by and about the Animal Liberation Front and us - the ALF Support Group. This newsletter also hopes to be a forum for discussion - on the ways to bring about liberation and freedom for animals; on the merits of various direct action tactics; on the use and terminology of "violence"; etc. These are your pages as well as ours, and we look forward to your letters, articles, comments, and suggestions! This first issue is being sent out to a wide range of individuals and groups with the hopes of gathering support for animal liberation. For a minimum donation of $10[*], you can receive F.L.N. by mail for one year, and for a minimum of $20 we'll send you the SG Newsletter from England as well! We hope FRONT LINE NEWS informs you, encourages you, and most of all, inspires you!!

[*] (more if you can/less if you can't)

HALLOWEEN ACTIONS

"All Hallows Eve" provided excellent cover for actions on the streets of Toronto, as masks were on hand in the event of a fast escape and disappearance into the disguised crowd.

The night began at the Toronto Stockyards where we spent at least 2 hours in amazement and disgust surveilling the huge yards. They are broken up into stalls which could hold about 12 cows each. We figured the yards could hold at least 2500 cows when full, all waiting to be murdered! There were only about 200 when we visited. The unloading docks can accomodate about 24 transport-trailers at one time, and the night we were there had about 40 in total at the docks and at the parking area. After overcoming our feelings of hopeless-

ness, the 3 of us went to work on 2 trucks, slashing tyres and spraypainting the sides.

When we left, we came across a fur store where we left our mark with paint on the front and with plastic steel in their locks

Our third action was a planned one on a small slaughterhouse on Clinton St., in the middle of a residential neighbourhood. We left them totally immobilized for the next day as 9 tyres on their 3 trucks were slashed, as well as giving them a new paint job!

Our final jaunt for the evening was in the fur district on Spadina, where we hit 3 stores with plastic steel and spraypaint. One store -Paul Magder Furs- received extra paint on his signs and a mural, and as well had his window smashed!

-The Halloween Maskeraiders

"Fighting in the front lines for Animal Liberation"

FRONT LINE NEWS is published periodically by the Animal Liberation Front Support Group (Canada), and is available by mail for a minimum donation of $10/year. Material in F.L.N. has been passed on to the Support Group anonymously. All our records of authors and activists are automatically destroyed. Support Group members do not take part in illegal activities; we pass on ALF news for informational purposes only!

The ALFSG (Canada) is an autonomous organization informally affiliated with the international network of ALF activists and Support Groups. Our mailing address is: P.O.Box 915, Stn. F, Toronto, Ont. M4Y 2N9.

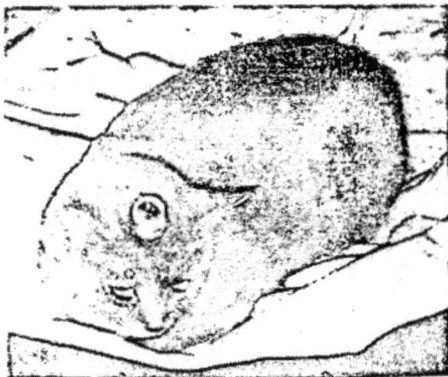

ANIMALS NEED HOMES!

Finding good, **reliable** homes for liberated animals, like the cat pictured above, is an essential part of the Support Group's work. Our responsibility doesn't end after the labs are raided. Rescued animals don't just disappear; we **urgently** need homes for cats, dogs, rabbits, and other species. These must be **stable** and **secure**, with **responsible** people, and must offer a pleasant, relaxing atmosphere. Most laboratory and abused animals have been through hell and absolutely need an environment that allows for their mental, physical, and spiritual healing.

If you are able to share your home with one, two, or more of our friends in the near future, and can provide these necessary requirements, please contact the Support Group **as soon as possible**. Small animals such as mice and other rodents, and animals that have not yet been abused, may not require as much time or attention as others, so long as the individuals are responsible and caring. Tell your friends and help us find the animals homes!

ALF TREATED SERIOUSLY

In June of this year, 10 animal activists in W. Germany were caught attempting to set a fire to a new lab. Not only were they charged with attempted arson, but also with "belonging to a terrorist organization" for being in the Animal Liberation Front. This move by the State is probably not surprising for those in Europe and England, or at least not as surprising as it is for us here in North America. Government repression has occured with much more frequency and regularity throughout this century across the ocean than it has here in White-middleclass-yuppiedom! But we should see those charges as an important indicator of how they want to deal with the ALF, and not pass it over by saying it can't happen here.

The level of direct action animal activism in England is at least a thousand times more than it is here in Canada. As with other protests and more militant factions of other movements, Canada falls well behind in most catagories. But from what we can see regarding the animal movement, direct action tactics are definately on the upswing. Regular actions take place in Montreal, Vancouver, and Toronto. So we have to assume that the CSIS (the Canadian Security Intelligence Service)is watching this upward trend as well, and are monitering it with open files.

Animal activists who choose direct action methods must realize and follow the most basic rules of security: Don't use phones for anything; Don't hold meetings in houses or known meeting places; Write down as little as possible on paper, etc. etc. There are literally hundreds of precautions to be aware of, so basically use common sense and your brains when planning.

The other point of this article is to say that we have brought the animal movement to a point where the police and State are taking us seriously. We can see this as a good sign as this 'importance' will help bring us ever closer to ending all forms of animal abuse. But we know it can't happen for a while yet; more people must get involved in direct action, especially in Canada.

Organise yourselves into small groups and plan in total secrecy. I can't stress that hard enough! Only those involved (anywhere from 3-8 are good numbers, depending on the scope of the action) should know anything at all about the plans. Only work with people you know and can trust. 'Outsiders' and new eager faces are great candidates for being infiltrators. So the underlining message here is: Be Careful!

-Ann Ayelefer

ANIMAL ACTIVIST GETS 6 DAYS

During a protest in the summer at a hotel in downtown Toronto against a vivisectors conference inside, Lyn Allen was arrested and charged with mischief to private property after a stinkbomb was thrown inside during their awards (sic) ceremony.

Her trial on Nov. 1 was before an extreme right-wing judge who said that he wanted to make an example of this activist. Despite this being a first offense of any kind; despite the defense asking for a discharge and the prosecution only asking for probation; despite this "offense" being something closer to a highschool-type prank; the judge handed down a sentence of six days in jail!!

The defense had tried to get an acquital based on a technicality - the crown didn't prove that the convention hall inside the hotel was private property. But the judge chose to ignore that. The two sides had also made a prearranged deal that a statement of "facts" would be agreed upon (even though some of this information was incorrect); and that the crown would also ask for a discharge. The crown reneged on his part of the deal by asking for probation instead, although it's questionable whether it would have made any difference.

There is some suspicion that the harsh sentence was a result of the group being stinkbombed - CALAS; the Canadian Association for Laboratory Animal Science. Having such an authoritative sounding name could have influenced the judge.

An appeal was launched immediately to avoid any time at all being spent in jail. This is also a critical case for Lyn because she is in the middle of immigration procedures and has been denied status once already, even though she's been living in Canada for 15 years. A conviction and especially a jail sentence could have serious effects on the outcome of those hearings.

One important lesson to be learned from this experience is: Don't hang around the "scene of the crime" even if you think no one saw you or if you have a group of people to (supposedly) hide in! We can also learn from this trial that, were an ALF member caught and tried, or any other animal activists for larger and more serious offenses, we should assume the harshest of sentences to be handed down.

But this should not stop us from acting! In England, the latest ALFSG newsletter lists well over 50 people either in jail or awaiting trial. Fear of jail is of course a real fear, but having decided to take action, we have as well decided to take the risk of a jail sentence. What does this mean? Just this - Plan Well and Don't Get Caught!!

Donations to help with Lyn Allen's upcoming appeal and legal fees should be sent to the ALF Support Group. Please attach a note mentioning the appeal.

-Miss Trial

S.G. FUND-RAISING BAZAAR!!!

The Supporters Group is launching its fund-raising campaign with a Bazaar on Saturday, March 22nd, 1986. The location will be Trinity-St. Paul's United Churches, 427 Bloor Street West from 10 a.m. - 4 p.m. Spadina Subway Station is only a five-minute walk away.

Your participation is VITAL if we are to make this event a success!! We require donations of TIME, ENERGY and SALEABLE ITEMS. The latter must be clean and in good condition - anything less than this simply will not sell!

We are in the process of finalizing plans for a storage space for Bazaar donations. Eventually, when we have this 'drop-off' point, it would be a tremendous help if you could deliver the items yourself.

For the present, write to the ALF Supporters Group, P.O. Box 915, Station 'F', Toronto M4Y 2N9, and let us know if you can help, either by volunteering your time or making a donation of articles.

PLEASE REMEMBER - ANIMAL LIBERATION COSTS MONEY! Your support will be used directly to assist in ending the imprisonment and torture of animals! Thank you!

CONTRIBUTORS WANTED

Dear friends,

I'm a political activist in Toronto who is editing a book on the topic of animal liberation as it relates to other social change movements. I'd like as many people as possible to contribute to the book; my role will be mainly as co-ordinator/editor, putting it all together. My vision of the book includes not only theoretical articles but also any or all of the following: writings from personal experience, fiction, poetry, song lyrics, artwork, etc. Of course, the book will take shape according to what comes in, but some of the areas that I think would be valuable to deal with include:

* Animal liberation and nonviolence.
* Animal liberation and feminism: the womyn/nature parallel, etc.
* Animal liberation and anarchism.
* Animal liberation and vegetarianism in the punk movement.
* Vegetarianism as a form of noncooperation.
* Capitalism and animal exploitation: the commodification of animals.
* Rationalizations of animal exploitation in organized religion.
* Animal liberation and positive spirituality (This could focus on Neo-Paganism, Native American spirituality, etc.).
* The role of multinational corporations in animal exploitation.
* Misrepresentation of the animal liberation movement in the mass media.
* Parallels between speciesism and racism.
* Animal imagery in pornography (Not only actual portrayals of animals, but womyn portrayed similar to animals: what this says about our culture's attitudes toward both).
* Animal abuse as spectacle/entertainment.
* History/theory/practise of the ALF and other groups using direct action against animal exploitation.
* Is violence justifiable in animal actions (e.g. the Hunt Retribution Squad)?
* Animal liberation and Lesbian/Gay liberation.
* Animal liberation and abortion: Can you be anti-animal abuse and pro-choice? Or does valuing all life mean being anti-abortion?

Of course, these are only suggestions; the choice of what to write about is up to you. I only ask that you try to approach topics that haven't yet been dealt with too extensively. For example, I'd like to stay away from straight factual articles about factory farming, vivisection, etc. as so much work has already been done on these topics.

Any financial contributions would be much appreciated as the actual process of publishing the book will cost me quite a bit. And any suggestions anyone has would be welcome (especially ideas for a title).

Send your articles, poems, lyrics, art, suggestions, donations, etc. to:

Lynna Landstreet
P.O.Box 1031, Adelaide St. Stn.
Toronto, Ont., M5C 2K4, Canada.

If you want to, you can include a few lines about yourself or your group/publication/whatever, which I will put in a "Contributors' Notes" section at the back. For those doing graphics: I am tentatively planning to have the book printed in 8½×11 format so keep that in mind. Either full page artwork or smaller pieces to accompany articles, lyrics, etc. are welcome. I hope to publish the book within the next year, so please respond as soon as possible.

In solidarity,
Lynna.

"WE ARE THE LIVING GRAVES OF MURDERED BEASTS
 SLAUGHTERED TO SATISFY OUR APPETITES.
 WE NEVER PAUSE TO WONDER AT OUR FEASTS,
 IF ANIMALS, LIKE MEN, CAN POSSIBLY HAVE RIGHTS.
 WE PRAY ON SUNDAYS THAT WE MAY HAVE LIGHT,
 TO GUIDE OUR FOOTSTEPS ON THE PATH WE TREAD.
 WE'RE SICK OF WAR, WE DO NOT WANT TO FIGHT--
 THE THOUGHT OF IT NOW FILLS OUR HEARTS WITH DREAD,
 AND YET WE GORGE OURSELVES UPON THE DEAD.
 LIKE CARRION CROWS, WE LIVE AND FEED ON MEAT,
 REGARDLESS OF THE SUFFERING, FEAR AND PAIN
 WE CAUSE BY DOING SO, IF THUS WE TREAT
 DEFENSELESS ANIMALS FOR SPORT OR GAIN,
 HOW CAN WE HOPE IN THIS WORLD TO ATTAIN
 THE PEACE WE SAY WE ARE SO ANXIOUS FOR.
 WE PRAY FOR IT, O'ER HECATOMBS OF SLAIN,
 TO GOD, WHILE OUTRAGING THE MORAL LAW.
 THUS CRUELTY BEGETS ITS OFFSPRING--WAR!"

                    George Bernard Shaw

FRONT LINE NEWS needs news to publish!
If you have any ALF or related news or
actions to report, please send it along
to us anonymously or use a pseudonym.
Remember: Actions aren't news until
          they're reported;
       and News doesn't happen until
          it's created!

          BE CREATIVE!!

A.L.F. CANADA
FRONT LINE NEWS

issue no. 2

P.O. Box 915, Station F, Toronto, Ont. M4Y 2N9 Canada

Sports Huntsmen: Lyrics By: Social Suicide

you go out in the woods today you're in for a big surprise,
you go out in the woods today you'd better go in disguise.
every hunter that ever there was will gather there for surely because,
ay's the day that sportsmen have their picnic.

you go out in the woods today you're in for a big surprise,
you go out in the woods today you'd better go in disguise,
'd better wear your orange jacket,
'd better wear your orange jacket,
rts, sports, sports, sports huntsmen.

If you go into the woods today you'd better stay on the path
Step on a twig or make a noise you've got lead up your ass.
Their trigger fingers are happy
Their trigger fingers are happy.
Sports, sports, sports, sports huntsmen.

Picnic time for teddy bear, the little teddy bears are having a lovely time today
If you went down to see the bears today you should've stayed home instead,
'Cause the hunters got up real early today and now Teddy Bear is dead.
It's beddie-byes for Teddy Bear,
It's beddie-byes for Teddy Bear,
Sports, sports, sports, sports huntsmen,
At six o'clock their mommies and daddies tuck them into bed, because they're tired
little Teddy Bears

"Fighting in the front lines for Animal Liberation"

Well, we've made it to Issue #2 of Front Line News, and as you can see we've grown quite quickly since our first issue. As usual, we are requesting a (minimum) donation of $10 per year, to receive the newsletter. This amount will barely cover printing and postage costs, so if you can afford to give more (and I know some of you can) please do! The more money we have for F.L.N., the more we have for the animals.

Some of you have begun receiving the British ALF-SG Newsletter as well, for which we asked a minimum of $20 per year. We now have to ask for a minimum of $25, as they have increased their newsletter by over 50% (in terms of pages), making our reprinting and postage costs that much higher. We recommend their newsletter as a vital source for news, critique, actions, and inspiration!

Thanks go out to all those who helped on this issue - from writing to typing, to layout and xeroxing. Also, thanks to everyone who came out to our recent benefit, and to those who helped make it the success that it was. We are now gearing up for our Bazaar, to be held in April, for which we need your continued support. (See notice in this issue).

What we're working toward, is a good solid base, in terms of finances and support people, from which ALF actions can continue and thrive from. With your help, more liberations will be able to happen, and more animals will be free from torture and death.

*Front cover graphic by Paul Yardley-Jones

FRONT LINE NEWS is published periodically by the Animal Liberation Front Support Group (Canada), and is available by mail for a minimum donation of $10 a year. Material in F.L.N. is either written by S.G. members or passed on to us anonymously. All our records of authors and activists are automatically destroyed.

Support Group members do not take part in illegal activities; we pass on ALF news for informational purposes only! The ALF-SG (Canada) is an autonomous organization informally affiliated with the international network of ALF activists and Support Groups.

FLN welcomes your articles, graphics, letters, comments and critiques, action reports, etc. Address them to the S.G. at P.O. Box 915, Station 'F', Toronto, Ontario M4Y 2N9.

S.G. NEWS

ALF Benefit Success!!

On Saturday, January 18th, the S.G. held a fundraising benefit for the ALF, at the Starwood Club, the first ever of its kind in Canada, and perhaps the first in North America. Without a doubt, the show was an amazing success, raising over $1,350 (after expenses) for the animals and ALF Activists. (Including a $100 donation).

There were many people involved who helped in all areas; from those who took control of the door and literature tables to the bands and soundman. I'm sure we couldn't have pulled it off without the co-operation and help from everyone.

Four bands played: Violence and the Sacred opened, followed by Was Ist Los, Mike Marley and the Sailors, and closing the show were Social Suicide. Basically, the music was hardcore punk with some "rock-n-roll" coming from Was Ist Los and theatrical-industrial performances from Violence and the Sacred. On an unfortunate note regarding the latter band, we couldn't get it together enough to record the concert, of which Violence and the Sacred were to release their live recording on a tape.

Cont'd.

Experimental videos were shown before the show and during the first set. The controversial video "Faces of Death" was shown, one which the Animals' Agenda notes in their Jan./Feb. 1986 issue as "vile...that graphically documents incidents of human and animal torture and death...". The controversial aspect of the video is the suspicion that some scenes of animal torture and death "appear to have been created specifically for the production...". By showing this video (with the sound off), the S.G. is in no way condoning this kind of atrocity happening for the sake of film or "art". We felt that quite the opposite would be conveyed; that people would get angry and outraged at what they viewed.

The ALF/PETA video "Unnecessary Fuss" was shown at 11 p.m. Unfortunately, the wires enabling us to put the sound through the main system were taken away (for unknown reasons), so only 40 or 50 people were able to hear the soundtrack off the machine. About 100 people watched the video.

An S.G. member from Kitchener came down bringing video equipment, and recorded about 40 minutes of the show. This footage will be part of a documentary he is putting together about the ALF and the S.G. (See the "Video Notice" elsewhere in this publication.)

For those interested in numbers, I would say about 400 people attended the benefit, all being given leaflets and other literature. The literature tables brought in about $250, mostly from the sale of T-Shirts. (Thanks to the people who donated original ALF T-Shirts at cost!)

Publicity and postering before the show was really excellent. It was mentioned in two Toronto alternative/entertainment publications (Now and Nerve), plus being mentioned in the Toronto Star's "What's On" section. CKLN-FM 88.1 gave us good support, with individual D.J.'s mentioning the show. It was listed on their entertainment listing, and we had interviews on two different shows. (I'd like to note that we received insignificant support from the Hardcore Show, a show one would expect great support from, given the political nature of our event.) We also had mentions on York University Radio (an S.G. member's show) and as well, in the Ryerson Eyeopener newspaper.

Posters for the show were noticeably ripped down a day after being put up, but since we had people constantly putting them up again, it made little difference.

Back to the show -- The atmosphere was amazing as people knew what they were there for, obviously agreeing with animal liberation. A couple of fights broke out outside the club including a certain group of "skins" (macho teenagers) who were not a part of the benefit. These fights plus a housefire nearby brought a couple of cops inside, prepared to assert their authority. One got particularly aggressive when he was asked to pay the cover charge, by two people in succession! He was quickly calmed down with reason, logic and bullshit! They left after ten minutes without getting any further than the front door and without getting anyone's real name or I.D. in their Big Brother notepads. One also received a lesson in punk-politics compared to skinhead-politics!

When the bar ran out of beer and then started to run out of hard liquor, the owners figured it was a good night for them and asked one of our organizers to "do more of these shows!" So, benefits on a semi-regular basis could be a reality in the near future. (If anyone is SERIOUSLY interested in benefits-organizing, contact us!) As well, some people are talking about setting up literature tables at gigs not organized as benefits, but just to get the information out.

All in all, it was a success in every way, and sincere thanks go out to all those who helped out. It was a night of major direct-action out-reaching, one which we can do quite a few more of!

Freebird

S.G. NEWS
Cont'd....

Support Group Video:

The ALF Support Group is making a video. The 20-minute video will consist of information about the Support Group, reasons why the group was formed and information on how to become involved in animal liberation.

However, I can't do this video without your help. What I need are fairly safe locations to film examples of abuses, and information about abuse in different areas. Also, if you have access to any film or slides dealing with animal liberation, they would be appreciated. New ideas are always welcome!

If you are interested in this project, I can be contacted through the ALF Supporters' Group. Remember, this is your video; the Support Group can't grow without your help. I'll look forward to hearing from you!

Padlock Politics, Producer

LAB ANIMALS/ANTI-FUR PROTESTS

For those interested in taking part in symbolic actions and protest, there will be an organizing meeting for World Day For Laboratory Animals and Anti-Fur Action at the Church Street Community Centre (519 Church Street) at 1 p.m. on Saturday, March 8, 1986.

"BIRD" NEEDS A NEW HOME!

Is there anyone who has an aviary, or a similar large structure, who is willing to house a male Ring-dove? This beautiful white bird is approximately 4 years old, was born and raised in captivity, and is now seeking a residence (larger than the four square feet he now lives in.) He needs a home where he can fly around, as he has been deprived of using this natural ability all his life, and subsequently needs lots of practice. If you think you are able to help out, please write to "Bird", c/o the Support Group.

A.L.F. SUPPORT GROUP BAZAAR

As mentioned in the first issue of Frontline News, the S.G. Group is planning a Bazaar in the Spring. The date of the event has been changed and is now (DEFINITELY) Saturday, April 5, 1986 at Trinity-St. Paul's United Church, 427 Bloor Street West.

The response to our request for help has been minimal, to say the least; only four people; the response to our request for saleable items has been even less!

People, perhaps you cannot make a public speech on behalf of animal rights, or take part in a demonstration, rally, or civil disobedience. But is it too much to ask that you clean out a closet to donate one item or stand behind a table for a few hours during the Bazaar? That is all we are asking you to commit yourselves to for the animals — not too much, is it?

We also have the Church from 7 p.m. to 10 p.m. on Friday, April 4th to set up the tables. Help would also be welcomed then. Nearer the date the S.G. will distribute a flyer, which you can post to advertise the event.

We have a storage area for items! Please write and tell us where we can make pick-ups, or if you can deliver your donation yourself. **Remember this is not for us, it's for the animals!**

It's disgusting that five animals die of neglect and this poxy store stays in business.

ANIMALS HAVE RIGHTS

By: Freebird

It is true that the animal "rights" issue is receiving more publicity in newspapers, and more magazines, as well, are devoting pages to the issue. Looking over the last few months, three magazines have given space to the issue: a very supportive editorial entitled "Torturing Animals: What's Next?" (By Peter Worthington) appeared in the November 1985 issue of Influence magazine; a liberalish, pro-legislative article entitled "The Fur Trade: Must It Die of Shame?" (by John Dyson) appeared in the December 1985 issue of Readers' Digest; and a ridiculously ignorant article appeared in the January 1986 issue of Saturday Night magazine entitled "Monkey Business" (By Robert Fulford).

Peter Worthington has previously made known his support for animal "rights" in earlier articles, so his editorial comes with little surprise. He makes some excellent and strong remarks that one doesn't usually see in any mainstream, glossy publications. Although he "accepts the need for some research using animals", his editorial touches on the horrors of cosmetic testing, the use of baboons at the University of Western Ontario, pain research and the Head-Injury Laboratory and break-in. He describes the labs as the "Auschwitzes and Belsens of modern society", and asks these questions; "(Do researchers) develop a self-protecting callousness? Just as those who performed medical experiments in the Nazi era became hardened to human suffering....do animal researchers develop a similar immunity to the pain of others?!" At the end of his editorial he notes the parallels between speciesism and racism, and gives support to the new book "In Defense of Animals" (edited by Peter Singer, and available from the S.G. for $6.95).

John Dyson's article in the Readers' Digest gives the reader good information on the kinds of traps used and supports the banning of the leghold trap. He believes that the economic benefits

are more important than animal lives, and he uses the (tired) argument of "native people clinging to subsistence lifestyles" to defend his point of view. Here are some of his more ludicrous comments: "A good trapper can plan his harvests, like a wildlife farmer", or "Unless the brutality is eradicated, the Fur Market will wither to nothing". How do you take the brutality out of murder? With "nice" traps?! The article did give publicity to some of the actions and campaigns that have happened and the following are those excerpted paragraphs:

Anti-fur activists seem to be shifting from a policy of conservation and wise use of animals toward protection and no use. One million British households have been mailed appeals by the Royal Society for the Prevention of Cruelty to Animals (RSPCA) for help "to take the cruelty out of fashion." The immediate aim is to cut demand for fur by one third. The RSPCA's chief wildlife officer, Stefan Ormrod, says: "A moral revolution is sweeping Europe, and I'm afraid the fur trade will be its victim."

The campaigns in Europe are bolstered by Canadian groups. In June 1985 the Ontario Humane Society (OHS) dropped its long-standing commitment to work toward more humane trapping and called for abolition of all trapping. "The cruelty on the traplines in just one day exceeds ten years of the seal hunt," says president Tom Hughes. "It's nonsense to imagine it will ever become humane, so the only answer is to ban it." Says George Clements of the Vancouver-based Association for the Protection of Fur-Bearing Animals, whose film Canada's Shame was recently shown widely in Europe: "Our aim is to tell consumers how every soft pelt that makes a fur coat bleeds and hurts before it dies."

The feeling against fur is fueled by other animal-rights campaigns. In Britain fox hunts and angling contests have been disrupted, and there have been assaults, including a firebomb attack, on scientists using animals for cancer research. Animal-rights splinter groups have sent a parcel bomb to Prime Minister Margaret Thatcher and — apparently to protest the seal hunt — an explosive device to the Canadian High Commission in London. In Europe furrier shops have been vandalized, fur farms attacked and animals released. Women wearing furs have been spat on or spray-painted in the streets.

In Toronto last April fur merchants Andrew and Steven Goodman found "No More Death" spray-painted over their windows, and red "blood" streaming from the doorway.

But fur trapping, this oldest and most traditional of Canadian enterprises, is threatened with extinction. The same strident international protest movement that effectively killed off the Newfoundland seal hunt is intent on wiping out the fur trade. The president of the Fur Council of Canada, Victor Topper of Toronto, says: "The fur industry is in a fight for its life."

A giant Greenpeace billboard that was displayed on British streets showed an elegant woman trailing a fur coat, its hem streaming a river of blood. The caption: "It takes up to 40 dumb animals to make a fur coat. But only one to wear it."

Anti-fur campaigns played a major role (along with other market factors) in reducing direct exports of Canadian raw fur to Europe from $159 million in 1981 to $77 million in 1984. Europe is the market for Canadian wild fur, because that is where 85 percent of pelts are ultimately retailed as garments. The Fur Council's Topper says: "In three years we've seen the Swiss market decline by a third, West German sales by two thirds, and in France, Holland and Belgium the market has virtually dried up. Now the U.K. is on the hit list."

THWAP! The sudden night noise in the marsh is followed by a squeal and a splash. A muskrat has stepped on the trigger of a leg-hold trap, springing the jaws shut on a forepaw.

Steel jaws locked on its paw, the muskrat in the trap dives for safety into the water. The trap slides down the wire and a device prevents the creature from returning to the surface for breath. Its nostrils, ears and mouth close to block out the water and within about four minutes it is dead of carbon-dioxide poisoning. The muskrat's pelt will fetch about $8, ultimately becoming the 40th part of a coat retailing for $1,800.

Cont'd on page 13

ALF Members Fined, Restricted

Following the raid on the City of Hope National Medical Research Centre last year, two people were arrested on burglary and stolen property charges after the police received a tip. Carole and Brude Jodar pleaded "no contest" apparently due to Carol's declining health (she suffers from Multiple Sclerosis). They admitted harbouring 12 rabbits taken by the ALF from the Medical Centre.

The judge gave them both probation sentences (rather than three-year jail terms). ordered Brude to do 360 hours of community service and ordered Carol to pay a $10,000 fine TO THE CITY OF HOPE RESEARCH CENTRE! On top of this outrageous sentence is the equally disgusting ruling that the Jodars are not allowed to affiliate with an animal rights organization for the next three years! We don't have any further news, but we hope that the Jodars will appeal their sentences.

How To Avoid Speciesist Words And Phrases

The Blacker Family in New York has sent out a letter addressed to "All Animal Rights Activists" regarding the use of words in our movement, and how to use them to our benefit. Not only should we use them to advance animal liberation, but we should be bringing reality into clearer focus; the era of Big Brother's "Peacekeeper" nuclear missiles, the "Free World" and smiling bureaucrats is also the era of "animal resources", "medical research" and smiling McChickens on your TV.

The following has been slightly edited, without altering the Blackers' ideas:

SPEAK AND WRITE ABOUT ANIMALS WITH UPLIFTING (NOT DOWNGRADING) WORDS THAT INDICATE RESPECT FOR THEIR RIGHT TO LIVE IN PEACE AS LIVING BEINGS.

Never refer to humans as the animals' "owners" or "masters". Humans are the animals' "companions".

Animals are not "things", "property" or "slaves". So, let's stop referrin to the animal as "it"... because tha implies something inferior to a living feeling creature. Instead, refe to the animal as "she/he" or "her/his" even if you don't know the sex o the animal.

Don't call animals "living things" They are "living beings".

Let's stop saying "that" or "which" when we should be saying "who".

Refer to non-domestic animals as "free-roaming... not "wild".

WHEN YOU REFER TO ANIMALS' SUFFERINC AND DEATH INFLICTED BY HUMANS, USE PAINFULLY EXPLICIT WORDS THAT REVEAL THE TRUE, GRISLY FACTS.

Stop using the following evasive, misleading words: "Euthanize", "Put To Sleep", "Sacrifice", "Destroy" - all favourites of brutal experimenters-on-animals, pounds and even shelters. "Cull", "Harvest", "Manage", "Thinning out the herd", "maximum sustainable yield" (MSY), "Optimum sustainable population" - favourites of hunters, trappers and their ilk. All these words mean "KILL" and "MURDER", so say "KILL" and "MURDER".

Instead of saying "take" animals, use the understandable words, "hunt, harass, maim, kill, capture" animals.

Humans try to cover up their horrifying cruelties against animals with deceptive euphemisms (like the preceding). Don't let them get away with their attempts to lull unsuspecting people into misunderstanding their barbaric crimes. Say it like it is so that people will realize the horrors that humans inflict on animals.

On a final note: To quote Vicki Miller of ARK II (as mentioned in the Jan./Feb. 1986 issue of the Animals' Agenda), "...over the next decade, I expect that the term "animal rights" will be replaced by the less esoteric one, "animal liberation..." Let's hope so!

Why I Care

(This article is dedicated to all those who know me but don't understand why I give my time and effort for Animal Liberation.)

It was at a Mobilization For Animals literature table in a shopping mall when the animal rights movement first entered my life. A poster of a cat in a restraining device, in God only knows how much pain, had drawn my attention. All the feeling had left my soul; I felt ashamed of being human. I felt hatred toward those who had caused the suffering. Wanting to do something, it was then that I became involved.

The helplessness of that cat had made me see something I wasn't aware of. I stared at the poster for a long time, sorting out a lot of feelings. I left for home after making a donation, taking some literature and with a changed attitude.

That scene haunted me! It wasn't moral. A cat is a free creature by nature, independent and proud. To restrain such an animal like that, I felt, just wasn't right.

I had taken in a stray only a few weeks before and the thought of my new friend in a torture device like that scared me into rethinking my personal views of the animal rights issue. It involved changing my lifestyle to the same degree as my new thoughts of morality.

To my family, friends and neighbours I preach animal rights. Making the pitch for the cause. Nothing is as sweet as helping a friend to see the light.

The use of animals is so widespread - touching almost all aspects of human existence - that it is not surprising to find attitudes that differ so much, even among those on the same side of an issue. The dreams, goals and realities of animal liberation vary from individual to individual.

I have seen small differences in policy come between very committed people. Any forward step, even a small one, is a positive step towards the final goal. We must continue to pull together. There has to be a feeling of being committed; it helps one to keep going to meetings, demonstrations and direct actions.

And I dream, I dream often. I dream for the future. A time when the word trapline falls into disuse, when all food is born of the soil, when 'sport' no longer involves the death of one participant, a time when the laboratory walls no longer echo with unheard screams. I dream for the judgement day!

I am involved in this cause to end the suffering. And someday I know we will succeed. But I became involved when an image of horror shook me from complaceny.

P.S. The FRONTLINE NEWS is a special paper. I know all of you who read it care very deeply. God bless you!

David J.

Pet rat defends woman's honor

JULY 10/85

FRANKFURT (Reuter) — A pet rat defended her owner against a body search when it bit a policewoman reaching under her blouse, police said yesterday.

The unidentified young woman was searched during a regular Sunday walk-about protesting a new runway at Frankfurt airport, a police spokesman said. When the policewoman reached under her blouse, "the rat apparently got aggressive" and dug its teeth into a finger, he said. Young people from the punk scene carrying pet rats in the streets have recently become a common sight in West Germany.

Research Fraud Continues

Consider the following: One set of "researchers" intentionally cause cancer in hampsters by injecting them with derivatives of nicotine, in an attempt to "reduce the risk of cancer" for smokers, former smokers and non-smokers forced to breathe the smoke. Another set of "researchers" cause cancer in rats in an attempt to find a cure for ulcers, by giving them doses of chemicals 500 times the norm over a two-year period. They claim it won't cause cancer in humans.

Cont'd....

In another "research" project, rats were given access to unlimited amounts of heroin and cocaine, by way of tubes in their necks, in order to determine that cocaine is more deadlier based on the amount of dead rats.

Do these seem like worthwhile projects to you? Or are these more examples of "make-work/make-money" projects for a supposed well-meaning profession, expertly duping an all-believing, consumerist public?

In the first example above, the researchers at Laval Hospital in Quebec City are trying to find a way to reduce the risk of cancer for smokers and those affected by cigarette smoke. In this waste of money and animal lives, they are ignoring the obvious solution - spend more time and energy on publicizing the killer effects of cigarettes and the whole cash-crop, deforestation industry and attack the huge multi-national tobacco companies that are exploiting and killing us with their products. Reduce the "risk" by not smoking.

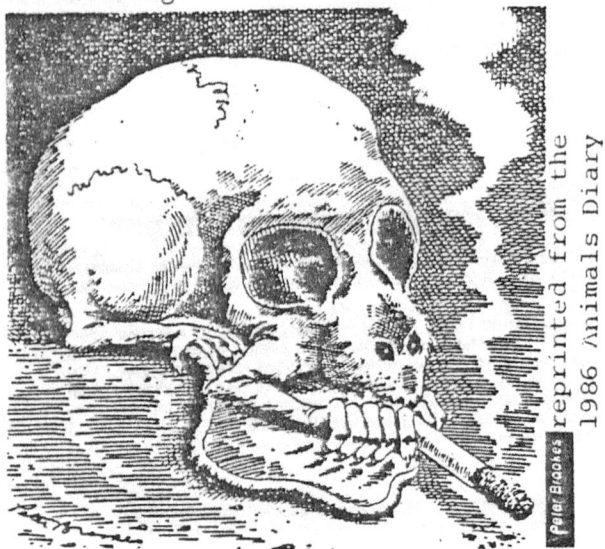

reprinted from the 1986 Animals Diary

Peter Brookes

In the second example, Astra (a Swedish Pharmaceutical Company) is trying to market its anti-ulcer drugs claiming that the cancer caused in rats as a result of their experiments will not appear in humans. These companies spend a lot of money telling us how animal "research" is necessary and valid, but when their tests reveal cancerous side-effects, they will quickly turn around and say that it's a different situation, as Astra has done. Anyone with common sense can foresee disastrous side-effects with doses 500 times the norm. Astra is desperately trying to maintain its hold on a $3 billion market with "new-and-improved" drugs, regardless of its research results.

In the third example, money and animal lives are spent trying to determine which of two poisons will kill rats faster, and they say this study applies to humans. Another ludicrous make-work project! Have you seen anyone with pure heroin or cocaine being continuously injected via a tube in their neck, walking down the street lately?

In a July 7, 1985 article in the York Sunday News, (York, PA), Dr Peter Gott lists quite a few vivisectors who have produced fraudulent studies based on "Fixed" research. He lists 6 "researchers" with a combined total of 162 papers or experiments that have been found fraudulent or suspect, including cancer immunology and heart experiments. Frauds have occurred at Columbia University, Yale and Harvard Medical Schools, and numerous other hospitals and research centres. These are the obvious and blatant examples of fraud. The not-so-obvious frauds, the ones in fact staring us in the face, are ones like the three examples listed previously - useless research that benefits only the vivisectors, universities and hospitals, and the multi-national drug companies.

Dr. Gott's last line in his article is the most important; "...we will end up being victims of any con artist with a typewriter and a laboratory full of rats."

Freebird

Sources:

The Economist, May 4, 1985: "People are not rats"

The Toronto Star, November 30, 1985: "Fighting effect of cigarettes Scientists aim"

York Sunday News, July 7, 1985: "Doctors Can Fall Victim to Research"

Unknown source and date: "Cocaine three times deadlier than heroin"

Copies of these articles are available by sending a stamped, self-addressed envelope.

ACTION REPORTS

Oak Ridges, Ontario: December 1985

ALF Activists raided the yard of an old house in Oak Ridges and rescued eight dogs from deplorable conditions. Because the "owner" is a known animal abuser, a warning was painted on his fence as well as slogans. The dogs were successfully adopted within two days.

Toronto Actions

December 13, 1985:

Several fur stores had their locks jammed with toothpicks and superglued.

December 14, 1985:

A two-foot hole was cut in a fence caging Arctic Wolves at the Toronto Zoo, allowing 13 wolves to escape. All were eventually recaptured. A $10,000 reward was posted for the capture of the "vandals". (This action was unclaimed.)

December 21, 1985:

Two fur stores had locks glued.

A Kentucky Fried Chicken outlet had locks glued and was spray-painted with blood-red "Meat is Murder" slogans. The "bucket" sign had a hole smashed in it by a brickbat.

January 3, 1986:

Seventeen fur stores had their locks jammed with pieces of broken toothpicks. One store, Victory Furs on Bloor, had been hit once before and now has a notice on the door warning that its door and windows are now electrified with 120 volts when closed! Don't be fooled by this ridiculous claim.

January 20, 1986:

A pile of cat excrement left on doorstep of Victory Furs. **The kitties' revenge!!**

Zoo Frustration

On December 14th, 13 Arctic Wolves were set free from the Toronto Zoo, where a two-foot hole was cut in the fence. Although this action was unclaimed by any persons or group, considering that they would have had to walk five kilometres and climb a fence to get to the site, it seems unlikely that it was mere "vandals" as the press and zoo officials claim.

In my opinion, I'm glad whoever did this did not claim it on behalf of an animal liberation group. It was definitely an animal liberation action, but they never completed the job. How can you let the wolves escape from their prison into the general population? They should have been herded into a vehicle and transported north or to an isolated area. It's like rescuing animals from labs without any homes for them to go to. The wolves were pretty lucky that the zoo officials did't shoot them, as they were suggesting they would, even though they admitted the wolves posed little danger to the public. They were all recaptured within eight days.

Regarding the effect on the wolves, author Farley Mowat summed it up pretty well: "They all must be very confused right now. These are desocialized wolves living in abnormal conditions, but they are responding to instinctive patterns."

The "vandals" were also branded "terrorists" by the zoo chairman, and a $10,000 reward was placed on their capture and conviction.

Unquestionably, we have to oppose zoos for the inhumane prisons that they are, the laboratory breeding grounds that they are, and the degrading and cheap "entertainment" for the pathetic human primates that support this establishment. But let's hope people have more sense when undertaking these types of liberations! If you can't do it right, don't do it at all!

Ann Ayelefer

ACTION REPORTS Cont'd....

NEW ALF CELL FORMED

A new cell of activists has been formed in southern Ontario for direct action activities against those who profit from the pain and death of animals. No significant actions to report yet, other than jamming sharp objects into the radiators of a couple of fur-delivery trucks and the usual graffiti slogans in high-traffic areas. No immediate plans, but stay tuned for a report in the future. It's worth the risk, but don't get caught!

Suburban Existentialist

LETTERS

To Whom It May Concern:

While I am in full support of the ALF Movement, I do have difficulty in the area of Animal Liberators destroying equipment and paint-spraying offices and/or labs. Don't get me wrong! I understand the anger and frustration one feels towards these establishments and the experimentors BUT should we not stop for just a minute and think of the effect of this action being reported to the general public whose tax dollars are paying for this damage and the replacement of equipment? Personally, I feel that a well-worded note (no abuse) left in the lab would do more good in terms of public relations for the ALF Movement. I really think the ALF would achieve more in terms of public support and respect by resisting the urge to destroy what the public sees or is quickly told is their property. I realize that sometimes it is hard to curb our tongues and actions when we see something which makes us feel extreme anger, but we must never allow that anger to over-ride our main aim, which is to educate the public to these abuses, which, in turn, will liberate these animals we all care about so much.

Anonymous in Toronto

In response to the above letter, I can only say that while your concern for the "image" of the ALF in the public eye is well-meaning, you have missed the entire point of the direct action tactics of the ALF. Although we agree that public education of the atrocities committed by vivisectors is important and desirable, these issues are largely unresolvable in the short-term. Our view is that the torture and killing must be stopped NOW! While thousands of animals are in peril daily, we do not have a lot of time to consider the ramifications of P.R. - Good or bad. To go into a laboratory or an office and leave a note addressed, "Dear Experimentor", is redundant at best. Believe me, if any group of people is aware of the horrors of vivisection, it is the vivisectors themselves! I am convinced that mere words would have little effect - actions speak louder! The ALF's purpose is the cessation of experimentation on animals. This not only requires that we rescue the victims of experimentation, but also that we destroy the means of torture. The animals are easily replaced - an endless supply of innocents for slaughter is bred, bound and bartered in a barbaric trade - but laboratory equipment is not so easily replaced. By destroying the tools of torture, we are buying time for the victims.......time to plan, time to act, time to save lives. The time is now!

   2T

As a further note to the above, in the latest ALF-SG Newsletter from England (#17) in an article entitled "As a Protest?", the author makes some important points.

"To be truly effective, ALF action must go beyond and be seen (especially by those who carry it out) to go beyond, mere acts of protest. The ALF must exist and see itself to exist, not just as another protest group but as an organization whose actions are intended to **directly** bring about change.

Animals should always be rescued whenever possible, but the main aim of ALF actions must not be protest, but economic sabotage."

He ends by saying, (and with my full agreement), "Not minimum damage but **maximum destruction**."

Freebird

The following letters appeared in the Toronto weekly "Now" Magazine during November and December of 1985. It started when I wrote the first letter complaining of the two images shown in the November 7th issue. What followed was a short debate that lasted for a total of eight weeks, ending with the Support Group placing an ad on the 'Letters' page. With circulation of 65,000 and an estimated readership of 120,000, (mostly a politicized readership). The use of the letters section in this and any newspaper is an excellent way to educate and outreach.

Photo stance anti-animal

NOW: *Nov 14/85*

I would like to protest the anti-animal stance your last issue seemed to take. As I opened the magazine to your first two pages, I was shocked first to see the utterly disgusting picture of a murdered moose and a leering woman on page three and then the TV Ontario ad with the rat in the measuring glass on page two.

The page three picture is an atrocious affront to any sane, feeling person. Blood sports are cruel and sadistic; the glory of killing a live, beautiful animal with a high-powered rifle is a mental sickness in our society.

Perhaps the TV Ontario ad is harder to complain about, as no obvious harm is being done to the rat. But the underlining implication that vivisection (animal experimentation) is "okay" or "rewarding," is well obvious. Millions upon millions of animals die at the hands (and instruments of torture) of so-called researchers every year. Researchers bolster their egos by having their "research" published, thereby having better chances of receiving more grants and donations for more "research," abling themselves to kill more animals for "science," and getting richer in the process. All in the name of "science" and "it's good for mankind." If they could only feel the pain they cause the animals.

Animal science and blood sports are no longer things to "oooh" and "ahh" about; they are two more of *mankind*'s sick traditions that must be stopped.

David Barbarash
for the Animal Liberation Front
Support Group
Toronto

Animal fans know nothing about moose

NOW: *Nov. 21/85*

Reader David Barbarash might have done well to swallow his "shock" at NOW's recent page three picture (Letters, November 14-20). A closer examination of the murdered moose was not, nor had

Explorations in Science.

From animal instinct to artificial intelligence — explore the issues and discoveries of science and technology. Watch nights on TVOntario.

TVOntario
Truly rewarding television.

the deceased ever been, a moose. It looks more like an elk, *Cervus canadensis*, a rare find in local parking lots. I have a sneaking suspicion that it is also plastic, and that it never was a "live, beautiful animal."

The Animal Liberation Front might consider hiring a new spokesman, one who actually knows something about the animals to be liberated. But that hope, too, is perhaps in vain. The animal rights group has shown off its colours once more; it is an urban-based movement of effete, sheltered aesthetes, who have never drawn water from anywhere but a tap. Where were they when real conservation groups were trying to get the province's wolf bounty lifted? On the strength of Barbarash's letter, it would take little to convince me that the movement knows little, and cares less, about animals.

By the by, the white thing in the beaker is a mouse.

James Whyte
Toronto

Of enemies and allies

NOW: *Nov 21/85*

I would like the opportunity to respond to David Barbarash's self-righteous attack on my photograph of the woman in the car with the caribou head tied to the roof.

In his letter last week Barbarash claims that my photograph has an anti-animal stance. Surely he cannot believe that the photograph advocates that people race out with high-power rifles so that they too may decorate the roofs of their cars with dead animal heads.

The people in the car were poor migrant workers in northern Florida. I was drawn to the image not because it was a stylish advertisement for blood-sports but because it presented an ironic encapsulation of the American Frontier Myth — a myth gone awry at the side of an expressway, shabby and sad, yet humourous when viewed ironically.

For irony to work in an image a certain ambiguity needs to be present. Perhaps it is this ambiguity which has confused Barbarash. A good photograph, it seems to me, has ambiguity implanted in it like a Rorschach design. The viewer's response tells more about his mind than about the photograph itself, which is a template from reality. Barbarash's indignant anger is, I believe, well justified; but not against my photograph. He would do well to more carefully discern ally and enemy in the subtle battle against barbaric greed and technological dehumanization.

I would like to thank Barbarash, however, for the strength of his response to my photograph; it is precisely what I seek as an image-maker — to arouse and question, to entertain and engage.

Lawrence Acland
Toronto

Animal lib too romantic

NOW: *Nov 28/85*

Animal liberationist David Barbarash's recent analysis of the motivations of researchers (November 14-20, 1985) showed remarkable confusion about what scientific research is all about.

Researchers don't publish in order to "bolster their egos" any more than potato farmers grow potatoes to bolster their egos. The job of a researcher is to provide new scientific information; this is done in published papers. Any academic scientist who doesn't publish is not doing his or her job. Also, Barbarash should realize that researchers aren't able to enrich themselves as their research grants grow larger. The person's salary is unchanged; the grant money goes toward lab supplies, business services and the funding of employees and students.

The thing that gets me about Barbarash's "researcher-as-ogre" motif is its blatant romanticism. I'm against cruelty towards animals (and don't do animal-related research myself), but there's something fundamentally corrupt about Barbarash's distorted portrayal of the medical research in which animals are used. I can't help but feel that Barbarash's fight is really against a particular destiny-controlling attitude that many people

have (including many people who are *not* cruel), and that the lab animal represents for him the same poor, suffering icon of uncontrolling "innocence" that the fetus represents for the anti-abortion movement. I'm in sympathy with Barbarash's legitimate concern for animal welfare, but I'm opposed to his romantic political agenda for humans.

Richard Summerbell
Toronto

Readers are specieist

NOW: *Dec. 5/85*

I have been labelled an "effete, sheltered aesthete" who "knows little and cares less about animals" by James Whyte (November 21-27, Letters); "self-righteous" by Lawrence Acland (November 21-27, Letters); and a confused romantic with a "corrupt" portrayal of vivisection by Richard Summerbell (November 28-December 4, Letters).

How could an animal liberation letter (November 14-20) cause such angry and defensive reactions from these three people, who all subtly suggest that they are in fact pro-animal?

How nice.

So how come they all feel compelled to attack me and the animal liberation movement? Why the hypocrisy? Could it be because of the radical nature of the group I belong to — the Animal Liberation Front Support Group (not the Animal Liberation Front)? Would they be happier if I were to join a "real (sic) conservation group" like Whyte implies?

I would rather support a group of people who liberate animals *now*, and cause financial damage and loss to animal abusers and institutions, rather than give my bucks to lobby groups who sit on their ass and money to support their bureaucracies and hierarchies (like the Toronto Humane Society which sits on $7 million that doesn't move, or the Massachusetts SPCA which sits on $50 million!). And then they wait to see if they can please the powers-that-be enough to get a law passed or changed, or set up an official so-called animal welfare group like the Canadian Council on Animal Care which has 14 anti-animal people (including the pharmaceutical industry and the Department of National Defence) and only two pro-animal people (from the Canadian Federation of Human Societies).

Well, no thanks! The liberation of the three cats and a (non-herpes-infected) monkey from the University of Western Ontario last New Year's Eve was worth 1,000 hours of lobbying and boot-kissing to our so-called representatives. Let's represent the animals ourselves; certainly they can't do it alone or with governments. If an animal is being tortured in a lab, well let's free it! How long would it take you folks to do it if it were a human primate instead of an animal primate? What's the difference?

This gets to the crux of the issue — Whyte, Acland and Summerbell will all suggest that they're really concerned about animals, but will do nothing more than attack a person who speaks out against two portrayals of animal abuse. Why? Because they're *specieist*. It's the same as racist. Remember the

Cont'd..

"nigger lovers?" Now we have "animal lovers." First we were fighting for equal human rights (which we still don't have), and for the past 100 years we've also been fighting for animal rights and equality, and we're still viewed as nutcases and fanatics. As the underground railroad liberated thousands of slaves in past times, the Animal Liberation Front is liberating thousands of animals here and *now*. Humans will always have their own voices; animals never.

If researcher Summerbell is "in sympathy," why doesn't he speak out against his colleagues? Or is he more concerned about getting grants or having his work published, as dissenting voices are always suppressed? If photographer Acland is an "ally," does he take pictures of animals in their natural surroundings? Or only dead ones on top of cars (for the irony, of course)? And if academic Whyte is concerned about the wolf bounty or other issues, why is he so strong in his attack of the animal liberation movement? Or does he think that being smart (i.e. knowing Cervus canadensis = elk) and writing a letter to NOW is enough?

Why all this hypocrisy? Let's have more action and less complaining of the animal movement!

David Barbarash
for the ALFSG
Toronto

Animal supporter

DEC 12/85

NOW:

Re: Letters, December 5-11/85 & November 21 through to December 5/85.

Three cheers to David Barbarash of the AFLSG for his apt response to anti-animal liberationists James Whyte, Lawrence Acland and Richard Summerbell.

In the past several weeks (since moving to T.O.) I have tried in vain to locate and become involved with just such an *action-oriented* animals rights group. If NOW could pass my name and address on the ALFSG, or else give me a number to contact for more info, I would be eternally grateful! (Despite your lack of judgement in printing Acland's revolting photo, that is.)

Cyndi Bazan
Toronto

Beside this final supportive letter on December 7th, I received two phone calls; one after my first letter on November 15th asking for more information about the S.G., and one on November 22nd after my second letter by an unknown man who left this message on my answering machine: "Hi! I just want to say 'Thank You' for that letter. In particular, for introducing the concept of speciesism. Thanks a whole lot!"

Our ad brought in approximately 15 letters of enquiry.

Dear Friends:

I don't know how I got through it, but in order to be able to debate more intelligently, I read "Animal Liberation" and have just finished "Slaughter of the Innocent".

I really believe the tactics of the ALF are the most important in order to effect change. When I grew up in Maryland, in a suburb of Washington D.C., I was right there with Martin Luther King's famous speech, gathering all those people together. I saw it all and he was a wonderful leader in the same way that Gandhi led his people.

Unfortunately, King's tactics can only work when you gather a very large group (in the thousands) and take to the streets. This brings news coverage and therefore, you can make your point by peaceful means.

What makes me mad is that if we counted all the animal organization memberships in the United States, Canada and everywhere else, or just North America, we have thousands, but none of them can get together to do an action or take to the streets in order to gain a lot of news coverage. Maybe someday there will be one animal rights leader equal to Gandhi and King to get us all united in action and we'd pounce on the scene so dramatically that we would cause changes.

This hasn't happened, and since it hasn't, we need the ALF, because that is the only other way to get our message spread.

All through reading "Slaughter of the Innocent" I was out for blood and would have loved to see a vivisectionist get the same torture he gives the animals. But after thinking about it for some days after finishing the book, I feel that the ALF would lose support if, by accident, an innocent person was killed as a result of an ALF action. I do believe in any destruction of research property and the taking of animals from labs. Liberating animals, destroying property

Cont'd

LETTERS — Continued

and writing slogans on walls will make people think about the ANIMALS and ask questions. Any real violence towards people or their children, i.e., poison candy, even if only a scare, will make the public only see terrorists and not think of the animals.

The ALF is the best thing that has happened to the animal movement since it started hundreds of years ago. I realize one important thing; that many really dedicated animal activists in the more conservative movements, without even realizing it, could still have remnants of speciesism. When you talk to them about breaking and entering or smashing property and stealing animals, they put up a guard and say, "we can't do that", yet, if this was in World War II Germany, the same people would have no hesitation in forming an underground to save the human animals in concentration camps. Therefore, these conservative animal activists are seeing animals as having less importance than the human animal, but thank God for the ALF for seeing them as having equal consideration.

Joanne Schwab. Toronto

"All that is necessary for the triumph of evil is that good men (and women) do nothing."

Burke.

Trapping indefensible
Re, Joe Hermer's letter defending trappers (Jan. 9). It seems ludicrous to claim that slaughtering animals, leg-hold trap or not, is humane and compassionate.

Killing or maiming a dog is considered cruel and is illegal, but do other sentient, fur-bearing creatures have no right to live?

This cruelty only continues because of the selfish and vain people who wear the animals' corpses as a status symbol. They deserve to step into a leg-hold trap. Furs are for beasts.

DEBORAH FISHER
Toronto

"Stop worrying, Sophie! They're a lower species, they don't feel things the way we do."

Inhumane treatment of animals must end
Re, the story, Barbaric leghold trap silences lonely call of Niagara's wolves (Dec. 2). I wish there was something I could do besides cry about the inhumane treatment of animals.

I guess I just have to wait for the human race to become more civilized. They're making great progress in other areas — discouraging smoking where I'm eating, dealing harshly with drunken drivers.

But what can I do in the meantime to alleviate all that suffering?

DONNA CUTHBERTSON
Islington

Sitting idle won't stop suffering of animals
Re, Donna Cuthbertson's letter (Dec. 16), which asks what she can do to help alleviate animal suffering. If she decides to just "wait for the human race to become more civilized." I believe she's in for quite a wait — a few centuries, perhaps.

Donna Cuthbertson, and every other person who loves and respects animals, can do many things right now to help eliminate animal abuse and suffering on all levels in 1985. You can join groups pushing for legislative change, or you can take direct action to stop this abuse.

The point is, don't sit around crying about animal suffering, do something about it! Anything.

DAVID BARBARASH
Toronto

Cont'd from page 5

In the final article we're looking at, we start off with a graphic showing a photograph of a monkey, with a research device added by an "artist" to the monkey's head, set on graph paper with a new-wave look. Pretty sick! Robert Fulford begins with a sensible comment, that we seek "nothing less than a basic change in human thinking..." This is true! Unfortunately, the article deteriorates rapidly. It continues by giving a rundown on the campaign and tactics used regarding B43 at the University of Western Ontario, calls us cranks, and insinuates that the ALF "frightened" B43 to get good pictures!

In the second half of the article he gives a brief historical overview of the movement citing Peter Singer as starting the modern-day activism, and, as Peter Worthington does, remarks on the parallels we draw in our arguments. But Robert Fulford does not accept the speciesist argument. He states that our logic breaks down when he asks the question, "is there any difference between a child and an animal?" Without offering any (speciesist) answer, he claims there is a difference.

We all know that humans and animals are of differenct species, but we all feel pain, emotion, hunger, etc. I don't think Mr. Fulford feels anything but elitism and superiority!!

(Copies of these articles are available from the S.G. for a stamped, self-addressed envelope.)

Dear Friends of the S.G.:

Here's a bit of foreign correspondence for you. I recently heard on the news that Scotland Yard has set up a special squad to keep an eye on certain animal rights activists. Ronnie Lee, spokesperson for the ALF, said this will in no way deter the direct action tactics of the ALF members. He said that not everyone is willing to face imprisonment for a cause they believe in, but there are a lot of people who are and the number is growing all the time.

More News: Bombs were planted in four locations around the country. (Vivisectors' homes) In one case, the bomb was planted under a car belonging to a "doctor" doing research into epilepsy; he uses primates (which were shown in the news rocking back and forth in their 2' x 2' cages). Apparently, it wasn't certain that the bombs had been set to go off. Either the police or vivisectors had been warned beforehand, so the Bomb Squad was sent in to detonate them. It seems they believe that at least one bomb was set to go off. The group claiming responsibility is called the "Animal Rights Militia". It seems they caused a bit of a stir about three years ago, only I'm afraid that that particular incident has slipped my mind.

(Ed. Note: The ALF-SG Newsletter from England (#17) has the communique from the Animal Rights Militia regarding their actions. This newsletter is available from us for $2.00.)

While I'm all for employing scare tactics against these torturing bastards, I'm not so sure about using bombs (that are set to go off), as long as there's any risk of someone getting hurt. If that ever happens, it's going to strike a big blow against the animal rights movement. It seems to me that by employing methods such as these, we are lowering ourselves to their level. These tactics will be construed as fighting violence with violence. If we are to gain support, the public must see us as being of a different calibre to those slimebags out there!

Anyway, when it comes right down to it, all I really want is to end this madness as soon as possible - (like NOW!!) Sometimes, when I think of all the sick things done to animals I almost don't care what methods are used to stop the atrocities.

Tarah for now,

D.H., England - (On Assignment!)

Hello! Thanks for your letter and support. Here's the latest list of prisoners. Quite a few people were given stiff sentences last month - (at least compared to the ICI sentencing where the longest prison sentence was 3 months with another 6 suspended).

We did hear from friends of Angus McInnes that he had received a letter from you and was pretty pleased about it. Sorry, we cannot help you as to whether the others got their letters as we're not in direct contact with them, because of the limited number of letters they can send out. Thanks for writing to them all. Hope you can send support to all the new prisoners. Keep in touch. Love and anger,

H. Steel for S.A.R.P. (Support Animal Rights Prisoners), Box 101, 84b Whitechapel High Street, London E1, England.

(Ed. Note: S.A.R.P. aims to help and provide for animal rights prisoners in England. If anyone has knowledge of such prisoners in North America, please send all the details to the Canadian Support Group at our P.O. Box.)

GENERAL NEWS OF PRISONERS:

John Curtin received a 9-month sentence with 3 months suspended. He had already served this time on remand and has now been released, as he was given bail for his charge connected to digging up the grave of the Duke of Beaufort.

Steve Symonds and Graham Mitchell have been released on parole. Dave Babbington and Carlo Hanshaw, if not released already are due out very soon, (no up-todate information on them)! Andrew Horbury, Steve Burrows, Paul Harvey, Dave Callender and Robin Smith have also been released. Cont'

Mark Houghton, Martin Gomez (who both received 3 months) and Helen Sinclair (1 month), sent to prison for damaging meat lorries, have all been released.

Shirley Clarke, Julie Edwards, Brett Jackson and Mike Hayes who were each sentenced to 6 months for going equipped to cause arson at a building that was going to be used to keep animals for vivisection at Leeds University, have all been released.

Note: For more information about the Wickham Trial and prisoners, or to make donations, contact: Wickham Defence Fund, Enfield Animal Rights, P.O. Box 133, Enfield, Middlesex EN3 6DS, England.

LIST OF PRISONERS - December 1985:

Iain McCann (J92353) - Serving a four-year sentence for an arson attack on vehicles at Cottage Patch Kennels at Fareham, Hants. (The kennels provide dogs for vivisection).

Gordon Bryant (J92309) - 21 months, 9 suspended.

Kevin Williams (J92279) - 6 months, 3 suspended.

Mike Nunn (J92297) - 3 years.

John Quirke (J92284) - 18 months, 9 suspended.

All of the above can be reached at HM Prison, Romsey Road, Winchester, Hants. SO22 5DF, England.

Sally Miller (D22865) - 18 months, 6 suspended.

Sue Baker (D22862) - 9 months, 4 suspended.

Sally and Sue are located at H.M.Y.C.C. and Prison, East Sutton Park, Sutton Valance, Maidstone, Kent, ME17 3DF, England.

With the exception of Iain they were sentenced on December 4, 1985 after being convicted of conspiring to burgle Wickham Research Laboratories and associated premises.

Materials Available From the S.G.

From Freedom mazagine: "An ALF Special", (May 1981) - 40¢

From PETA NEWS: "The City of Hope Medical Centre Raid" - 15¢

From the Animals' Agenda: "The Head Injury Lab Break-in" - 25¢

From Kick it Over: "Sharing the World with Animals" and the New Year's Eve raid in London, Ontario - 30¢

Animalines: "Stop the Machine" - Free

From England: ALF Action Reports, Issue #1 - Free

From ARK II: Various leaflets dealing with alternatives to and the use of animals in experimentation; dissection, psychological experiments, information on cruelty-free products, etc. - Free

From ARK II Activist: ALF Editorial - Free

From England: The ALF-SG Newsletter, (#'s 4, 6, 8-16) - $1 each. #17 - $2

From England: Direct-Action Animal Bulletin (#5) - $1

Front Line News: (#1) - 25¢

"In Defense of Animals": Edited by Peter Singer - $6.95

"1986 Animals' Diary: loaded with graphics and useful information with room to write notes - $7.95

Buttons: $1 each

Vivisectors are Scum
Boycott Zoos
Meat is Murder
ARK II
Animal Liberation/Human Liberation
Against Pound Seizure
ALF Supporters' Group

"Support The ALF" T-Shirt - $6 unemployed or $8 employed.

Ceramic Figures: The ALF Liberator Series, Limited Edition - $5 each

Please add extra money for postage

A.L.F. CANADA
FRONT LINE NEWS

P.O. Box 915, Station F, Toronto, Ontario, M4Y 2N9 Canada

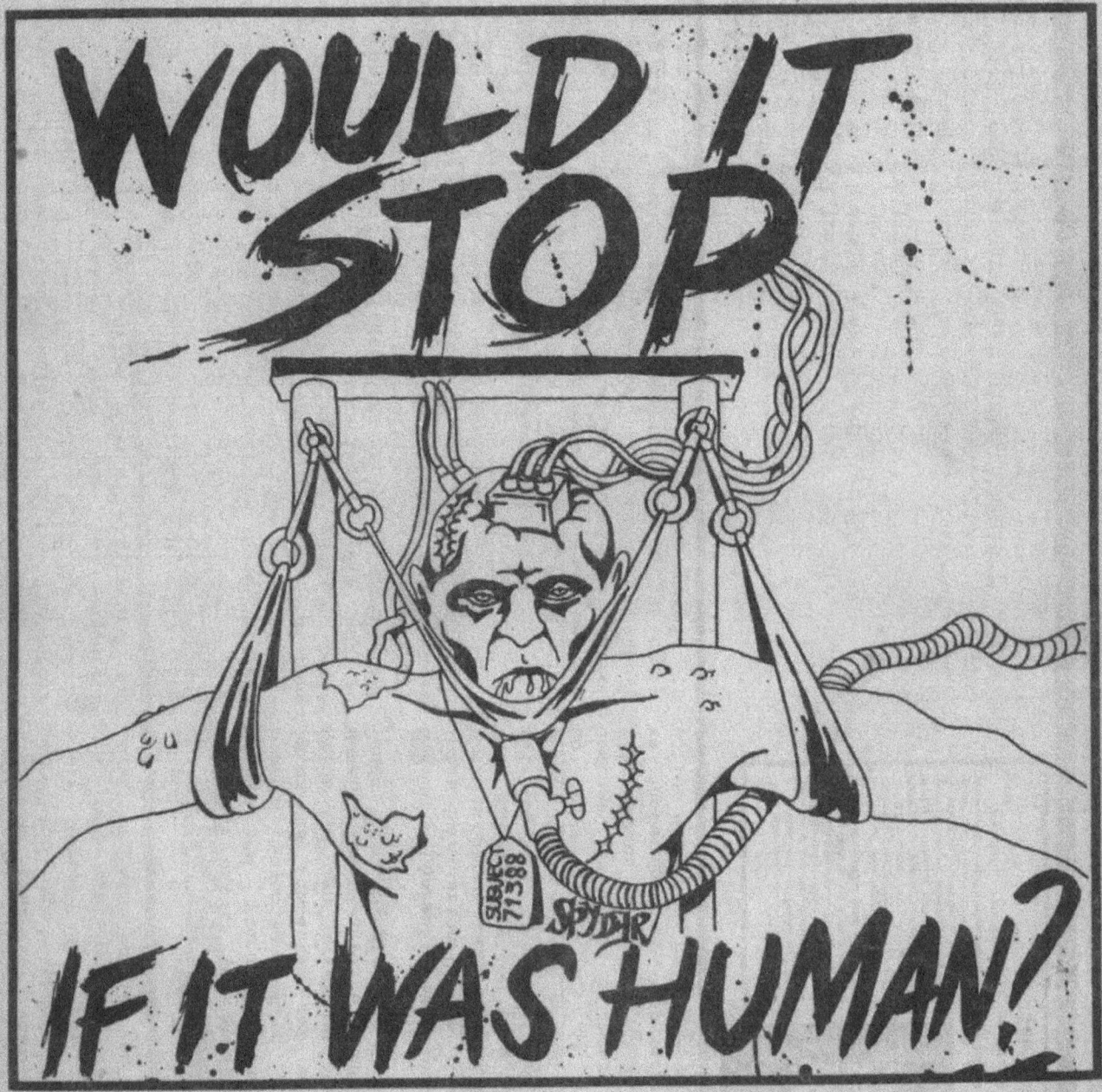

"Fighting in the front lines for Animal Liberation"

WORLD DAY FOR LAB ANIMALS

April 24, 1986, World Day For Laboratory Animals, was a tremendous day for Toronto! A great undertaking by the animal rights movement occurred. A great day indeed! Though the event did not go off as had been expected, this type of commitment from all who participated has never been seen here before.

More than a protest, a day when all the odd assorted bits of Freedom Fighters banded together to assault the worst of their horrors - VIVISECTION!

Connaught Laboratories under seige! The opportunity to show the world a group of caring individuals, not just social deviants and old women in sneakers!

The members of the various animal rights groups, brought together by the cohesion of ARK II, put on a great show. A needed lesson. The labs at Connaught produce a polio vaccine from animal tissue (primates). 300 primates a year die needlessly in this process.

The demonstrators made it clear that there is an alternative to this mass slaughter - the human diploid cell. Connaught officials said that type of vaccine production is not approved for use in Canada. Yet it has been used for many years in other countries. This is clearly a case of the usual bureaucratic inertia which enables Connaught to avoid the changeover to a humane method of vaccine production. Typical of the animal abuse on this planet - ethics of finance and lethargy.

Attack this horror again and again! Conscience can only rest when all the creatures of the Earth are free!

Bless you all! Your great deeds shall not be forgotten!

Attention All Armchair Activists!

The courage and strength shown by Merlin Andrews at the assault on Connaught Laboratories shows that age is not a factor in the fight for animal liberation.

It takes a lot more than a bunch of Connaught Goons to frighten a person like Merlin, who has devoted her life to the struggle for human and animal rights.

On August 25, 1984, Merlin made a speech at the Festival For Animals in Nathan Phillips Square - a speech which moved everyone who heard it.

The following is a small excerpt:

"..These pseudo-scientists who live off public money. These men and women who so cheerfully sacrifice what they term the 'lesser creatures' are MORAL TROGLODYTES. They suffer from amnesia of the conscience, from a massive and terminal deterioration of personal and collective integrity. The show these inept and callous clowns put on for the benefit of the public would be hilarious if it were not so sad.

When the last animal is clubbed, skinned, dissected or driven mad; when the last blade of green grass is burned and poisoned by the scientific maniacs, when nothing stands between Man and eternity but a barren, sterile, radioactive wasteland in which nothing but greed and cruelty can prosper - what then? Do we stand back and slavishly applaud the lunatic architects of our own and our planet's destruction?"

(N.B. Despite being knocked to the ground during the Connaught demonstration and suffering a concussion, 72 year old Merlin is once more 'fighting fit'!)

Nighthawk

ALF-SG Bazaar Report

Following a very successful benefit concert in January at the Starwood Club, there came another rousing success; a fund-raising bazaar held at Trinity/ St. Paul's United Church on Bloor Street.

In the last issue of the Front Line News we reported that only four people had donated saleable merchandise. Only a miracle can explain the fantastic response that resulted in the Gymnasium at St. Paul's being absolutely packed with goods for sale.

Vegetarian food was available - and it was damn good! Information tables were also set up by several organizations which provided educational materials for the shoppers. Judging from the response, it was, for many, a terrible shock to learn the truth about what is happening to the animals. Little by little, day by day, one by one, support grows for the animals.

To top off a wonderful day, there was coverage by City TV. (It is unknown as to whether or not they purchased anything!)

Thanks to all those organizations who accepted our invitation to distribute literature or sell cruelty-free cosmetics, and, of course, special thanks to all those who donated merchandise, mileage, baking and time. Without your help (and our customers) this event could not have been the success it was.

David J.
A special 'Thank You' to the members of Action Volunteers for Animals who volunteered their time and efforts to assist at the Bazaar - this despite several members of the AVA Executive Committee who voted not to have a table at the ALF-SG Bazaar because they felt it placed them at some kind of 'legal risk'.

ALF-SG Benefit Report

The ALF Support Group here in Toronto held its second fundraising benefit show on the 28th of June. It was held once again at The Bridge on Bloor St. and this time five bands donated their time and energy! Many thanks go out to Puppet Show (from London, Ont.), Stig Mata Martyr, Death of God, Was 1st Lost, and Social Suicide. It was the second time for the latter two bands as well! The SG decided not to show any films this time, instead deciding to hold an educational evening some time in the near future where the content of films and videos could be better absorbed. We did have literature tables set up as usual, and thanks to ARK II for coming out with their literature. The show went off without any problems thanks to the work of the organizers! It seems the only unfortunate note of the whole evening was the

club's decision to put a person at the front door to check people's i.d.s (you have to be at least 19 years old to get into a Toronto bar). Many people were turned away because they weren't the right age or simply didn't bring i.d. with them. Due to this, we didn't make nearly as much money as the first time, but we did make enough to get this publication out, and increase the numbers printed! Perhaps next time we'll rent a hall ourselves and take care of everything ourselves.

The next project the Support Group is working on, is a picnic in mid-August here in Toronto. It will be an educational event with workshops and discussions, and it will also be a chance to share thoughts and ideas. If you're interested in coming out to it, drop us a note for more info.

'Chicken-Tossers' Charged

Two University of Alberta students face criminal charges in connection with tossing chickens from a second-level balcony at the University, after first painting the birds red and black.

The local SPCA Shelter Manager, Kathy Wakeford, said she is discouraged by a lack of co-operation from University officials during the investigation, which includes trying to find out who the three other students were who took part. Officials, meanwhile, have made it clear that they do not believe the 'prank', as they call it, to be a very big deal. 'After all, they are only chickens!'

The five chickens survived the fall but were very seriously injured and were killed by other students at the scene. The bodies of the birds have not been found.

Reginald Shandro (22) and Earl Greenhough (21), both agricultural students, could face a maximum of $500 fine and six months in jail if convicted.

(Think they'll get what they deserve? No way! It's MUCH MORE SENSIBLE to

throw people who are trying to stop cruelty to other species in jail for years!

Let's hear it for the big, brave, brain-damaged neanderthals - Yeah for Reggie and Earl!#%&?!*#!

Front Line News

FRONT LINE NEWS is published periodically by the Animal Liberation Front Support Group (Canada), and is available by mail for a minimum donation of $10 a year. Material in F.L.N. is either written by S.G. members or passed on to us anonymously. All our records of authors and activists are automatically destroyed.

Support Group members do not take part in illegal activities; we pass on ALF news for informational purposes only! The ALF-SG (Canada) is an autonomous organization informally affiliated with the international network of ALF activists and Support Groups.

FLN welcomes your articles, graphics, letters, comments and critiques, action reports, etc. Address them to the S.G. at P.O. Box 915, Station 'F', Toronto, Ontario M4Y 2N9.

Support Animal Rights Prisoners

The following letter and information was sent from S.A.R.P. in the U.K.:

Dear ALF-SG:

Thanks for sending us the S.G. Magazines and for printing information about the prisoners in them. As you can see from the list enclosed, there are 26 people in prison in Britain now for animal liberation activities. It seems like the authorities are having a big clampdown and trying to stamp out the Direct Action side of the movement. SOME CHANCE!!

Well, thanks again. I hope you can send them letters of support as it makes quite a difference to a prison day to get such a letter, especially from abroad.

If there are any animal rights prisoners in Canada let us have the details and we'll get people to write.

Love and anger,

'Helen'

(N.B. The following list of prisoners and information is the one to which 'Helen' referred. Thank God, as yet, we do not have any activists in jail but inevitably that day will come! We urge you to write to any one or all of those prisoners listed. There can only be one thing worse than being an animal rights activist in prison, and that is to be a forgotten animal rights activist in prison.)

S.A.R.P.'s aims are:

Distribution of up-to-date information on prisoners to enable those outside to write to the prisoners, and also to the governors of the prisons demanding that the prisoners are given vegan food, toiletries and clothing without having to be members of the Vegan Society.

To provide funds for magazines, newspapers, books and radios for prisoners and for travel costs of visitors on a low income.

Please send any donations you can afford to provide funds for the above, to: S.A.R.P., BCM Box 5911, London WC1N 3XX.

Note: ALL LETTERS TO PRISONERS ARE OPENED AND CENSORED. DO NOT DISCUSS ANYTHING THAT COULD JEOPARDISE FUTURE ACTIONS OR SOMEONE'S FREEDOM.

Note also that prisoners are very restricted in the number of letters they are allowed to write. Therefore, they will want to write to friends and family, so do not be disappointed if you do not receive a reply — remember, the idea is to let them know that they have our support and solidarity.

PRISONERS:

Sally Levitt (D27314), Lesley Phipps (D27315), Beverley Cowley (D27316), Virginia Scholey (D27317) — letters (individual ones please) can be sent to them at: H.M. Prison, Parkhurst Road, Holloway, London N7 ONU.

Duncan Thorpe (N41997), Jim Snook (N41998), Nick Sweet (N42186), Alistair Fairweather (L64804) can all be contacted at: H.M. Prison, St. Loyes Street, Bedford MK40 1HG, England.

Peter Anderson (L64805), Eric Marshall (L64806), David Carre (Duggs) (L64807), Paul Watkins (Mo1) (L64779), Nigel Crouch (N42186) can be reached at: H.M.Y.C.C., Glen Parva, Saffron Road, Wigston, Leicestershire LE8 2TN, England.

The preceding thirteen prisoners, plus Sally Miller who is already serving a sentence for the action against Wickham Labs, etc., are in prison awaiting sentence, after being convicted

of conspiring to burgle Unilever Laboratories on 19/08/84. They are due to be sentenced some time in May or June.

Roger Yates (VO2605), Ronnie Lee (VO2682), Kevin Baldwin (TO2959), Gary Cartwright (TO2960), Ian Oxley (TO2961) are all being held at: H.M. Prison, Hedon Road, Hull, North Humberside HU9 5LS, England.

Julie Rodgers (P34407) is in: H.M. Remand Centre, Warrington Road, Risley, Warrington, Cheshire, England.

The six activists mentioned above are on remand charged with conspiring to cause damage in Sheffield (Yorkshire) and London, in relation to incendiary devices planted in department stores which ignited at midnight and resulted in sprinklers being activated, causing smoke and water damage to the fur departments.

Brendan McNally and Vivien Smith have been released on bail.

Iain McCann (J92353) is serving a four-year sentence for an arson attack on vehicles at Cottage Patch Kennels, Fareham, Hants. The kennels supply dogs for vivisection. Iain can be written to at: H.M. Prison, Cornhill, Shepton Mallet, Somerset BA4 5LU, England.

Shaun Ellis (H25078) was sentenced on February 27, 1986 to nine months for causing damage worth $17,000. to a Lancashire meat firm. Write to Shaun at: H.M. Prison, 69 Hornby Road, Liverpool L9 3DF, England.

Sally Miller (D22865) received 18 months (6 suspended) after being convicted on December 4, 1985 of conspiring to burgle Wickham Research Laboratories and associated premises. Sally is being held at: H.M.Y.C.C. and Prison, East Sutton Park, Maidstone, Kent ME17 3DF, England.

Also sentenced for the same action were: Gordon Bryan (J92309) — 21 months, 9 suspended; Mike Nunn (J92297) — 3 years; John Quirke (J92284) — 18 months, 3 suspended. All can be reached at: H.M. Prison, Romsey Road, Winchester, Hants. SO22 5DF, England.

Terry Helsby (P85326) is also at the above-mentioned Winchester Prison on remand for alleged damage to butcher shop windows and alleged involvement in digging up the grave of notorious huntsman, the Duke of Beaufort.

PLEASE REMEMBER ALL THESE ACTIVISTS WHO HAVE GIVEN UP THE MOST VALUABLE THING THEY POSSESS FOR THE ANIMALS — THEIR FREEDOM.

Perhaps we can't all scale walls, climb fences, lie in ditches or break and enter to liberate animals, but WE CAN ALL PICK UP A PEN AND WRITE. LET'S DO IT!

Phoenix

STOP PRESS — LATEST ON ANIMAL RIGHTS PRISONERS (ENGLAND)

Ronnie Lee is now being held without bail.

Gordon Bryant has been released.

Roger Yates is awaiting trial — his bail was set at $25,000!

Nancy Phipps — D28005, Debbie Smith — D28007, Delia Lowick — D28008 are all in Holloway Prison, London, England.
H.M. Prison
Parkhurst Road
Holloway, London
N7 ONU

Karl Garside — L65137
H.M.Y.C.C.
Glen Parva
Saffron Road
Wigston, Leicestershire
LE8 2TN

Giles Eldridge — E74944, Carl Egan — E74945, Boris Barker — E74946, Gary Allen — E74947, Keith Griffin — E74948, Nike McKrell — E74949, Julian Webster — E74950 and Alan Cooper, E24960 are all at H.M. Prison, Welford Road, Leicester, LE2 7AJ, England.

The activists accused of digging up the Duke of Beaufort were sentenced to 2 years each.

(Thanks to S.A.R.P. for this update!)

Letters

We received a terrific letter in our mail from Ursula Crabtree, Ph.D. in California. Ursula sent copies of this letter to ARK II, U of T Campus Newspaper, U of T School of Dentistry, major Toronto newspapers and Prime-minister Mulroney, as well as to at least nine groups in the States. We thank Ursula for her letter and reprint it here in its entirety:

To: The Office of the President, University of Toronto

Re: Animal Experiments/February ALF Raid, School of Dentistry

I have been associated with the American Animal Rights Movement for a number of years, and I have read a lot of ghastly stories regarding the use and abuse of animals in research through-out the world. However, I must say that nothing has ever jolted me as deeply as the news item I read in the May 1986 issue of The Animals' Agenda.

According to this news item, the Canadian Animal Liberation Front (ALF) tried to break into the tightly secured University of Toronto's School of Dentistry to rescue some experimental animals from pain studies conducted there. The news item mentions that the activists' only knowledge of what is going on behind locked doors stems from studies published by researchers, as 'the peer review system for monitoring the welfare of lab animals in Canada is closed to public scrutiny although it is taxpayer-funded."

According to these research publications, this is apparently what is going on behind those doors:

The animals, mostly monkeys and cats, are used in taxpayer-funded pain studies in which paralytic drugs and stereotaxic devices (mechanical restraining devices used in precision experiments) are used to keep the animals still. Anesth-etics are used only during preparation for experiments, such as the implantation of electrodes into the animals' brains, according to Vicki Miller of ARK II, the Canadian Animal Rights Network.

In addition to experiments in which facial pain and paw skin pain are induced, Miller described a typical dental pain experiment in which wires are implanted into animals' tooth pulp through which experimenters send electrical impulses and measure the speed with which pain impulses reach the brain. Monkeys are used in chronic pain experiments and are probably kept in restraining chairs, she said. (The Animals' Agenda)

Let me put it this way. Since these occurrences happen behind tightly guarded doors, it will be easy for the School of Dentistry researchers to disclaim any allegations of cruelty. If the researchers admit to any pain thresholds at all, they will no doubt defend their work in the name of science, for the good of mankind. That is exactly what the researchers at the University of Pennsylvania Head Injury Lab said before some illegally obtained videos showed the enormity of the sadism and brutality that was going on in this bastion of science (as praised by the U.S. National Institutes of Health (NIH) in an earlier report on excellence in research).

So let me put it another way. I AM SICK TO DEATH OF RESEARCH FREAKS WORKING OUT THEIR PENCHANT FOR SADISM ON ANIMALS UNDER THE GUISE OF DOING SOMETHING WORTHWHILE FOR THE HUMAN RACE. I have a Ph.D. myself, and I know the power struggle to get grants and excel. I am at the point where I feel that the goddamned human race does not deserve any amenity that comes from the brutal suffering of defenseless animals - AND THAT INCLUDES ME! I applaud the work of the ALF and will send them as large a cheque as I can afford to help them further their activity: they didn't succeed in the last raid on the dentistry lab, but there is always hope for the next time.

Don't I know that demolishing university property is against the law? Haven't I heard that breaking into restricted areas of a building is against the law? Don't I know that trying to rescue those animals is really a form of theft, since they are the rightful property of the university? And haven't I ever heard that violence begets violence, and that mankind will only survive if we, as individuals, learn to live with each other in harmony, allowing for our inalienable right to be different?

Of course I have heard the above argu-ments, and, in some cases, they may even be true. However, my world view has progressed to a point where I no longer feel the need to excuse the inexcusable just because a human being happened to be involved in it somehow. I feel no compunction what-soever to say that anyone making a living off the torture of other living things - be they animals or people - deserves AT LEAST a dose of the same medicine. This goes for anyone extracting information from prisoners in military dictatorships to fledgling scientists in research labs playing around with totally defenseless creatures to test such exotic news items as whether it does hurt to hit raw nerves in any part of the face, be it for 'tooth pain' or tic douloureux. There ARE a few respectable scientists, and those among them are slowly acknow-ledging the existence of alternative methods of testing pain or any other commodity in the field of medical science. There are computer models, and there are math models. And, above all, some of the findings have already been known since the dawn of mankind: they are merely being repeated to reach 'degrees of sophistication' in a given study area and/or ensure the 'redundancy' so important to the hearts of scientists.

Many of these tests and studies continue to be done for only one reason: to bring individual academic or other success/glory to the person doing the research while amassing as much funding to carry out the research as possible. This approach is at the heart of the academic research system, no matter in which country, and that is the greatest evil. IT LEADS TO THE PHILOSOPHY THAT THE END JUSTIFIES THE MEANS!

As for the researchers themselves: all I can really say is that I regret that I do not have the power to evoke a higher power to step in and give them their just due. It should be an eye for an eye, a tooth for a tooth - apparently benighted mankind, despite its bragging that it is the superior species, understands little except the most primitive laws of the universe. I do wish that someone would get hold of them, put them into one of their own stereotaxic devices, preferably clamped to a couple of the most sensitive areas of the body, and then, in the style of Sir Lawrence Olivier playing a mad scientist/Nazi doctor gone berserk in the movie, Marathon Man, drill through every one of their own teeth till they croaked from the combination of shock and pain.

Such a fate, to me, is regrettable, but well-deserved. Break-ins in the style of the ALF are also regrettable, but equally well-deserved - in fact, I would call them acts of civil diso-bedience that even Thoreau would have been proud of. Until the universities learn to open their doors for public scrutiny of the research that is going on, and especially when taxpayers' money is involved, they are asking for groups such as the ALF taking matters of justice into their own hands.

I often despair over the slow progress that the animal rights movement is making, but as long as I still have a voice to speak - unlike most of those animals whose vocal chords have been conveniently cut out so they cannot protest on their own - I shall speak out. This is a message, if you wish, from one animal rights activist for the cause of better treatment of animals in America. I am not merely singling out Canada - I am sure that the same stuff is going on in innumerable dental and other research labs the world over. In the U.S. it has been perfected into a fine art. The point is that the evil of using animals for the sake of science without even acknowledging that they might have rights of their own as living things is THE cancer - all-pervasive - in research communities, be they academic or private. However, to me, as an academic myself, the fact that univ-ersities continue to be some of the worst offenders in this area is THE most shameful aspect of all.

Ursula Crabtree, Ph.D.

P.S. Incidentally, since I am sending your government a copy of this letter, for whatever it is worth. I should not forget what a refreshing sign it has been to some of us not only interested in the welfare of animals but cultural differences as well, that Canada has managed to outdo its more barbarian neighbour, the good ole U.S., in terms of poor taste.

I am referring to the glossy ad for Grizzly Beer (Canadian Lager, brewed by Hamilton Breweries in Ontario, importec by Van Munching in New York) that has been appearing in U.S. magazines. The sparklingly clean and fresh bottle of frothy beer is tightly hugged (encircled) by an old-fashioned leg-hold trap, with the slogan, 'Capture Canada's Bear of Beers'. I have already personally complimented the brewery for their 'good taste' in advertising, but let it be further said that it strikes me as highly ironic to see Canadians capable of the same sin that they are so fond of levelling against the U.S. - vulgarity. The theory of rugged individualism and brute strength gone haywire, crass commercialism, ABOMINABLE taste.

(Ursula went on to say she was not anti-Canadian, just anti-cruelty.

We thank her for her great letter and generous donation!)

Dear ALF-SG:

I have a protest! Being a vegetarian and getting repulsed by the sight of fur, I'm all for you, upfront. But I think that you're going about it the wrong way.

There was an anonymous letter in your last issue, where someone finally voiced their concern on your violent approach. You came back at them with saying that violence is the only way to turn peoples' heads. You're wrong! Instead of destroying things that you are only going to have to pay for in your taxes, why don't you make yourself known!? The more people that know about you, the more support

you'll get. So! Get some smarts dudes! Start telling people to tell other people - friends, family, acquaintances. Put out leaflets and flyers, get out on those streets and let people know that you exist!

JUST DON'T ENCOURAGE VIOLENCE! And, remember, folks, that you can't destroy violence with violence. Only with peace and patience!

Anonymous in T.O.

Dear Anonymous in T.O.:

I'm mystified by the views expressed in your letter to the Support Group condemning the so-called 'violent' approach by the ALF.

What violent approach are you talking about? As far as I am aware, no-one has ever been injured by the ALF in Canada. If you are referring to the damage of instruments and property within the torture chambers of research facilities, then let me make it clear that neither the ALF nor the ALF-SG regard such destruction as 'violence'.

If someone had plotted to destroy the chambers of death at Dachau or Belsen Concentration Camps during WWII, would you have vetoed the plan as being too violent? Believe me, there is no difference!! And, as for my taxes paying for the damage done to laboratories, they are already being used to torture animals - what could horrify me more than that?

There are many activists 'spreading the word' throughout Canada, the United States, Great Britain and many other

overseas countries. What are you doing? I did not notice a request in your letter for flyers to be sent to you so that you could distribute them, or an offer from you to go onto the street and spread the word yourself. What I saw reflected in your letter was the kind of negativity activists don't need to hear - namely, that those out putting their backsides on the front lines for the animals are doing it all wrong!!

IF YOU WANT TO AFFECT CHANGE FOR THE ANIMALS, JOIN US AND DO SOMETHING!!

We have tried peace and patience for hundreds of years and where has it got the animals? Millions upon millions upon millions of them tortured, living in agony for weeks, months and even years until they are finally murdered and death brings a release from their torment!

Vivisectors are scum!! To hell with patience. THE TIME FOR ANIMAL LIBERATION IS YESTERDAY - NOT TOMORROW!!!

Phoenix

RE. LETTERS RECEIVED BY THE ALF-SG

Please be patient - it may take a little time, but all letters will be answered. If not in person, then via this section of the FLN. Thank you!

'A Scenic Harvest From The Kingdom of Pain'

JUST WHEN YOU THINK YOU'VE HEARD IT ALL! - Welcome to the insanity, horror and lunacy of SCIENCE RESEARCH LABORATORIES.

Science Research Laboratories is based in a dingy foundry on the outskirts of San Francisco. There, Mark Pauline, Mattie Heckert and Eric Werner create 'art'. Art, which incidentally has now something of a following. The locations of the 'art shows' are always secret and when you read on, you will understand why.

Among their 'exhibits' are the following:

. a device which looks like a stainless steel spider. It jumps around when it is turned on. It will be modified so its movements will correspond to the movements of a guinea pig named Stu. (Short for 'stupid') who is slipped into a jacket that holds him in place inside the device. Stu is then wired so that the spider machine will mimic his effort to get free.

. a box (still in the planning stage) that will house 3 chickens with their heads coming through holes in the top. the box will first decapitate them and then the front will open so that their headless bodies will come running out.

. a laser-activated merry-go-round with rabbit and cat carcases instead of bobbing wooden horses.

. a dead rabbit (the 'rabot') manipulated to walk in place while a female assistant lobs oversized darts at it from a pneumatic catapult.

The list of 'artworks' by these three sicko's is endless. The crin has been accepted by the San Francisco art scene and in 1985 they held shows in Los Angeles and New York - to much critical aclaim!!!

They've even appeared on national television during a segment of 'Believe It Or Not' about strange artistic pursuits and Target Video sells a video of their show called 'A Scenic Harvest From The Kingdom of Pain'.

SO WHAT CAN BE DONE TO STOP THESE SCUMBAGS?

Start sending letters to the following:

The Northwest Association of Animal Protective Agencies
2608 Centre Street
Tacoma, Washington 98409
U.S.A.

(It is located near Seattle)

The Humane Society of the United States
2100 L Street N.W.
Washington, D.C. 20037
U.S.A.

Buddhists Concerned for Animals
300 Page Street
San Francisco, California 94102

Write to Target Video telling them you will boycott their videos.

To all of you near the location, you might try to get to one of their 'Art Horror Shows'. The last listing we could find was the Center on Contemporary Art (COCA) presents Survival Research Laboratories in Seattle. The show was dated for last May 24th at a 'top secret location.' For more information they requested you call 624-6394 (Seattle number.)

FOR ANY AND ALL ALF MEMBERS NEAR SEATTLE WHO MAY HAVE BEEN UNAWARE OF THIS GROUP OF SCUMBAGS - Well, no more need be said.

Thanks to D.B. in Vancouver for sending us this information and an accompanying article.

Phoenix

Animal Emotions

ABOUT THE ARTICLE ON Survival Research Laboratories. This group of sickos call the incredible cruelty and torture of animals *art*? I can't describe the anger and disgust I feel from reading that article. I can tell you that this letter is not the last word I'll say about this — this "event" must be stopped. Mark Pauline, Mattie Heckert and Eric Werner have to be the most revolting human beings on this planet. I thought the idea of art was to create!
Diane Barbarash
Vancouver, B.C.

U of T Dentistry Raid

In the early morning hours of Sunday, February 16, 1986, a group of ALF activists entered the University of Toronto's Faculty of Dentistry Building in an attempt to liberate some of the imprisoned animals who were being tortured in pain experiments.

Surveillance of the building had taken many months, and all of us had been inside at night on at least two or three occasions, so we had put together extremely detailed maps of the upper floors.

The target research laboratory was a major problem! First, we knew that the time between guard rounds was very short, secondly the response time by police had been estimated at approximately two minutes, which meant we'd be trapped in the building if we accidentally triggered an alarm and thirdly, the doors and the inside of the lab were under 24-hour video coverage. Despite all these obstacles the lab was felt to be such a hell-hole, that those involved in the planning voted unanimously to go ahead with the raid!

So, that Sunday morning, as soon as it was felt to be safe, we made our way, in one's and two's to the point of entry. Those who were on watch outside would remain in close contact via the C.B. Radio.

Once inside, we made our way to Sessle's office, (the bastard in charge of the pain studies) intending to get documentation on the research. Unfortunately, our tools were not strong enough to break the lock and so, as time was running short, we decided to go to the fifth floor where an attempt would be made to enter the lab via the window of an adjacent

meeting room and then from there, across the roof.

We discovered very quickly that the window glass was shatterproof, which, naturally increased our determination to smash through it! Once that was done, we discovered a second shatterproof pane behind the first one!

Again, determination enabled us to break the window — but it cost us an enormous amount of time (again lack of proper tools — damn!) and the noise was incredible! We were so concerned we chanced breaking radio silence to check with the activists outside to see if the sounds of crashing glass could be heard from the street!

Once through the window there was an 8-foot drop to the roof and a 10 yard sprint across to the lab wall. Two of us stayed in the main building, manning the radio, handing out tools to those on the roof and watching and listening for both guards or movement from the three main elevators. The rest of the group made their way across to the laboratory.

A quick examination of the laboratory roof and walls made us realise that we would have to try going in through the wall. Several layers of material were ripped away with more brute force than finesse, but when our time-keeper noted that we had been inside the building for more than three hours, it became apparent that we were not equipped to complete the break-in to the lab in the time we had left.

THE FRUSTRATION AND RAGE ONE FELT AT BEING SO CLOSE TO THE ANIMALS AND UNABLE TO GET TO THEM WAS INDESCRIBABLE! THE THOUGHT OF GOING OUT WITHOUT THEM TORE US ALL APART!

With some difficulty, and by lowering chairs onto the roof, we managed to get the group back through the jagged hole in the window without injury. Then, we all decided to return to Sessle's office where we daubed the area with ALF slogans.

After this we wandered into some adjacent areas and smashed some equipment and defaced the walls with slogans. Economic sabotage is hardly as satisfying as liberating animals, but we were to feel much more satisfied several days later when we learned the damage amounted to at least $10,000.00!!

By now we had been inside the Dentistry building for over four hours and our time-keeper was getting really edgy, to say the least, and so we decided to get out while we could.

We made our way to the exit point where we left, again in two's and three's, after checking with our outside contacts that all was clear.

It may have been four months since this action, but all the activists involved are spiritually still inside that building. How can we find peace when we still think of those we left behind!

ALF Canada

(N.B. Perhaps those who wonder why the Support Group solicits donations will understand more clearly after reading the above account of the raid! Without the proper equipment, the ALF can do nothing. And, without homes for liberated animals, they can do even less!)

Dentistry break-in

Vandals who broke into the Faculty of Dentistry sometime during the weekend of Feb. 15 and 16 broke equipment, sprayed graffiti and smeared paint on floors, walls and elevator doors on the fourth and fifth floors of the faculty's old and new wings. Damage is estimated at $10,000. The office of Dr. Barry Sessle (above), associate dean of research, was a particular target of the vandals, who identified themselves in the graffiti as the ALF (Animal Liberation Front). They also sprayed graffiti around the entrance way to the animal facilities. James Kenyon, director of the Division of Laboratory Animal Science, says dentistry has at most 50 animals for research. Because of incidents such as that at dentistry, Kenyon says security costs have escalated to $100,000 and it has become more difficult to get some animals.

A N N O U N C I N G . . . . .

SCUM OF THE MONTH AWARD !#$&?!

Congratulations to Dr. Barry Sessle, Assistant Dean of Research at the University of Toronto's Faculty of Dentistry and recipient of our 'SCUM OF THE MONTH AWARD'!

Sadist Sessle is using primates in research on facial pain and jaw movements after first using a paralytic drug on the animals.

Both Sessle and that other scumbag, Faculty Dean Richard Tencate, should be bloody well appearing in Ripley's 'Believe It Or Not' fairly soon because, according to them, they are measuring the levels of pain experienced (as the result of torture inflicted!) by primates who (and I quote Tencate) are under anesthetic and feel no pain!

Measuring pain where no pain exists! See what a good education and a degree gets you? Everything but intelligence!

On second thought — I think as well as 'Scum of the Month' award, both Sessle AND Tencate should also be awarded 'LUNATICS OF THE MONTH AWARD'!

Phoenix

Interview With The

Under tight security, a member of one cell of the ALF Canada agreed to be interviewed for the Front Line News.

For purposes of the interview this person shall be identified only as Robin.

How did you come to join an ALF cell and why?

'Getting involved was inevitable after doing a lot of investigating and finding the system allows and even encourages goons, crazies and Frankensteinian creeps to gain and profit from the torture and humiliation of helpless animals. I CAN'T JUST STAND BY AND NOT DO ANYTHING ABOUT IT and happily neither can a lot more of us who want to put an end to animal abuse.'

How do you find laboratories to target?

'There are MANY animal concentration camps of one sort or another with willing employees who don't like what they see, and so come forward anonymously with information. That, combined with our own methods of investigation, gives us a good idea of what's going on where.'

Do you draw the line at physical violence? What is your reaction to the Animal Rights Militia's tactics, e.g., letter-bombs?

'After witnessing the worst kind of violence I have ever seen in labor stories, slaughter-houses and traplines,

I understand and experience the passionate rage the Animal Rights Militia feels. However, for the time being my personal anger manifests itself in taking part in raids. It is obvious that support for the ALF is here in Canada and growing rapidly. Violence may set us back — it's a big risk.'

Suppose you remove a laboratory animal; won't it be replaced by a new one who will have to suffer the ordeal of the experiment as it is repeated from the beginning?

'They will repeat the experiments anyway, and keep repeating them ad infinitum. The only way any animal gets out of a lab under normal conditions is when it is dead. At least this way, the ALF gives some a chance to survive, and that is, after all, our main goal, as well as removing incriminating documents and evidence that will put these places out of business. I'd be amazed if anyone thought I could walk out of a lab and leave all those animals behind!'

How do you carry out surveillance? *

'With a warm coat and a hot thermos!'

How do you guard against infiltrators?

'That's not easy when you live in a society that pays you to fink on your neighbours. Mostly by being as careful as we can; also the format of the ALF means that individual cells

are encouraged to develop independently. Therefore, one is not known to the other.

When did the first Canadian ALF action occur and what was it?

'The first MAJOR action carried out by the ALF in Canada was June 15, 1981 at the Hospital For Sick Children. (Sick kids sharing the same roof as the torture labs!) 21 animals were liberated, including the earless cat that got so much media coverage.'

What equipment is needed for a break-in?

'Jack-hammers, Helicopter and a Wrecking-Ball!' *

Any other comments you'd like to make?

'Yes! Carrying an animal away from daily terror is worth the risk of possible future penalties or imprisonment. I'm not a fanatic, a terrorist or a misguided misanthrope. I'm just enraged at a society that forces people to go outside the law to defend helpless animals. With the support of other animal rights activists and groups, we will expose the horror that so few of us see.

Finally, I urge everyone out there who has a home for a liberated animal to please let the support group know. This is our most vital need right now!'

* For security reasons Robin preferred not to answer these questions!

ALF Infiltrated

Eleven from Huddersfield got away with conditional discharges after pleading guilty to criminal damage to shops involved with animal abuse. But costs and damages came to $5,000, so they're organizing benefit gigs, etc. But "the whole case was bound up with the fact that our animal rights group/hunt sabs group was infiltrated. A bastard called Robert Walker, who is in several local hunts, a butcher,

etc., managed to get involved in our group over a period of 1 1/2 years, so much so that we trusted him. He was pretty clever, never pushed himself forward, never asked questions, etc. He was accepted so much that he was involved in the action in question. He, of course, grassed us up and the police caught us.

He even contrived to come to the group

after we were all arrested (he was arrested too that night — the police wanted him to carry on infiltrating). However, we thought it was too much of a coincidence to almost all be caught, so we started 'investigating'. After a confrontation, he confessed!"

Penny Pitstop (England)

Article courtesy of The Green Anarchist.

ACTION REPORTS

Local

March 1986 - Oak Ridges

The ALF made a return visit to 'Farmer Brown'. They found two dogs chained up and whimpering with fear.

As Farmer Brown hadn't learned from the first visit, one liberator took the dogs to safety while the others checked the barn. The barn was empty, so it was torched.
Good day, 'Farmer Brown'.

Toronto - April, 1986

Van belonging to Victory Furs had its tyres slashed, was spraypainted with the words, 'SCUM', 'MURDERERS' and 'ALF'. Windscreen wipers were bent and the windscreen was smashed.

Toronto - April 19, 1986

Locks glued and windows defaced with glass-cutters at Weissman Furs, Frankel Furs and Furs by Finn

Toronto - April 27, 1986

Cooks Meat Market and Cowiesons Meats decorated with 'Meat is Murder' slogans and locks glued.

June 9, 1986 - Toronto

A follow-up action was taken against Dr. Tencate, head vivisector at the

U of T's Faculty of Dentistry. A visit was made to the building's underground parking lot where Tencate's car was parked. ('Dr. T' on the license place, no less!!)

A swift daylight action took place, resulting in approximately $1,000 worth of damage to the car. Just a small reminder to Tencate that the ALF haven't forgotten him!

June 6, 1986 - Newmarket

One cell from the Northern ALF raided the premises of Chester's Chickens in Newmarket.

In order to get into the main chicken concentration camp, we had to cross a huge field which was overlooked by the Highway. In order to escape being 'picked-up' by headlights we had to crawl on our faces for most of the way. The farm itself was well-lit by floodlights and surrounded by two fences. We quickly cut our way through these and made our way into the main building.

Inside we stopped, mesmerized by the sight of thousands of chicks — so many that they covered the entire floor of the building. It was like looking at a living yellow carpet with bright lights beating down from the ceiling!

We immediately began to liberate chicks — 106 in all, and before leaving sprayed slogans everywhere — mainly 'Chicken Lib' and 'Scum'. In two's and three's we left the building, separated, and came together later at the designated meeting place.

The chicks have all been placed in good homes where they now get to go to sleep in the dark at night!!!

International

Australia:

July - December, 1985

Four rats, due to be gassed and used for dissection, rescued from school.
Numerous attacks on butcher shops, windows smashed, locks glued and graffiti painted.

Numerous attacks on fur shops, sheepskin shops and gunshops. Again, locks were glued and stores were covered in graffiti.

Vivisection labs covered with graffiti.

New Zealand:

October, 1985

Several thousands of dollars worth of damage done to the Deerstalkers Association when four molotov cocktails were hurled through the open windows of the empty building. Outer walls were covered in graffiti.

France:

1985 (No date)

Bulldozer that was used to destroy wildlife habitat was damaged.

Attack on a meat company resulted in three trucks being damaged and one being burned.

(Our thanks go to the Australian Newsletter - Direct Action For Animal Rights - for the previous information.)

ALF Toulouse (France)

December 2 and 3, 1985: Eight meat lorries and a car damaged: 'ALF' painted on, windscreens smashed, wipers bent off, tail-lights broken, etc. Two butchers' windows broken.

Farm Freedom Fighters

The following press release was sent to the Support Group for immediate release:

Animal Liberation at Mid-Atlantic Factory Farm!

On Wednesday, June 4, 1986, the Farm Freedom Fighters liberated 25 laying hens from a Mid-Atlantic battery egg operation. According to Farm Sanctuary, the spokesgroup for the liberators, this is the first direct farm animal liberation ever conducted in the United States.

Farm Sanctuary was alerted to the liberation when an anonymous caller contacted the group early Wednesday morning and identified himself/herself as a member of the Farm Freedom Fighters. A videotape of the actual liberation,

photographs and a detailed description of the liberation was left for Farm Sanctuary. The videotape contains footage of the liberators, the battery egg operation, and the hens. The tape also shows the liberators spray-painting slogans such as "Animal Auschwitz" and "Battery cages are torture chambers" on the walls of the hen warehouse. A note was left for the egg producers urging them to stop using battery cages. (Copies of the videotape and photographs are available upon request - contact: Farm Sanctuary, P.O. Box 37, Rockland, DE 19732, U.S.A.).

The Farm Freedom Fighters targeted the egg industry because it is one of the largest abusers of farm animals. Over 95% of the eggs sold today are produced in the battery cage system where four to five laying hens are crammed into a bare wire cage commonly

measuring 12" x 18". The extreme overcrowding results in extensive feather loss, skin damage, and feet malformations. The raising of laying hens in these stressful conditions poses serious health hazards for humans as well. The birds are fed enormous quantities of antibiotics to reduce the high disease and mortality rates resulting from intensive confinement systems. Many medical experts fear the rampant use of antibiotics is creating antibiotic-resistant bacteria in humans, a condition which renders life-saving drugs useless.

According to a statement made by the Farm Freedom Fighters, "This action is the first of many farm animal liberations. Our war against farm animal oppression will continue until all farm animals are free from the brutality of factory farms."

ALF PRESS RELEASE

EARLY THIS MORNING, MEMBERS OF THE ANIMAL
LIBERATION FRONT MADE ENTRY INTO THE
ANIMAL CONCENTRATION CAMP OF THE U OF
T'S DENTISTRY BUILDING.

MESSAGES WERE LEFT FOR THE CHIEF
ANIMAL TORTURER, COMMANDANT SESSLE,
AND HIS NAZI COHORTS.

SESSLE IS A SPECIALIST IN ADMINISTERING
CHRONIC PAIN BY IMPLANTING ELECTRODES
IN THE TOOTH PULP OF PRIMATES AND
SUBJECTING CATS AND RODENTS TO MASSIVE
FACIAL MUTILATIONS AND OTHER
MINDLESS CRUELTIES.

LAB AREAS SUSTAINED EXTENSIVE DAMAGE
AS PART OF THE ALF'S ECONOMIC
SABOTAGE CAMPAIGN AGAINST THE SCUM
WHO TORTURE ANIMALS.

FEBRUARY 16, 1986

ALF

SAVED!!

The clinical silence, at last was broken
that Sunday afternoon.
Our cages echoed,
The bars rattled
As the noise ricocheted
In the laboratory!

And then we saw them ...
The figures
Our saviours -
Men and young women,
All moving in quick, expert,
organized action!
All working as one -
With the same intention
Pliers - swiftly cutting the bars of our
Hated prisons!
Their concentrated toil worked wonders ...
They risked all -
They freed us all -

One lovely human, warm and caring,
Cut the bars of my torture chamber -
She pulled them aside -
And her loving hands
Reached into my cage,
She picked me up and took me out.
She freed me!!!
She held me in safety,
Held me against her warmth -
And I, never having known such love -
Felt .... Oh, so happy!
Having known only pain and brutality
I snuggled into her arms,
Burrowed into her arms,
I didn't want to lose her
I didn't want her to lose me!
I didn't want to lose Freedom.
I didn't want to go back and be hurt
EVER AGAIN!

Reprinted from 'The Isle of Wight
Animal Preservation and Action Group'

Group claims responsibility for damaging U of T lab

A group called the Animal Liberation Front is claiming responsibility for a weekend break-in at the University of Toronto's dentistry faculty, where medical research using animals is done.

Vandals damaged laboratory equipment and spray-painted graffiti on walls and doors on the fourth and fifth floors of the faculty's Edward St. buildings at the weekend. Metro and university police are investigating.

The vandals did not get into the laboratory where research using monkeys and other small mammals is carried out, said Dr. Richard Ten Cate, dean of dentistry.

Ten Cate estimated damage at $10,000, including $1,000 to $5,000 damage to a laboratory device that measures the acidity of liquids.

Animal rights protesters linked to U of T damage

The Globe and Mail FEB. 18/86

The Animal Liberation Front has claimed responsibility for damaging areas of the dentistry building at the University of Toronto during the weekend.

The group said in a news release that the laboratories of the "animal concentration camp" in the building at 124 Edward St., were severely damaged as part of its "economic sabotage campaign against the scum who torture animals."

The statement said the group is protesting against the use of animals in experiments conducted by the Faculty of Dentistry.

Metro Toronto Police Staff-Sergeant Graham Everdell of 52 Division said the damage, estimated at $1,000, was limited to the fourth and fifth floors of the building and was mostly graffiti spray-painted on elevator doors.

The dean of the faculty, Dr. Richard TenCate, said the damage could run from $4,000 to $10,000, depending on how difficult it will be to get the paint off doors and walls.

"They were trying to get into the animal faculty we have up here, but they didn't make it," Dr. TenCate said. "So, instead, they damaged some other labs."

The Toronto Sun, Tuesday February 18, 1986

RESEARCH 'WILL CONTINUE'
Lab raiders fail

By B.J. DEL CONTE
Staff Writer

A U of T assistant dean said yesterday he will not halt his research because of threats and a destructive weekend raid on his lab by animal-rights activists.

The raiders caused an estimated $6,000 damage by splattering red paint and smashing at least one piece of test equipment at the lab at 124 Edward St.

Among the spray-painted slogans were 'A.L.F.' — signifying the handiwork of the Animal Liberation Front — 'scum', 'torture motel' and a warning to Dr. Barry Sessle that the raiders would be back.

Sessle, assistant dean of research at the faculty of dentistry, is using about a dozen monkeys in research on facial pain and jaw movements.

Sessle said the warning made him "uneasy," but would not stop his research.

Faculty dean Richard Tencate said Sessle's animals are anesthetized during research and feel no pain. "I wouldn't tolerate them being in the building if they did," he said.

Vicki Miller, spokeswoman for animal rights group Ark II, disputed Tencate's claims but said her group wasn't involved in the weekend raid.

"It seems from the published material that most of the stuff coming out of (Sessle's lab) involves pain experiments," Miller said.

Research labs aren't subject to public scrutiny and raids are the only way to find out what's happening in them, she said.

THE TORONTO STAR,

U of T gets orders to clean animal labs

The University of Toronto has been ordered to clean up some of its animal research facilities or close them by September. The order comes from the Canadian Council on Animal Care, which can freeze research grants if the order isn't met.

Professor David Mock, spokesman for the cash-strapped university, blamed antiquated buildings and the high cost of security for the problem and said it could cost up to $1 million to rectify.

CRUSH THE HEADS OF VIVISECTIONISTS

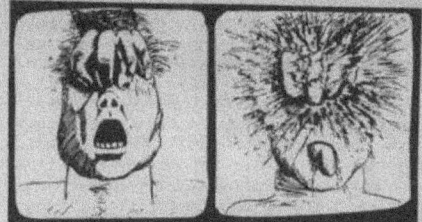

GEORGE BERNARD SHAW'S CLASSIC DEFINITION OF THE VIVISECTOR

"These poor little dullards," said Shaw, "with their retinue of two-penny Torquemadas,* wallowing in the infamies of the vivisector's laboratory and solemnly offering us as epoch-making discoveries their demonstrations that dogs get weaker and die if you give them no food; that intense pain will make mice sweat; that if you cut off a dog's leg, the three-legged dog will have a four-legged puppy. I ask myself what spell has fallen upon intelligent and humane men (and women, Ed.) that they allow themselves to be imposed upon by this rabble of dolts, blackguards, imposters, quacks, liars and worst of all credulous fools."

* Spanish Grand Inquisitors

(Reprinted from the American Anti-Vivisection Society Magazine, February 1986)

The Enemy Within?

(The following article was published in the British ALF-SG Magazine - #3.

Until recently, the ALF had only very limited facilities to answer irrational condemnations thrown at it. When the group makes a statement to defend itself - it is accused of 'attack' and yet whenever anyone else attacks the ALF, no objections are heard. The ALF will defend its position and hopes that SG members will assist it to do so. It is ironic that the ALF, deemed by many to be the 'hard man/woman' of the animal rights movement does in fact, by its actions, shows more compassion, more sensitivity and more respect for life than many others. Again, something to think about.

ALF actions result in the IMMEDIATE PREVENTION OF ANIMAL ABUSE and statements condemning the ALF do not harm the ALF - but they do harm the animals! The ALF clearly strives for ANIMAL LIBERATION, not division within the movement, and those who participate in words or actions which cause division are clearly no friends of the animals.

The ALF works for the liberation of animals - defending its actions uses up valuable time. While time is wasted, animals are dying!!!

While Animal Rights/Welfare Organizations condemn, criticize and argue against the ALF and among themselves, the ALF will be busy continuing with its work.

"As long as animal torture is lawful in this country, we must act outside the law." (E.C.)

Over a three-day period, ALF activists attacked Joseph Fox Fur Shop in Sheffield England. Expensive plate-glass windows were smashed, other windows were damaged by glass-cutters and anti-(animal) cruelty slogans were painted on the premises. The total damage was $5,000.

Later that month, Jean Pink of 'Animal Aid' stated: "This action does more harm than good..."

What or who does this damage exactly 'harm'? Not the animals for sure!

The ALF expects inane statements from animal abusers but NOT from people who claim to be members of the Animal Rights Campaign. Animal Aid, with other organizations, educates the public, and without any reservation,

the ALF supports this and considers this a WHOLLY NECESSARY part of the campaign. It is distressing to note the condemnation of the ALF action - and this is not the first one - that Jean Pink has made. No harm to life occurred - simply damage to animal abuse property which will result in animals being saved. That is, the money spent on repairs and extra security measures will come from money allocated for investment in animal cruelty. How can such an action be wrong??

It is perhaps worth thinking about which animal rights organization has saved the most animals? Which animal rights organization spends all the money it receives on animal liberation? And which animal rights organization has done the most to publicize the horrors of animal abuse and bring it to the Press and Television? It is indeed worth thinking about these questions the next time you send money off to an animal rights organization. It is pathetic indeed that the group that has saved the most animals and taken the greatest risks survives, literally, on a 'shoestring'.

Lifeforce's Peter Hamilton Smears ALF

In a recent article in the London (Ontario) Free Press (May 20, 1986), Peter Hamilton of the group Lifeforce denounced the Animal Liberation Front and tactics they use in the struggle against vivisectors and research. In reference to raids last year on the University of Western Ontario (where one rhesus monkey and three cats were liberated), Peter Hamilton rejected the use of militant tactics to expose cruelties and said such tactics "tarnish the image" of activists! One has to now wonder whose image Peter Hamilton and Lifeforce are more concerned with! In many cases, the only way to expose the 'image' of the vivisectors is for the ALF to break into the labs and find out for themselves what's going on. Two such examples are the Head Injury Lab in Pennsylvania where 60 hours of the researchers videotapes were stolen in a raid, and the University of Western Ontario where photos and videotapes were taken by raiders previous to the liberation raid. Peter Hamilton/

Lifeforce now 'own' these latter photos and tapes, and make money from their distribution. The videotapes can't be shown unless Lifeforce has a part in their showing.

So Mr. Hypocrite Hamilton now denounces the ALF even though he makes money as a direct result of their actions. He further says that the ALF 'cause more damage to our campaigns than anything else', even though it is well-proved that without the clandestine raids the animal liberation movement would have never gained the awareness it now has among socially-conscious peoples.

We in the Support Group have, as one of our goals, the desire to unite all the forces in the animal liberation movement. Aside from our obvious support of the ALF and their tactics, we recognize that attacks against the animal exploitation industries must come from all levels - everything from liberations to saying 'Pretty

Please?' to useless government officials. We will not tolerate people like Hamilton and their animal welfare businesses making money and publicity at the expense of radical groups.

Hypocrites and profiteers like Peter Hamilton must reassess their position within the movement and decide whether they want to further animal liberation or help set us back back to when it was safe for vivisectors behind locked doors. The London Free Press article was certainly a good PR piece for them!

We urge all our readers and supporters of the ALF to withhold funds from Lifeforce, and to write them and tell them what you think of their ignorant, false and misleading comments. A copy of the article is available on request.

Write to them at P.O. Box 3117, Main Post Office, Vancouver, B.C., V6B 3X6, Canada.

Freebird

WORLD VETERINARY WEEK: The Princess and Animal Protection

(Translated from a French veterinary journal)

At the last British Veterinary Congress in Exeter, Princess Anne declared that a balance must be found between the excessive use of animals in research and the 'extreme violence' (Wot? -

Ed.) of animal protection groups in England. According to the Princess, English animal protection groups are very active and laboratories are forced to become veritable fortresses to repel the regular attacks organized by 'perfectly trained commandos'. (Tee-hee! - Ed.)

More recently, near London, 'non-violent' protesters created a diversion by picketing in front of the entrance

to a laboratory while a small team went in to destroy equipment and release all the animals. The financial burden on the laboratories of such operations is very heavy. In effect, a study on the carcinogenicity of a drug could last two years; the release of the animals to the wild means the experiment must be redone from the beginning. This means that millions of francs are lost, not to mention the loss caused by the delay in obtaining results.

Networking

One of the most gratifying things that has happened since the inception of the ALF-SG in Canada, is the rate at which our membership has grown! As well as having members from all over North America, we correspond with activists from Germany, Holland, France, New Zealand, Australia, Italy, and of course, Great Britain.

This makes us realise that ANIMAL LIBERATION IS TRULY HAPPENING AT THE INTERNATIONAL LEVEL. VIVISECTORS BEWARE!!!

In future issues we hope to bring you news of actions in some or all of those countries. We have begun an exchange of newsletters, so that activists everywhere can see that they are not alone out there. Someone else is doing something too.

This brings me to an important issue – NETWORKING!!

It has become apparent from letters written to us by activists in the other provinces and throughout the United States, that there are many people who are fighting for this movement on their own. Many of you are practically next door to each other, yet say they wish there was someone else they could get together with. Obviously, for security reasons, the S.G. does not, under any circumstances, give out anyone's name or address to anyone else. However, if we are to grow and become more effective, then you all have to be put in touch with one another.

We would welcome any letters on how this could be done. One suggestion

we have is that anyone who is PRESENTLY ON THE MAILING LIST and who would like to become a contact for activists to come together, write to us and let us know. The next step would be to get yourselves a P.O. Box and, then send us the address, telling us at the same time, what code name you wish to be called. We could then publish that, for example, we now have a contact in Prince Edward island. Anyone out there who wishes to contact other activists should write to the S.G. and we will forward the letter. The contact person will then be responsible for doing the rest.

Anyway, its a thought! But we do have to get you working together. There is strength in numbers, and the animals need ALL of us, not just SOME of us.

Phoenix

DLN - The Animal Activist Information Network

The DLN Network is not just another organization. It's a network of activists from all over who help each other to be effective in animal welfare/ rights work. All types of actions and all levels of involvement can move us closer to our goals, as long as the common philosophy that respects the value of the individual animal life - regardless of it's 'usefulness' in human terms - is an underlying ideal in our efforts. The network exists to pass on knowledge of what worked and what didn't work for each of us, to exchange any sort of information that can help other activists who are doing similar things. The DLN Network wishes to link up with individuals, organizations or networks with common interests and goals for the purpose of exchanging practical information and ideas.

The network is NOT set up as a corporate organizational structure. There are no leaders and no hierarchy. The purpose is to help to spark the real sharing of ideas and resources. The purpose is to encourage people to trust their own creativity and trust their own set of priorities, while keeping the larger ideal of animal and human rights as the vision we're all working towards. The purpose of the network is to free people from the feeling of the uncertainty that their own action and animal rights involvement must first in some way, be 'authorized' by someone else, by some 'leader' some 'big group' and so on.

Everyone has the choice of whether they want to act individually, or work with an organized group – or both. The network can help people to know that they, themselves, are in control of their own actions and a person always has the choice to work with a group, rather than for a group. The network is a support for individuals, and not an entity that individuals are asked to support. The network is a way to empower individuals - a way to free people to trust in their own ideas and to take responsibility to try out their own actions and outreach in what ways they feel most comfortable. With the literature and educational tools, with the confidence that comes from self-education and by taking responsibility to act on our own beliefs more and more things can start to happen directly for animals.

The DLN Network does not have 'memberships' and the only time that money's exchanged is when you are helping to cover xeroxing and postage costs of requested materials. DLN has no paid staff and does not produce expensive promotional literature such as brochures or flyers. DLN is here to help you with your campaigns and to let you help others with theirs.

Since we're great believers in the 'snowball effect', we anticipate that many people will have their own network of contacts as well. People can photo-copy information and send to their own contacts - thus reducing costs and reducing the need for people to

send money to any central location or mailbox on any sort of regular or required basis.

A main post office box has been established for practical reasons – and as a central clearinghouse for information exchange. The only publicized address within the network is:

DLN NETWORK
3421 M. STREET N.W.
SUITE 1329
WASHINGTON, DC 20007

Practical how-to information sheets and kits are needed for virtually every aspect of animal rights work. If you can develop an information sheet or kit or if you just have a useful suggestion or idea – send it to DLN.

DLN will assist in circulating photos, films and videos, slides, records, books, anything where the primary focus is education and not the promotion of an organization. If you have clippings of actions, campaigns, demos, etc., please send them to DLN.

N.B. An Animal Liberation Front (ALF) Ideas/Information/How-to Booklet has been prepared and is available through the network by writing to the DLN mailbox. If you can include a small amount of cash – $2 or $3 or so – to cover the costs of xeroxing and postage, it would be most appreciated. All orders will be confidential and we encourage you when ordering direct action materials to use an alias.

Attention - Polio Victims

R. Yves is attempting to form a group of polio victims who are against animal-based polio research.

There is already such a group in the United States and the Quebec group is forming quickly. These groups could become a powerful force against the vivisection community. You can reach the groups at the following addresses:

Quebec:

R.Yves, Breton C.P., 95 Stn. Place D'Armes, Montreal, Quebec H2Y 3E9.

United States:

Gazette International Institute, c/o Polio Network News, 4502 Maryland Avenue, St. Louis, Missouri 63103, U.S.A.

From Freedom magazine: "An ALF Special",
(May 1981) - 40¢

From PETA NEWS: "The City of Hope
Medical Centre Raid" - 15¢

From the Animals' Agenda: "The Head
Injury Lab Break-in" - 25¢

From Kick It Over: "Sharing the World
with Animals" and the New Year's Eve
raid in London, Ontario - 30¢

Animalines: "Stop the Machine" -
Free

From England: ALF Action Reports,
Issue #1 & #4 - FREE

From ARK II: Various leaflets dealing
with alternatives to and the use
of animals in experimentation; dissection, psychological experiments,
information on cruelty-free products,
etc. - Free

From ARK II Activist: ALF Editorial
- Free

From England: The ALF-SG Newsletter,
(#'s 4, 6, 8-16) - $1 each. #17 -
$2

From England: Direct-Action Animal
Bulletin (#5) - $1

Front Line News: #1 - 25¢, #2 - $1.00

"In Defense of Animals": Edited by
Peter Singer - $6.95

"1986 Animals' Diary: loaded with
graphics and useful information with
room to write notes - SPECIAL PRICE!
-- ONLY $2.95!

Buttons: $1 each

Vivisectors are Scum
Boycott Zoos
Meat is Murder
ARK II
Animal Liberation/Human Liberation
Against Pound Seizure
ALF Supporters' Group

"Support The ALF" T-Shirt - $6 unemployed
or $8 employed.

ORDER FORM

Send me the following items:

1) _____ $ _____
2) _____ $ _____
3) _____ $ _____
4) _____ $ _____
5) _____ $ _____
6) _____ $ _____
7) _____ $ _____
8) _____ $ _____
9) _____ $ _____
10) _____ $ _____
                 Sub-Total $ _____
              10% Postage $ _____
                   Total $ _____

(Cheques payable to: ALF Support Group)

Please Print Clearly

NAME: _____
ADDRESS: _____
CITY: _____ PROV./STATE: _____
COUNTRY: _____ CODE: _____
PHONE NO: _____

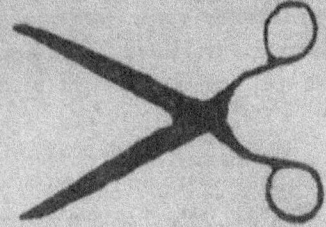

ANIMALS NEED HOMES!

Can you take in one or more abused and/or
liberated animals? These animals need
good, responsible homes and people, to
help them live out their lives as peace-
fully as possible. Let us know if you can
help out.

Type of Home: Apt.___ House___ Farm___

Animal(s) Capable of Providing Home For:

_____

Animal(s) already sharing your home:

_____

SUBSCRIBE TO FRONT LINE NEWS!

___ One year for only $10 (more if you
             can, less if you can't)

___ One year for only $1 million (special
     rate for vivisectors, hunters, butch-
     ers, furiers, multi-nationals, cops.)

HELP OUT THE SUPPORT GROUP!

___ I can help out with time and energy!

___ I have a "special" skill!: _____

___ I can help out by donating: $ _____

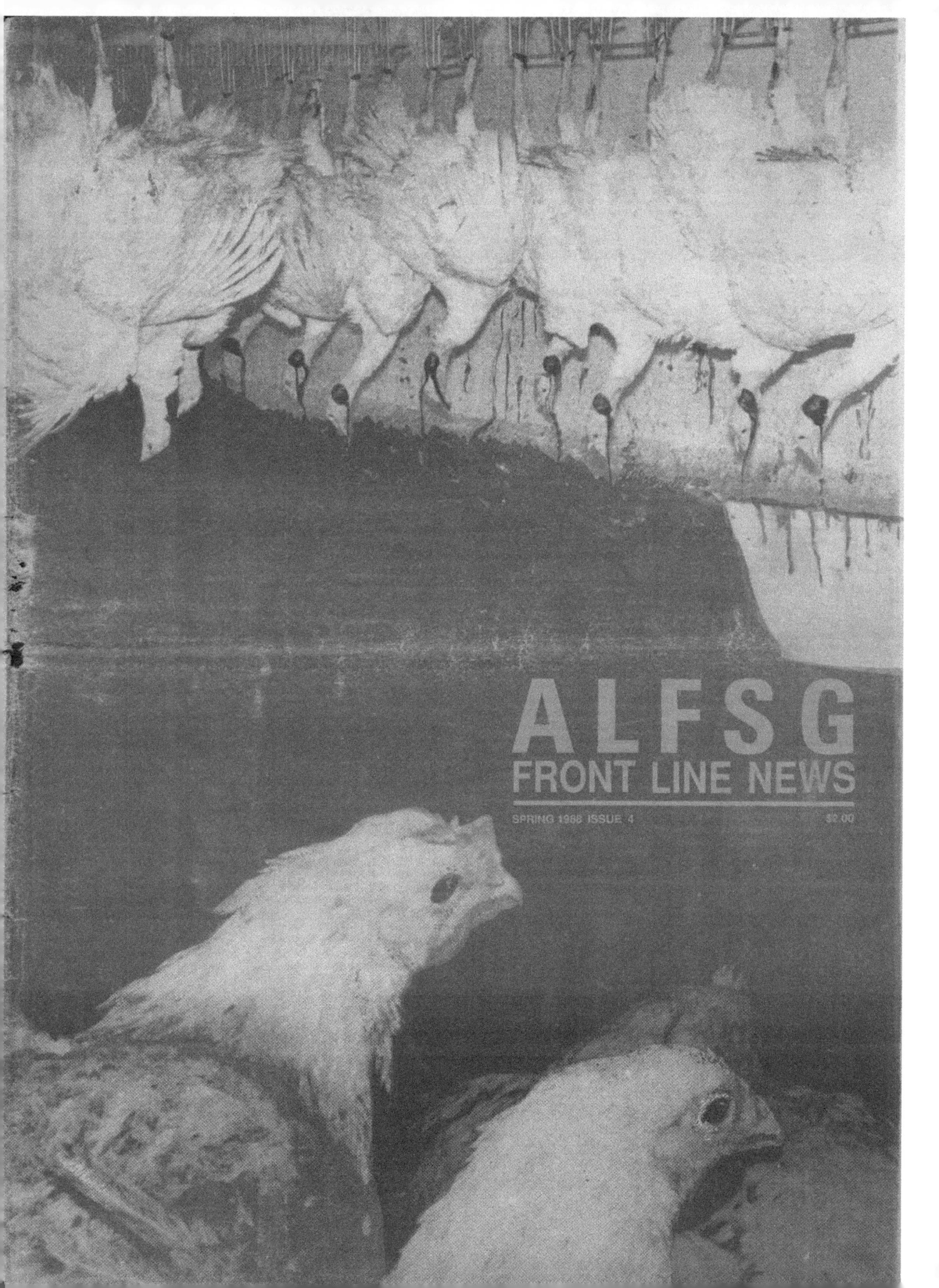

ALFSG
FRONT LINE NEWS

SPRING 1988 ISSUE 4 $2.00

WELCOME TO ISSUE NO.4!

Welcome to the fourth issue of *Front Line News!* It has been more than a year and a half since our last issue, and for this lengthy delay we send out our apologies. (Your patience is rewarded by this huge issue!) As many of you know, we've had our share of difficulties here in Toronto during this time, mainly dealing with the support for the five people who were arrested in January 1987. The arrests and subsequent, numerous court hearings and all the complications associated with that (which you will read about), have played a big part in our inability to foster enough energy to put out this issue. But, as we will always continue the struggle no matter what the state does, we continue our work in the ALF Support Group. In fact, we recognize now the even greater need for a Support Group, and an even greater need at this point in time for more people to get involved.

We have experienced some real practical difficulties in putting out this issue, also associated with the arrests. When the five were arrested, in their possession (and now as part of the 'evidence' against them), were some of the stories, letters and articles you will find in this issue. Other material which had been entered into the computer, was somehow 'lost' and had to be re-typed.

In this issue you will find an internal memo from the Department of Anatomy at Dalhousie University and an interview with an ALF person who went into the dentistry lab at the *University of Toronto*. Kenn Quayle is charged seperately with break and enter into the dentistry building in the February 1986 ALF raid (see *FLN #3*) even though Kenn was not even in Canada at the time of the action! The police, in their ambition to nail the five for as many ALF actions as possible, don't care about alibis or any real evidence. They will just present what they have to the courts, warp the information as best they can, and hope for the judge to agree with them. And so far the judge has. Not because the evidence is is believable, but because the judge recognizes the political case being made by the prosecution, and recognizes where he stands on the issues, which is obviously with the sleazy establishment.

It still comes as no surprise to us the number of charges for seperate ALF actions the five are facing. Toronto has seen a significant increase in direct action over the past few years, and it is the state's intentions to put a stop to it. One tactic used often around the world is to make examples of a few individuals. In their statement made to a judge to obtain search warrants for people's homes after the arrests, the police write in the first paragraph: "Since Oct. 1986 Metro police are closely monitoring the movements of a group known as the Animal Liberation Front. To date (Jan. 1987), 67 occurences have been recorded by the Metro police which through similar acts have been credited to this group." This calculation of 67 actions (though we have not received word about all of these) puts it at roughly 20 actions per month, during the period mentioned. By Toronto standards, this is a great deal of activity.

We hope you enjoy this issue, as we are all very excited and happy to see it finally published. We hope that your interest in the Animal Liberation Front and the Support Group's work is more than just a passive one, and that you will respond to the different ideas and information in this magazine.

Money, as always, is very much needed, and for those of you who haven't yet sent in your subscription ($10/year), or have not done so for a few years, we hope that you will be generous and help us out. Also, beginning with this issue there is now a cover price of $2.00. We would love to continue giving the magazine away for free, as we feel the information is unobtainable anywhere else in a single package, but we can no longer afford the cost of free distribution. Therefore, we are seeking your help in soliciting your local alternative/community bookstore or group to sell FLN on a consignment basis. Orders of 10 issues or more are available. The seller keeps fifty cents and sends us $1.50 for each copy sold. Individuals are welcome to place orders as well to sell or give away to friends and groups.

Over the past year there have been articles and information about the arrests, and pleas for money and support printed in numerous

FRONT LINE NEWS

Front Line News is published periodically by the **Animal Liberation Front Support Group - Canada (Toronto)**. The views expressed belong to the individual writers and do not neccessarily reflect the opinions of any or all of the members of the ALFSG. The information is for your general interest only; the ALFSG does not advocate breaking the law! All material is anti-copyright so readers are encouraged to reprint articles, giving proper credit. Submissions are very welcome - letters, action reports, articles, graphics and photos are requested. Subscriptions to Front Line News are $10/year; cheques should be made payable to the ALF Support Group, and mailed to: P.O.Box 915, Stn. F, Toronto, Ont. M4Y 2N9 Canada. See our Distribution List on page 29 for more information.

alternative publications. It is with the support of these papers which spread the views and information of the ALF that help the animal liberation community grow. We would like to say *thanks* to these publications by listing them here (in no particular order) with their addresses. If you want a sample copy of any you should send a buck or two to them.

Factsheet Five, 6 Arizona Ave., Rensselaer, NY 12144 USA; **Bayou La Rose**, P.O.Box 2576, San Diego, CA 92112 USA; **International Barometer**, 1025 Connecticut Ave. NW, Suite 707, Washington, DC 20036 USA; **The Thought**, c/o The Philosophers' Guild, P.O.Box 3092, Orange, CA 92665 USA; **Ecosystem**, 323 Grand Ave., Long Beach, CA 90814 USA; **Dialogue**, 916 Euterpe St., New Orleans, LA 70130 USA; **The Animals' Agenda**, P.O.Box 5234, Westport, CT 06881 USA; **Lomakatsi**, Box 633, 1377 K St. NW, Washington, DC 20005 USA; **ALF France News**, BCM 1160, London, WC1N 3XX, England; **Pagans For Peace**, P.O.Box 6531, Stn. A, Toronto, Ont. M5W 1X4 Canada; **Black Flag**, BM Hurricane, London, WC1N 3XX, England; **Kick It Over**, P.O.Box 5811, Stn. A, Toronto, Ont. M5W 1P1 Canada; **Earth First!**, P.O.Box 5871, Tucson, AZ 85703 USA; **Open Road**, Box 6135, Stn. G, Vancouver, B.C. Canada; **Vrienden van Let BDF**, (Friends of the ALF-Netherlands), Jan Blankenstraat 2, 2515 PP, 's-Gravenhage, The Netherlands; **Ecomedia Bulletin**, P.O.Box 915, Stn. F, Toronto, Ont. M4Y 2N9 Canada; **Androzine**, c/o B. Peuportier, B.P. 192, 75623 Paris, France; **Now Magazine**, 150 Danforth Ave., Toronto, Ont. M4K 1N1 Canada; **RFD**, Rt. 1, Box 127-E, Bakersville, NC 28705 USA; **The New Catalyst**, P.O.Box 99, Lillooet, B.C. V0K 1V0 Canada; **Faerie Home Companion**, Rainier B-1, 616 E. Thomas, Seattle, WA 98102 USA; **Anarchist Black Cross (Toronto)**, P.O.Box 6326, Stn. A, Toronto, Ont. M5W 1P7 Canada; **Anti-System**, P.O.Box 14156, Kilbirnie, Wellington, New Zealand; **Urgl-Orp**, P.O.Box 2541, Stn. D, Ottawa, Ont. K1P 5W6

Canada; **Wimmin Prisoners' Survival Network**, P.O.Box 6326, Stn. A, Toronto, Ont. M5W 1P7 Canada; **The Agitator**, P.O.Box 159, Eltham 3095 Australia; **Garbage In, Garbage Out**, c/o ALFSG Canada (Toronto), **Dr. Smith**; **Queer Anarchist Network**, P.O.Box 6705, Stn. A, Toronto, Ont. M5W 1X5.

We would also like to thank the following individuals for their work and support. Needless to say, we can't list everyone, but you know who you are! Thanks to Michael S. and **People for the Ethical Treatment of Animals** for their large, generous contributions to the Toronto Animal Rights Defence Fund. Thanks to Paul Avouris who is writing articles in Greek publications about the ALF,"...in a country where nobody seems to be interested." Thanks to Nicole for her work putting together a music benefit in San Francisco which raised $500. Also thanks to the people who donated their time and energy by playing there - *Christ On Parade, A State Of Mind, Caroliner Rainbow, Condemned Attitude*, and *Totentanz*. Thanks to Paul Watson, of the Sea Shepherd for coming to Toronto to do a fundraising lecture. He helped us raise $800. And a very special *Thankyou!* to Alice, who, as legal counsel and friend, enables the five activists to continue to get together to talk and share their lives, even if their time together is very limited.

Finally, a big *Thanks* to everyone who has contributed to the **Toronto Animal Rights Defence Fund** over the past year.

- ALFSG Canada (Toronto)

5 ARRESTS AS DIRECT ACTION INCREASES IN TORONTO

Over the past year, since the Fall/Winter of 1986, **Animal Liberation Front** activity has increased dramatically against the property of animal exploiters in Toronto. These actions have all been aimed at property destruction rather than the actual liberation of animals, but the effects nonetheless have left their mark on those involved in their slaughter, specifically for fur and meat. "Fast food" establishments have as well been on the receiving end, in particular, McDonald's and Kentucky Fried Chicken. It was outside the latter on a cold early morning in January 1987 when five activists were arrested, allegedly spray painting the walls. The five are: Kenn Quayle, Jacquie Rabazo, Gail Erno, Linda Cotnam, and David Barbarash.

Perhaps as a signal to the ALF, the police, being quite aware of this increase in direct action, are treating these arrests as one might expect them to treat most politically "subversive" activity. Investigators from Metro Intelligence were called immediately, and in the court, a special prosecutor was assigned to the case. Indeed, this is a "special" case for the political police. A poster for the five's defence campaign reads:

"What should have been simple mischief charges has turned into a situation where many, and more serious charges have been laid against them by the police... This is part of the current police intimidation campaign, where they are attempting to squash animal activism in any way."

The five are facing 46 charges combined, the majority of which are "mischief", connected to many ALF actions in Toronto.

When we speak of "direct action" for animals, of "economic sabotage", or "destruction of property", what are we talking about? And in what way do we expect these campaigns to be carried out? What types of actions fit into the ALF's guidelines of non-violence? Well, quite simply, the action must be non-violent; this means no loss of life or injury to any human (except in the course of self-defense against physical attack) or non-human. No action taken by the ALF in Canada has ever exceeded these guidelines, and there is no inidication that they will.

One charge facing the two men is "possession of a dangerous weapon". This charge involves nothing more than a slingshot. Another charge is "possession of explosives". This one though, might make a few flinch at the thought of bombs, explosions, fire, etc., but we should bring the use of this type of tactic into context with the animal liberation movement today.

Harsh Sentences In England

On February 5, 1987, in England, nine members of the Animal Liberation Front were convicted and sentenced to prison terms, with sentences ranging from nine months to ten years - four years being what most received. Ronnie Lee, co-founder of the ALF ten years ago and former **Support Group (UK)** media spokesperson,

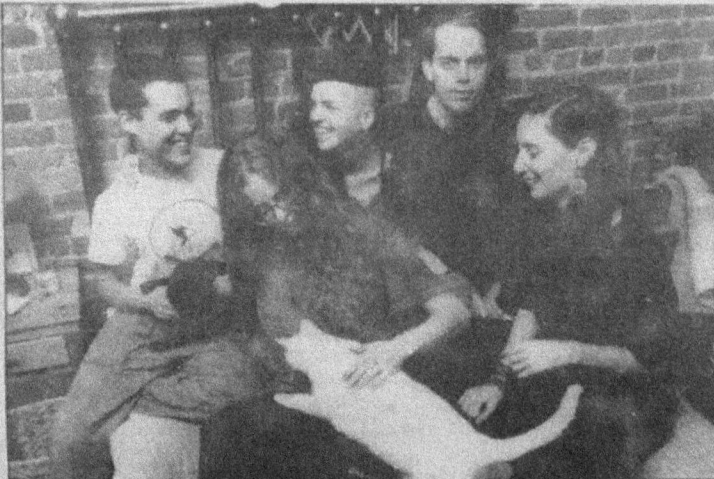

Arrestees David Barbarash (left), Gail Erno, Linda Cotnam, Kenn Quayle and Jacquie Rabazo say humans must protect other creatures.

received the harshest term of ten years. These were all in relation to fire-bombings which took place in fur depts. of stores in England over the past year and a half.

Ronnie Lee was convicted on charges of conspiracy to commit arson, committing criminal damage and inciting others to commit criminal damage, while most of the others were convicted of the conspiracy charge alone. One person, Roger Yates, did not show up for sentencing and is now underground, in hiding. In an interview with the London Observer, he states clearly that the fire-bomb campaign will contine: "It's a threat but it's not terrorism... The ALF's (so-called) violence is far less than the horrors of the meat trade and vivisection that it is fighting. Direct action pays. Most liberation movements have had to go outside the prevailing laws... The campaign is effective because it strikes at the heart of animal exploitation. If people have got no hearts to break then you can always break them through their profits."

Animal liberation action has increased in scope from simple spray painting to the destruction of property on a massive scale - millions of dollars of damage in England alone over the past year - and now we are seeing the use of fire on a rapid increase in the United States (*see the action reports*).

From the latest issue of the UK ALF Suporters Group newsletter, Ronnie Lee comments on this development. "I am in partial agreement ... over the gluing of butchers' locks and similar small-scale actions. Such actions can be effective over a period of time and, indeed, many butchers and other animal abuse shops have closed as a consequence. What concerns me is that it's obvious that many activists are carrying out such smaller-scale actions as a substitute for (instead of as well as) more effective and financially damaging raids on factory farms, vivisection labs, etc... Especially in recent

years many businesses and establishments involved in animal persecution have closed down following ALF actions against them. These include vivisection labs, factory farms, fur farms, and butcher shops."

The sentences in England are by far the worst ever for animal liberationists. Alongside our shock to their length comes the realization that the ALF are definitely recognized by the State as "dangerous terrorists", and are compared as similar to other urban guerilla movements such as the **IRA** or the **PLO**. But this is a false comparison. While most of the various (armed) human liberation struggles do not stop short of injuring or killing their own or other species, the ALF maintains its policy and commitment to non-violence. (This is not to belittle those who are involved with the struggles and resistance movements who carry out actions against people.)

We might agree that the ALF's stance is indeed a very noble and principled one, but the authorities couldn't care less. They refuse to see the difference or acknowledge this main point. But then again, perhaps they do. It doesn't take many hours of research to see that "crimes" against property are dealt with much more harshly than crimes against humans (or animals). This brings us to the crux of the issue, to the real motivation behind severe sentences against the Animal Liberation Front. The State recognizes two important factors:
1. Property is valued more than living beings, and
2. "Illegal" political action is the most dangerous and immediate threat to their existence, with all of their power and authority. And *we* know this too, which is why some of us choose to support, or engage in, "illegal" direct action.

With this perspective, we come back to the arrests in Toronto of the five activists. It is

now more clear as to why there is a real fear that even simple acts of (political) spray painting will bring down the force of the State. From their point of view, they must stop any and all direct action as quickly and as effectively as possible. One previous arrest in Toronto, where an activist threw a stink-bomb into a conference for vivisectors (effectively disrupting their awards ceremony and dinner in the summer of 1985), brought a six-day jail sentence. The conviction was eventually thrown out on appeal.

A letter dated Feb. 11, 1987 from the five arrested explains their situation:

"After being arrested and interrogated, the five of us sat in the police station for 16 hours before being moved to police cells. We were denied our legal right to see a "Justice of the Peace" within the 24-hour time period. We should have been released, but instead, Jacquie, Linda, and Gail spent five days in jail before getting out on bail ($2000 cash surety each), while Kenn and David were held seven days (before being released on $7500 and $10,000 property surety respectively). Our conditions for our release on bail are severe and amount to nothing less than psychological harassment. Aside from the cash and property sureties, the womyn must report to a Bail Officer once a week; the men twice a week."

All five were to maintain a curfew of 10 p.m. to 6 a.m. in their homes. They were also prohibited from communicating with each other, either directly or indirectly except in the presence of counsel, for the purposes of defence. The five write:

"Together the five of us have enjoyed sharing discussion (both critical and supportive) with the aim of creating an aware and responsible, sharing, co-operative community. We have prepared and enjoyed vegan meals together, again with the goal of educating ourselves, and in the spirit of co-operation. And our spirituality is based on our understanding that all life is sacred. To suddenly be denied any communication (outside our lawyers' offices), be it in person or by telephone is, to say the least, traumatic.

"Our friendship together is based on a deep love for each other, and a commitment to creating a better way for people to communicate. The future of this planet depends on human animals learning respect and honesty, and with this in mind we can move on to create a sharing, caring future - a global family, transgressing all boundaries imposed by human fear, competition, and mistrust. We are forced to deny ourselves contact with those who are the closest to us. Just a simple "hello" could be seen as a breach of our bail conditions, and could result in waiting for trial in jail. If even one of us were not able to contribute to the planning of our defence, it would create considerable problems for us all. It is extremely hard to live in fear, not just for ourselves, but for each other, and not have each other for support."

There are many examples of current and escalating harassment against the animal

Continued next page

Continued from previous page

liberation movement here in Toronto, the following being only a partial list:

- Attempts by the media to link **ARK II** (Canadian Animal Rights Network) to the ALF by use of implication and insinuation (ie: no facts);

- The non-stop barrage of attacks against the **Toronto Humane Society** in an effort to oust the legitimate, membership-elected Board of Directors, who happen to be activists rather than bureaucrats. These attacks include attempts by the media and a few THS Board members to link the activists Board members to the ALF;

- The **Ontario Humane Society's** attempts at convincing the Ontario government to seize control and funds of the THS, as well as a multitude of false claims and allegations made in the media in efforts to sway the public and government's opinions. (They have now withdrawn their legal participation but continue to be disruptive.)

- And most recently, a current federal government Senate committee investigation on "terrorism and public safety" interviewed a director of ARK II regarding ALF activity and animal activism in general.   This committee's report tries to link the ALF with right-wing fascists.

The list goes on and on. What this all amounts to, is a reflection on the progression of the animal rights and animal liberation movements in North America, and in Toronto specifically. Unfortunately this level of success (in terms of increased activity and the resulting public awareness) brings more attacks against the movement. These provocations can only make us stronger.

Quoting from the Toronto five's letter:

"We strongly maintain our commitment to animal and human liberation... There is no question that we must continue our fight on behalf of all non-human species on our planet. The survival of all life depends on it."

On March 16th, 1987, the five went to court for a Bail Review hearing. Their curfews were lifted, and Jacquie, Linda and Gail are now allowed to associate. Kenn and David, however, are still restricted from communicating with each other or any of the other three. The prosecuting attorney told the judge that the men "were obviously in a leadership role," and that their communicating could be a danger to the public! We would like to make it very clear that this

ALF bite back

sexist nonsense created by the prosecution is an attempt to divide the activists. This will not deter them - they were arrested together, and they will stick together until this is over.

Fortunately, in July, they retained a very supportive law student (through their lawyers) to meet with them on a semi-regular basis, and start working on more fundraising. She shows her support by working for a nominal fee - thus not incurring additional legal costs. Thanks to her, this has greatly improved their spirits and their ability to deal with their current situation.

Finally, we need to recognize that this case is a 'first' for Canada. It is imperative we send a clear and unmistakable message to all those who willingly enforce a code of laws encouraging the abuse, exploitation and murder of other sentient beings, that our support systems are firmly in place. Not only will we always provide the best defence for our people, but we will do whatever else is necessary to ensure that activism on behalf of animal liberation continues to grow in this country.

An Update on the Situation

The results of the Preliminary hearing have been, not surprisingly, disappointing. The Prelim is the time when the prosecution is supposed to convince the judge that there is enough evidence, for each individual charge, to take that charge to trial. After four days in court, spread over a month, Judge Mercer claimed to not need time to think about his decision (with five accused, and 46 charges!), and he committed the five to trial on all charges. The judge later refused to give his reasons for the committal.

At the outset, several charges were not contested by the defence, those being: the 'mischief' charge against all five relating to the night of arrest outside the Kentucky Fried Chicken outlet; the 'disguise with intent' charge against the Jacquie, Linda and Gail, also relating to the night of arrest, and; the 'possession of stolen property' charge against David relating to evidence seized during a police raid following the arrests.

A charge of 'possession of burglary tools' against Linda, Gail and Jacquie was dropped by the Crown Attorney, Ed Geller, before the Preliminary hearing began. It seems that even he was surprised that many more charges were not dropped.   A seperate charge against Kenn of 'break and enter' (relating to the Feb, 1986 raid on the University of Toronto Dentistry building) was heard on Jan. 26, 1988. Even though Kenn was out of the country during the ALF raid, the judge still managed to commit him to trial based on flimsy evidence. The activists were said to be in possession of material that connected Kenn to the raid. That material happens to be an interview with an ALF person who was involved in the dentistry raid, which is printed in this issue of *Front Line News*. It also happens that they were in possession of reams of material which was destined for the *FLN* . This is typical of the kind of (il)logic that the crown attorney and Judge Mercer have relied on throughout the Preliminary hearings.

Prosecutor Eddy Geller also insinuated that there was some sort of "central plan." The general argument was, that if the five were found guilty of one "crime", then it was somehow automatically reasonable to suggest that they were guilty of similar activities. To top this off, he attempted to lay 'conspiracy' charges against David and

Kenn for the same actions that they are already charged for under 'mischief'! But this idea was even too much for Judge Mercer who ruled that the five could not be charged with more than one charge for only one "transaction". Saved from further abuse by a legal technicality!

A 'Motion to Quash' the committals to trial (an appeal of the decisions make at the Preliminary herings) was filed, and heard on April 12, 1988. The Motion was denied, after the Judge held his decision for 2 days. April 21 was the day to set a trial date. The trial will take place November 14th 1988. The arrests were in January, 1987.

Bail variations have been granted for both David, Kenn, Linda and Gail at different times, allowing them to leave Toronto for short periods of time. Kenn was able to miss two weeks of his twice-weekly reporting condition in mid-October, and David was able to miss three weeks in November and Linda and Gail were able to miss 3 week of their once a week reporting, in April. Unfortunately, this has not turned out to be an easy process. New bail papers have to be drawn up each time there is a variation, which means hours in custody while the paperwork gets done. It also seems that the officials are finding it difficult to keep track of the changes. Officers at the Bail Office threatened to put out a warrant for David's arrest for not reporting, until lawyers reminded them of the variation. There is a tendancy to return to the original bail papers from last January, and now David is supposed to be living with his mother (his surety) and has a 10:00pm curfew. These conditions were lifted last spring! The earliest bail conditions required that none of the five communicate, but was changed allowing the three womyn to be together. Recently Jacquie, Gail and Linda were threatened with arrest when they went in to report together. It took another call from lawyers to straighten things out.

The Toronto Animal Rights Defence Group, which was set up to help support arrested activists, has raised about $20,000 toward legal costs. After the Preliminary hearing, they are about $5,000 in debt, and the trial itself still hasn't even begun. Almost all of the money raised so far has come from personal donations, and once again we ask you to help by donating whatever you can afford. Please send donations for the Defense Fund to:

Mary Bartley, Barrister and Solicitor
        11 Prince Arthur Ave.
        Toronto, Ont., M5R 1B2 Canada.
Please note on your cheque or money-order, *In Trust, Toronto Animal Rights Defence Fund.*

Donations for the ALFSG and *Front Line News* can be sent to:
        ALF Support Group
        P.O.Box 915, Stn. F
        Toronto, Ont., M4Y 2N9 Canada

Your encouraging letters have been very helpful in raising the spirits of all of us in this rather unfortunate situation.
        - Thank you.

bennett's view

Network of Defence Groups Proposed

Anarchists from across the United States and Canada will be meeting in Toronto July 1 - 4, 1988, at an **Anarchist Survival Gathering**, the 3rd annual North American anarchist conference. At a planning meeting held in Atlanta January 16 - 18, a proposal was put forward to set up a network of animal liberation activist defence funds. Animal liberation has rapidly gained acceptance as a serious struggle by anarchists over the past few years, and the Atlanta proposal is only a small indication of that growth.

Members of the ALFSG Canada (Toronto) attended the meeting and helped work on the idea. The proposal, which will be further discussed in Toronto in July, reads as follows: To establish Defence Funds to support animal liberation activists. Individual collectives in charge of funds will decide on distribution of funds on a case by case basis. In Toronto, a list of groups with ALF prisoner defence funds will be created, so that in the event of special needs, seperate groups can transfer funds.

A Statement of Principles was also agreed upon, which happens to resemble the Animal Liberation Front's principles. This comes as no surprise because the structure of the ALF, being decentralized, as well as their analysis of different struggles and the interconnectedness between them, does resemble anarchist theory and practice. The Statement of Principles reads: A 3-fold campaign: 1) liberating animals; 2) education; 3) economic sabotage. The principle of non-violence should be maintained where any action will not harm nor kill any life - human or non-human. The only exception may be in self-defence.

For further information about the upcoming *Survival Gathering*, write to **Anarchist Survival Gathering**, P.O.Box 435, Stn. P, Toronto, Ont. M5S 2S9 Canada.

Peter Hamilton Continues Smear Campaign

In Issue No. 3 of *Front Line News*, we reported on Peter Hamilton of the group **Lifeforce** denouncing the **ALF** and their tactics in a *London Free Press* article. He was reported as saying the ALF "tarnish the image" of activists by using militant tactics, and that the ALF "cause more damage to our campaigns than anything else." In the article we asked people to write to Hamilton to tell him what you thought of his comments, which some of you did. We heard through people who spoke to him, that he said that he did support direct action and that the press had misquoted him. He also sent us a letter suggesting that we were relying on false information and that we were spreading rumours. So we, in the **Support Group** weren't quite sure what to think, and sort of left the issue hanging. But now we have more news.

In the Fall/Winter (87/88) newsletter of the **Animal Defence and Anti-Vivisection Society** of B.C., an article appears on pg. 3 reporting on a lecture and film showing of the movie "Hidden Crimes", presented by Lifeforce on August 3, 1987. Some A.D.A.V. members attended and report: "We were not pleased with Mr. Hamilton's pre-interpretation of the Animal Liberation Front's participation in the film. Apparently, the portion showing the ALF was preceded by the remark, "now comes vandalism," and the portion showing the ALF rescuing animals was cut from the film."

This incident once again shows us that Peter Hamilton is lying. Mr. Hamilton and his pseudo pro-animal group Lifeforce are a profit-making venture, which makes money from the distribution of some photos and videos taken by the ALF. Once again, as we did in *FLN* #3, we urge our readers to withhold funds from Lifeforce, and to write Mr. Hamilton telling him what you think of his anti-activist views. We must wonder when people who are supposedly pro-animal continue to make statements similar to the research establishment. Who's interests is he serving?

ALF SUPPORT GROUP (UK) UNDER ATTACK

Over the past couple of months the police have been raiding, arresting and charging people who they suspect to have some connection with the **Animal Liberation Front**. A number of these people are members of the legitimate A.L.F. **Supporters Group**, an organization completely separate from the activist A.L.F. groups who work autonomously. So far, the person who has taken over from Ronnie Lee as national Press Officer has been raided four times since November 1986, and has recently been charged by Cardiff police for allegedly conspiring to incite others to commit criminal damage. He has had to surrender his passport, report to the police station twice a week and raise a £1000 surety.

Another arrest has resulted in a charge of allegedly conspiring to commit criminal damage and this person has similar bail conditions. Both appeared at Cardiff Magistrates court on August 10,1987, and face a prison sentence of 4 years each if found guilty. Ronnie Lee, co-founder of the A.L.F. was charged and subsequently convicted in February 1987 after being kept on remand for 10 months. He then received a 10 year prison sentence, yet was never proven to have had any direct link with illegal acts. Another worker at the Supporters Group received a 4 year sentence.

Those in a position of power, the Governments and the Multinationalists, consider the Supporters Group and Press Office as being one of the most damaging elements within the direct action movement. The Press Officer, for instance, often speaks to millions of people in one go and although the majority do not agree with some ALF actions, a certain amount are always educated as to the extent of animal abuse. The propaganda machine which is being run by those in power may be huge but even one live interview on television featuring the A.L.F. Press Officer can disrupt the corrupt business of abusing animals and the financial gain made as a result more than they care for. Imagine how powerful the meat industry must be when it makes a profit of £120 million a day. Many members of parliament are in some way connected with the meat, fur and vivisection industries, some own farms and many are keen blood sport enthusiasts. It is hardly surprising then that the ALF and the ALF Supporters Group have absolutely no faith in politicians.

There is far too much money at stake and anyway, the governments would never allow themselves to be put into such a vulnerable position and risk losing the support of the Multi-death companies involved in the killing of animals. The very fact that the Animal Liberation Front have posed such a massive threat to this financial empire makes them the most obvious targets. However, due to the fact that the ALF are autonomous makes it virtually impossible to arrest the activists. Therefore, the most vulnerable are the voluntary workers in the ALF Supporters Group who work entirely within the law yet are constantly being harassed by the police. All are under close police surveillance and their telephones are being tapped.

Since the convictions in February 1987, the Supporters Group have sought the advice of 2 independent solicitors and only literature which is considered legal is distributed, but this seems to have had little effect judging by the latest charge of incitement. By charging another Supporters Group worker, the police feel that they have made their conspiracy case complete. This is obviously a political case brought about because of a fear by those involved in big business afraid of losing substantial financial gains. When we consider that 800 million animals are slaughtered each year in this country (UK) alone we can begin to imagine just how much money is involved in the industries which abuse animals. Think of any large company and you can be sure that they are responsible for this slaughter because the very basis of society rests upon the exploitation of animals. The Ministry of Defence use millions of animals to not only test new weapons but to manufacture both old and new diseases for use in biological warfare. The list of horror inflicted upon animals is literally endless.

You can write to **Lifeforce** at P.O. Box 3117, M.P.O., Vancouver, B.C. V6B 3X6 Canada. We would like to extend our thanks to the people at **A.D.A.V.**, and you can write to them at P.O.Box 391, Stn. A, Vancouver, B.C. V6C 2N2 Canada. Send a buck or so for a copy of their newsletter.

The Animal Liberation Front, consisting of caring and compassionate individuals, have been the most effective direct action group to have campaigned against the persecution of animals. As a result, they have been labelled "terrorists" by the corrupt media. Since the conception of the ALF in 1976, the very strict rule of non-violence towards all living creatures remains intact and yet the courts refer to the few arrested activists as being public enemy no. 1. In actual fact, it is not the public who fear the actions of the ALF, but those whose vast profits are at risk. How can the torture and murder of animals ever be justified? Quite simply, it cannot! Alternatives to products derived from animals are available in abundance. Surely the greatest crime of all is to abuse an animal that has no way of defending itself. The callousness is overwhelming.

The forthcoming case reflects the latest move by the authorities to silence those who disagree with the injustices which are imposed upon the other species. A case such as this could effect the future of all groups who agree with the use of non-violent direct action, including **Greenpeace** and **Sea Shepherd**.

-Christopher Oakley, *Press Officer* (ALFSG-UK)

ALFSG - Montréal

There is now an ALF Support Group set up in Montréal, Canada. After a supporter spent the summer in Toronto and worked with us here, they returned to Montréal and established an SG. Actions are beggining to increase in Montréal, so it is an ideal time for its formation. Although their first priority will be to support Montréal and Quebéc-based activists, they will also help support and publicize actions happening in the rest of Canada and worldwide.

The Montréal SG has published the first issue of their newsletter with the focus being on McDonald's. To obtain a copy, send them a dollar, or you can subscribe ($11/year-more if you can, less if you can't). Send to: **ALFSG-Montréal**, Box 4007, Montréal, P.Q., H3Z 2X3, Canada.

PRISONER SUPPORT

Support Animal Rights Prisoners

S.A.R.P., BCM Box 5911, London, WC1N 3XX England

In this section of *Front Line News*, we list people who are imprisoned for animal liberation actions. We urge all our readers to write letters of solidarity to these people; even if you don't want to maintain correspondence with them, a small letter or note will do wonders for their spirits and morale behind the locked doors. We receive regular updates from S.A.R.P., and their latest list is printed below. If there is more than one person at a prison, please write separate letters. Please remember that ALL letters to prisoners are opened and censored, so obviously don't say anything that could jeopardize future actions or someone's freedom (including yours!). Please do not expect a reply as prisoners are restricted to the number of letters they can send out, and may have priorities such as family and friends. When you do write, include the 'prisoner number' next to their name on the envelope. Mail will be detained without this number. If you know of any prisoners that would like to be listed here please send us their names and addresses and any details you have.

"No, it wasn't—it was Jasper who went to a zoo. Eric became a cuddly toy."

U.S. Prisoner Wants Letters

John Clem recently sent us a letter from a youth detention centre in California, detailing his experiences over the past four years, and requesting letters from people he could correspond with. John's first action was four years ago when he and a friend were caught attempting to liberate monkeys from the San Diego zoo. They were caught and sent to a group home, from which they ran away. On the run from the police, they broke into the home of people who owned a dog food company, and vandalized their property. They were caught again and John was sent to a 'rehabilitation' program called "Vision Quest" which John describes as an "old time Wagon Train program" (christian fundamentalist??). John became angry at the treatment of the horses and mules used in this program, who were forced to haul heavy loads for long distances every day, with little food. The animals were also being harassed by other kids who were hitting them. John decided that he couldn't deal with it any more so he ran away from there as well. He was arrested again and has been locked up since February 9, 1987, and will be released in December, 1988, followed by 2 1/2 years of parole. John writes: "if you could find some people that can take a few minutes every now and then to keep me up so these people (in the prison) don't get into my head; I'd write back to anyone who writes."

John Clem #49896
Y.T.S., P.O.Box 800
Ontario, CA
91761 USA

S.A.R.P.'s aims are:

1. *Distribution of up-to-date information on prisoners to enable those outside to write to the prisoners, and also to the governors of prisons to demand that prisoners are given vegan food, toiletries and clothing on request.*

2. *To provide funds for magazines, newspapers, books and radios for prisoners, and for the travel costs of visitors on a low income.*

Please send us any donations you can afford, to provide funds for the above, and a stamped addressed envelope or two if you would like to receive further lists of prisoners.

List of Prisoners January 1988

Ronnie Lee V02682
H.M. Prison
Long Lartin,
South Littleton,
Evesham, Worcs.
WR11 5TZ

Kevin Baldwin T02959
Gary Cartwright T02960
Ian Oxley T02961
H.M. Prison
Lindholme,
Bawtry Road,
Hatfield Woodhouse,
Doncaster, South Yorks,
DN7 6DG

Brendan McNally T03014
H.M. Prison,
Acklington,
Morpeth,
Northumberland,
NE65 9XF

Vivienne Smith P34563
Julie Rodgers - now out!
H.M. Prison,
Cookham Rd.,
Rochester, Kent,
ME1 3LU

The above people were sentenced in Feb. 1987 at Sheffield Crown Court. The charges were: 1. Conspiracy to commit arson, 2. Conspiracy to cause damage, 3. Conspiracy to incite others to commit damage, 4. Conspiracy to 'steal' the Ecclesfield beagles.
Ronnie was sentenced to 10 years for charges 1, 2 & 3. Vivienne and Brendan were sentenced to 4 years each for charge 2. Ian and Gary were sentenced to 4 years for 1, 2, & 4. Kevin was sentenced for 4 years for 1 & 2. Julie was sentenced to 30 months for 1 & 2. Roger Yates was sentenced to 4 years in his absence (he absconded during the trial) for 2 & 3.

Andrew Clarke V50557
Geoff Sheppard V50730
H.M. Prison,
Coldingley,
Bisley,
Woking,
Surrey,
GU24 9EX

Andrew and Geoff are being held (since early September, 1987) awaiting trial on charges of conspiracy to manufacture incendiary devices and possession of various items with intent to cause damage, and causing damage to the value of over $18 million to Debenhams Dept. Stores in Luton, Romford, and Harrow in July, 1987. (The Debenhams chain of stores sell fur coats in some branches.)

Iain McCann J92353
B (2) Wing,
H.M.P. The Verne,
Portland, Dorset,
DT5 1EQ

Serving a 4 year sentence for an arson attack on vehicles at Cottage Patch Kennels, Hants.

Lesley Phipps T82697
H.M. Remand Centre,
Pucklechurch,
Bristol,
BS17 3QJ

Gari Allen W62615
H.M. Prison,
Winson Green Rd.,
Birmingham,
B18 4AS

Lesley and Gari are being held (since mid-December, 1987) awaiting trial on charges of criminal damage to Cocksparrow fur farms (by spraying foxes' fur with a harmless dye), and also conspiring to cause an 'explosion' with petrol (to damage the car of a poultry farmer).

Valerie Mohammed 369
Young Offender,
H.M.P.,Cornton Vale,
Cornton Rd.,
Stirling,
FK9 5NY

David Barr 4193
B Hall,
H.M.P., Saughton,
Edinburgh,
EH11 3LN

David and Valerie were sentenced in March 1988. They were found guilty of conspiring to further the aims of the ALF by criminal means, by placing stickers threatening contamination on animal tested cosmetics and making threats against stores selling furs and animal tested cosmetics, to the press and stores involved. David was also found guilty of planting an incendiary device in Jenners dept store in Edinburgh, but the jury deleted an allegation in the charge that he attempted to set fire to the store. David was sentenced to 3 years imprisonment and Valerie was sentenced to 9 months. Val should be out in May!

Diary of Actions #4

Liberating Self to Liberate Animals

David Firsching was arrested a few years ago on traffic charges, and placed in a local jail. His two golden retrievers were with him at the time and they were placed in jail as well, in the local pound. Unable to post bail, and fearful that the pound officials would kill his unclaimed dogs, David made an incredible escape from jail, went to the pound, and then liberated his dogs! In a letter to the editor in the March 1988 *Animals' Agenda*, he describes the ordeal:

"Employing chisel and hacksaw blade, I cut through the window and bars. Using a hand-braided rope, I lowered myself to the ground... Under the midnight sky, I raced to the animal shelter on the outskirts of town... Once there, I scaled two barbed-wire fences and ran down the row of kennels, wishing mightily that I could liberate all the unfortunates housed there. Spotting my girls, I unlocked their 'cells' and carried them over the fences to freedom. By the time my absence was discovered, Mannie, Helga, and I were enjoying a blissful reunion in a motel 200 miles away."

In an unfortunate twist, David was recaptured a short time later and sentenced to four years in the maximum security San Quentin prison, classified as an "escape risk". In a recent letter to the ALFSG Canada (Toronto), David says that "Not for one second have I regretted my actions. I couldn't live with myself if I had done nothing." He has been involved with animal rights for a long time, but this recent experience has led him to "strongly believe that direct intervention is the only way to do things..."

David Firsching will be released near the end of '88, and in the meanwhile would love to hear from ALF supporters, "to learn from, and share ideas with..." On a cautionary note he writes, "I needn't remind you and your readers that mail here is randomly screened (so) be discreet in any mention of incriminating specifics."

We suggest not to mention at all about anything illegal. You can write to the following address:

M.D. Firsching
P.O.Box 12009
Tamal, CA 94974 USA

TORTURE IN NORTH AMERICA

Over 3 billion chickens are killed annually in the U.S., and over 10 million in Canada for consumption by humans. Their slaughter is the culmination of a pathetic existence devoid of the smallest comfort; an existence totally alien to their natural instincts, survival patterns, needs and desires.

Hatcheries which produce 'egg birds' kill all the male chicks by such means as suffocating them in plastic bags. Their remains become fertilizer or food for animals raised for fur. Immediately after hatching, 92% of the chicks are sold to giant battery farming corporations such as **Pillsbury, Safeway, Kroger, Kentucky Fried Chicken**, etc. These battery farms house up to one million laying hens each. At ten days old the chicks are debeaked, which entails the removal of the upper mandible or the entire tip of the chick's beaks. They are debeaked a second time at 20 weeks of age. The chickens are debeaked because the conditions under which they are raised are so stressful that they will often peck at a cage-mate until she is dead; a weaker chicken has no means of escape. The chicken's beak is a very sensitive and important part of a chicken; apart from the pain endured during removal, the bird has thereafter lost an extremely helpful member. The removal of the beak adds greatly to the frustration suffered the rest of their lives.

Battery cages are packed in long rows, one above the other, four or five tiers high. They are constructed solely of wire mesh, with the floor sloping toward the front to enable the eggs to roll out into the collection tray at the bottom. The birds are packed so tightly in these cages (4 or 5 per cage) that they will have between 1/4 and 1/3 of a square foot each - less than the size of a record album cover. They must climb over one another to reach water and food. They spend their entire lives standing on a wire floor which produces painful malformation of their feet; their claws grow so long they will often curl completely around the wire, trapping the bird for her lifetime (or resulting in slow death by starvation and dehydration if she gets caught away from the food and water. Abscesses form on the birds' breasts and the tail feathers are usually rubbed away exposing red, sore skin. Even if they were alone in the cage it would still only allow enough room to stretch one wing at a time; if one chicken moves the others are compelled to do so. Many are lost through suffocation or being crushed by fellow inmates. Allowances are made by the producers for these losses - up to 20% death rate is normal under these conditions.

One person will usually be responsible for approximately 70,000 birds. The only individual care given is the removal of dead birds. Illness and disease go undetected in the massive units. They are plagued by parasites; flies are attracted to the strong smell of ammonia from the droppings which accumulate beneath the wire mesh floor of the cages prior to periodic removal (about once a year). Frequent use of insecticides is needed to combat these pests. The aforementioned points coupled with the high density of dust and poor ventilation are great contributing factors to the chronic respiratory diseases commonly found among the birds. The largest portion of deaths are credited to cancer (heart, lung, ovary, kidney), digestive and liver related diseases. A good percentage of the birds merely lose the will to struggle further, give up and die.

Food and water are automatically dispensed at the front of the cages. The food is comprised of various substances including recycled poultry manure and unsaleable parts of slaughtered chickens. The cosmetic Xanthophyll is added to the feed to darken the pale yolks of the eggs, and to increase the yellow colour of the chickens' skins, making them more attractive to the consumer. Small quantities of antibiotics are continuously fed to the chickens to promote growth, and at the slightest sign of disease the dosage is increased. When their laying days are over (about 2 years) the chickens' worn out bodies are suitable only for sale to soup manufacturing companies (often **Campbell's**) or for use in chicken pot-pies, etc. The natural lifespan of a chicken is about 12 years.

Apart from laying hens, another side of the business lies with so-called 'broiler chickens'. These birds exist under the same horrific conditions as the layers, but for a shorter period of time (about 9 weeks) before reaching the desired weight for slaughter. One of the largest producers of broilers is **Ralston Purina**. Here the object is to produce the biggest bird in the shortest possible time, at the lowest cost to the industry.

Lighting is used to simulate night and day, and is switched on and off at frequent intervals to encourage the birds to eat and sleep in quick succession, and thus rapidly gain weight.

Further exploitation of the hen is seen with the university studies to produce a featherless chicken. This would curb costs to the producer by eliminating the time consumed by feather removal after slaughter. If successfully developed, this would, of course, render the chicken's entire body vulnerable to sores and abscesses from continuous rubbing against the cage walls.

The industry's alternative method of broiler production finds the chickens uncaged but in a huge building with thousands, often tens of thousands, of other chickens. Chickens ordinarily have a highly developed social system, which humans term a 'pecking order'; the chickens can only manage, however, to maintain this system in numbers under one hundred. When housed in the thousands, the birds are hysterical, stressed, and often cannibalistic. When a human enters the house, all of the birds crowd on top of one another in the far end of the building, often killing those on the bottom of the pile by suffocation.

Sources: Feminism and Animals' Rights; PETA, Seattle.

FACTS ON K.F.C.

Today in Canada, virtually all of the poultry, eggs, pork, veal, milk and by-products (yogurt, cheese, ice cream, etc.) come from animals confined in grey, steel, mechanized, factory-like buildings that are scattered throughout the southern third of the entire country, from Victoria, B.C. to Charlottetown, P.E.I. Ten million confined laying and broiler birds are the 'meat' of Canada's poultry industry. The Ontario Chicken Marketing Board reports that in this province alone (Ont.) there are 700 commercial broiler farms and 804 egg laying operations. These flocks of 10,000 to 50,000 birds are all reared on feed which is totally foreign to their natural diets, and is laced with chemicals and growth-inducing drugs and hormones.

The broiler chickens spend their 8 week lives crowded together on slatted floors over manure pits, or, less commonly, stacked in cages like those of the egg laying hens. At first, bright lights flood the building to encourage feeding. Later, in the few days left before their slaughter, when each fully-grown bird has space about the area of a magazine page, the lights are kept very dim to reduce fighting. Crews of 'catchers' wade in and stuff them into crates, which they are held in during transportation. Arriving at the processing plant, they are removed, decapitated, bled, scalded, plucked, cleaned, dressed and packed for the supermarket or fast-food outlet.

Factory farming is capital-intensive rather than labour-intensive, and prefers chemical and technical hardware to human input. In the fifties, traditional farmers were caught in the industrialization of farming that forced many of them into 'bigness' - mechanization and specialization - or risk losing the family farm (which many did).

In Canada, Scott Restaurant Inc. is a perfect example of how agribusiness monopolism through "vertical contracting" - buying up and down the food producing, processing and retailing system - develops market muscle and farm control through restraints on competition. **Scott's**, which owns **Kentucky Fried Chicken** (as well as **Black's** and **Brown's Cameras**), also owns its own slaughterhouses and is buying farms as well as contracting with owners. Essentially, Scott's sets the price for chicken meat in Canada.

The shift from small mixed farms to huge multinational agribusiness corporations has resulted in the development of a cruel, environmentally destructive system that relies on living beings to produce enormous profits, in every step of the process that farms animals into food. Productivity and profit override any concern for the individual human or non-human.

In January 1984, Dr. S.P. Oldham, a federal meat inspector with the Department of Agriculture, produced an inspection report of a Scott's Poultry Packing Plant in Victoria, B.C., in which he cited: "...an employee urinating on a packing house floor ... another instructed to package condemned meat ... employees dumping one of their co-workers into a tank full of slush ... (and) another stabbing of a live fowl with a pitch fork ..." He concluded: "... the poultry is of questionable wholesomeness."

The intensive farming systems of 1987 are an issue that should concern everyone. While protection of animals is of growing interest to many, the destructive impact of agribusiness - from the factory farm to the fast food outlet - is a many-facetted issue, dealing with the environment, human health, humane treatment, sound farming, and ethical business practices.

-Animals' Diary 1986

SUPERMARKET SABOTAGE

This article was submitted to us by an ALFSG member in the U.S. Standard Disclaimer: The ideas expressed here are for your consideration and general interest only. The ALFSG does not advocate breaking the law!!!

Supermarkets are just cemetaries for dead animals. Pigs, cows, chickens and fish are wrapped in tight-fitting plasticized suits and placed in refrigerated coffins until someone plucks them up and prepares them for cremation in a kitchen oven, frying pan or food-processor.

Supermarkets are the last link in a long chain of animal exploitation for profit. If individuals can intervene in this process and force shoppers and store owners to question the value - ethical, ecological and financial - of continuing to consume and sell animal products, that action will translate into less suffering and death. During a lifetime, an average meat-eater will consume about 8 cows, 36 sheep, 36 pigs, 550 chickens, and half a ton of fish. Thus, hundreds of animals are saved each time someone switches to a non-violent diet.

Identify Animal Death

Tell people exactly what a hamburger, steak, or pork chop is. "Meat" is a nice, misleading way of saying dead animal flesh. When you're in a supermarket, take along a bunch of stickers that read:

> ## ANIMALS SUFFERED TO MAKE THIS PRODUCT

> ## WARNING: THIS PACKAGE CONTAINS DEAD ANIMALS.

Apply them to packages of meat, dairy items and products containing animal ingredients. Doing so educates customers and makes the managers, owners and butchers think about what they are doing and what customers want (or don't want). Employees will often open up the packages when they spot them to see if the product has been tampered with. That action seems pretty funny when you think about it because all you've done is identify the main ingredient in the product (a dead animal) or explained how it was produced (through animal suffering). It's equivalent to putting a label on a box of spaghetti which says, "This product contains noodles."

Instead of placing stickers randomly on animal products, you may want to target specific items. This approach has a number of benefits. First, you can call attention to products associated with the greatest amount of suffering, such as veal and battery eggs, and work to eliminate the sale of these items. In addition, the assault on the supermarket will appear to be more focused and you or a member of your group may be able to pressure the manager into removing the products from the shelf more easily.

Show them that Meat is the Message

Another good tactic is to load up hand baskets and shopping carts with meat and other animal products and then leave them sitting in a different isle in the store. The baskets and carts will only appear to be temporarily unattended as when someone goes to get an item which he or she has forgotten. Be sure to load up with fresh cuts of flesh because when these products sit for a period of time without refrigeration, they spoil and have to be discarded. You can quicken this process by slitting the cellophane wrapper with your fingernail, exposing the fish or meat to the air.

Whenever possible, it's good to put stickers on at least a few of the items that you've

sabotaged so that managers and employees will recognize the political nature of the action and not mistake it for a prank. Place leaflets about factory farming and vegetarianism (and veganism) in the carts and baskets to educate people further. Make certain that the flyers don't contain the name of an individual or group who might be held responsible for the action (or any fingerprints, if possible). You may, however, want to create a fake name to put on the leaflets.

Raising animals to be slaughtered and sold for profit *stinks*. So why not let supermarkets know that. Engage people's senses by creating a *real* stench. This can be accomplished by hiding fresh meat on the back of shelves behind paper towels, rolls of toilet paper, cat litter and other items large enough to block visibility. After a few days the meat will begin to rot and smell, and people will complain to the managers or, better yet, stop shopping there. Again, it's helpful to put stickers on the packages and, whenever possible, to tear part of the wrapper to expedite spoilage. Canned items can be sabotaged by using a small can opener to puncture an air opening in the lid.

Use Theater to Fight Murder

As you're leaving, you can call additional attention to the role of supermarkets in the chain of animal exploitation. Load up a cart full of meat and other animal products and then get in a check-out line. If you're asked why you're buying so much meat, say that you're planning a large cookout. When the cashier has totaled your "purchase", dig frantically in your pockets and then "suddenly" realize that you forgot to bring money. At that point, a friend or someone in your group could start telling everyone around about the animal suffering and death associated with the products in the shopping cart and mention the health dangers of eating meat, the waste of energy in production, the inefficiency of using grain to raise livestock, and so on. You can then show sympathy to these arguments and decide that you don't want the products after all. Your action may help to persuade others who are listening and watching the theatrics or at least make them think twice about what they are buying. In any case, it will raise awareness and inconvenience the supermarket when employees have to return the products to their original location. This is just one possible scenario for action. Improvise and experiment.

Suggestions

Lookout for store mirrors above the meat coffins and keep an eye out for employees who wander about restocking shelves. Many stores now have video surveillance cameras as well to catch shoplifters.

Switch to different stores temporarily if you think the ones that you have been acting in are on the alert. But keep continual pressure on as many places as possible.

Enter and exit the store by yourself or in small groups of two or three people so as not to attract attention. Most of the actions can be performed by yourself or with a single friend.

Choose days and times when the store is most crowded. That way you won't stand out as a shopper. Fridays and shortly after the work day has ended (5 - 7 pm) are usually good times.

Keep the pressure on a supermarket in as many ways as possible. Someone not taking part in the actions should meet with store managers in your area to discuss the animal products that he or she stocks. That person can provide the manager with information on animal exploitation, factory farming and cruelty-free products which the store could sell. The individual could also tell the manager that many people plan to boycott the store until it stops selling veal, battery eggs, or other chosen products. (If a store is being harassed then anyone approaching the manager may automatically be suspect and hassled by the police. Be careful!)

McDONALD'S FEELIN' THE PRESSURE

For the past 3 years, Greenpeace (London) - a group independent of Greenpeace Int. Inc. - has put out a call for a day of action against McDonald's on Oct. 16, also known as World Food Day. Activists from around the world have responded to this idea by utilizing tactics ranging from leafletting to smashing in their windows. The goal is to raise the public awareness about the destructive nature of this multi-million dollar corporation, and its harmful effects on people, animals, and the planet. Greenpeace (London) have also produced a leaflet entitled "What's Wrong With McDonald's?" which many groups and organizations, including the ALFSG Canada (Toronto), have distributed and reprinted.

Now it seems that McDonald's is a bit upset over the adverse publicity they're receiving. In England, where this campaign started, McDonald's has threatened many groups, including the BBC, with lawsuits unless they retract certain allegations made against them, and publish apologies. Greenpeace (London) has received similar threats but have ignored them without consequence.

One organization being harrassed by 'McDeath' is Veggies Ltd. of England. Veggies reprinted the Greenpeace leaflet, and were subsequently asked by McDonald's lawyers to retract the parts which referred to the destruction of tropical rainforests for cattle grazing and paper bags. The leaflet also mentions anti-union policies, the poisoning of people from the food, and the torture and murder of animals, among other issues.

A British magazine, *Peace News*, published an article about the 'McDeath' intimidation campaign against Veggies in their Oct. 30, 1987 issue, which also stated that Veggies is "researching the validity of the McDonald's case." In response to this article, and that statement in particular, McDonald's have issued new threats. Their lawyers' letter says, "In view of what has appeared in Peace News, the situation is obviously now more serious." They threaten High Court pro-

ceedings unless Veggies publish a retraction them to retract the allegation that McDonald's is responsible for the torture and murder of millions of animals! This is an incredibly ludicrous request, unless of course, their hamburgers are indeed not made from dead animals; though if it was discovered that they were all chemicals and nitrates, no one should be too surprised!

Veggies have decided not to give in to this multi-death corporation pressure and are prepared to fight a court battle. If they do, they will need a lot of money, knowing that in 1986 McDonald's made $1.32 million profit a day, and can afford to fight back their opponents.

In further news, *Animals' Agenda* reported in their Oct. 1987 issue that McDonald's have been forced to withdraw advertisements which claimed that their hamburgers were nutritious. The Attorneys General of Texas, California and New York threatened to sue McDonald's following a research project by a grade 3 class in League City, Texas, which discovered that McDonald's claims about the nutritional value of their food didn't match the facts. The students' research prompted action from Texas Attorney General Jim Mattox who said, "McDonald's food is, as a whole, not nutritious." When the two other states threatened lawsuits McDonald's withdrew the ads voluntarily.

The campaign to remove McDonald's advertising was co-ordinated by the Centre for Science in the Public Interest (CSPI), which was also successful in causing McDonald's to withdraw another ad claiming its Chicken McNuggets were made from 100% chicken. CSPI discovered that the McNuggets were cooked in beef fat.

Further information about McDonald's is available from the ALFSG Canada (Toronto), Greenpeace (London), 5 Caledonia Rd., London SE I, England, or CSPI, 1501 16th St. NW, Washington, DC 20036 USA.

The Politics Of Food

As animal liberationists fighting against the use of animals for the supposed good of the human species, we must be able to recognize that Western culture has traditionally attempted to treat the symptoms of its illnesses, be they physical, psychological, spiritual, or economic, rather than curing them at their sources. One of the most important sources is the food we eat. Given the obvious ethical reasons for not eating animals, we can begin to see food as preventive medicine. We are often responsible for our own diseases, for disease often results from our choice of food. According to what we choose to eat, we develop health or sickness. When we fail to supply the body with the proper nourishment it becomes weak, inviting disease. We then may turn to the medical establishment for drugs which have been researched on animals to treat mainly the symptoms of what could have been prevented with the proper diet. Such a diet is that of vegetarianism. This perspective also lends strong support to the argument in favour of Alternative Medicine such as Homeopathy, which is not tested on animals, but on human beings. Although too lengthy a topic to go into detail about here, Homeopathic remedies are not, except for a few exceptions, made with any animal products. Therefore, we can see the truth on many different levels, in the belief that life need not be destroyed to give life to another.

We assume that Animal Rights activists understand that it is hypocritical to have a diet that is not vegetarian while fighting for the liberation of animals. In speaking of vegetarianism\veganism, we see veganism as the goal of any serious and sincere animal activist. We cannot hope to end speciesism in others and continue to contribute to the oppression of animals in our own lives, no matter how small that contribution may seem in the context of the work we do.

A vegetarian\vegan diet is often assumed to be difficult to practice and receive the nutrients needed by the body. It is difficult in that one must de-construct socialized ways of eating and learn new ones. Animal liberationists have already begun to de-construct forms of socially sanctioned, subconsciously ingrained oppression.

Learning to eat cruelty-free should not be difficult as an extension of this awareness.

In the following paragraphs, we will provide the basic info needed to follow a nutritionally sound, total vegetarian diet. Firstly, we will go over some of the arguments other than the ethical ones that support vegetarianism. These will be divided into the subjects of health & practical reasons, world hunger, and the environment.

CHICKEN is a VEGETABLE #1

Some people think CHICKEN is a vegetable

So you're a vegetarian... you can eat chicken can't you?

Total Vegetarian or Vegan

A total vegetarian is one that does not eat animals or animal products in any form whatsoever. This diet consists of mainly fruits and vegetables, beans and whole grains, nuts and seeds, seaweed, etc. No dairy products are included in this diet. Those who include dairy products in their diet are ovo-lacto vegetarians, ovo - eggs, lacto - dairy. To be vegan is to follow a vegetarian diet and lifestyle using no animal products derived from leather, horn, or other animal parts. For ovo-lacto vegetarians who do not feel ready to make the step to a total vegetarian or vegan lifestyle, free-range dairy products are available at most health food stores. For those who are ready to eliminate dairy products and eggs from their diet, the following should be observed.

1. Have at least one serving of each of these foods each day:
Legumes - soybeans, pinto, kidney, or chick peas. etc.
Whole grains - rice, millet, oats, wheat, etc.
Leafy dark greens - spinach, chard, watercress, etc.
2. Have at least three servings of each of these foods every day:
Tofu or soy milk, soybeans, other soy products, almonds, cashews, sunflower seeds, sesame seeds, peanuts, raisins, dried fruit.
3. Have two to four servings of each of these foods every week:
Lecithin, nutritional yeast B, molasses (unsulphured).
4. Have at least once a week:
Cooked/raw carrots, broccoli or other green vegetable, cabbage or cauliflower, cucumbers, zucchini or green pepper, potatoes, onions, bananas, raisins, millet or other grains, molasses, engevita or 'good tasting' yeast, lecithin, acidophilus or tofu.

5. Eat three or more times a week:
Spinach or other dark leafy greens, lettuce, apples, oranges or other fresh citrus fruit, dried fruit, nuts and seeds (raw), brown rice or other whole grains, legumes, whole-grain cereal, natural oils, fresh 100% real juices, vitamin B-12 rich foods and calcium rich foods. (ed note: for more information on B-12, see "Why Vegan".)

Protein

Vegetarians worry about where to get their protein from. Every natural food except for sugars and oils contain some protein. The concentrated vegetarian sources of protein include legumes, soy bean products, nuts and seeds, leafy green vegetables, whole grains and dairy products if used. Many nuts and vegetables are nearly complete proteins in themselves, and when taken in combination with other certain incomplete proteins they become complete. Many bean and grain combinations have equal or more protein value than meat. The main functions of proteins in the body are to furnish energy, provide enzymes for digestion, provide antibodies and antitoxins for resistance against disease, and build and maintain the body cells.

Calcium

Calcium is a concern for those who eliminate dairy products from their diet. There are many sources of calcium in the vegetarian diet such as almonds, sesame seeds, dark leafy greens, soy products, seaweed, etc. And on a plant based diet one needs less calcium than on a meat based diet, because too much protein causes a depletion of calcium in the system

Continued next page

Vegetarianism and Health

1. The human digestive system and other bodily functions are in every way like those of fruit eating animals and very unlike those of carnivorous animals. Just like other vegetarian animals, the human digestive system is twelve times the length of the body, (in meat-eaters it is 3 times as long), we sweat through our skin (not our tongue), we drink water by suction and our tooth and jaw structure is vegetarian. From these physical facts it can be deduced that humans must have evolved for millions of years living on fruits, nuts, grains and vegetables.
2. The Journal of the American Medical Association has reported that a vegetarian diet can prevent 90-97% of heart diseases.
3. Over 50% of North Americans are overweight, while on the average, vegetarians weigh about 20 pounds less than meat eaters.
4. Meat moves extremely slowly through the human digestive tract which is not designed for a meat diet. The lack of fiber in meat has made chronic constipation a common problem in our society. Present research indicates that appendicitis, diverticulitis, cancer of the colon, heart disease and obesity are all reduced with a diet high in natural fiber.

5. Plants provide, on average, more than twice the amount of vitamins and minerals provided by meat and fish.
6. The kidneys of meat-eaters have to do three times the amount of work to eliminate poisonous nitrogen compounds in meat than do the kidneys of vegetarians.
7. When an animal is killed, the proteins in its body coagulate and substances called ptomaines are formed. These ptomaines result in the extremely rapid decomposition and putrifaction of the animal flesh. As it takes meat about 5 days to pass out of the body (vegetarian food takes only 1 1/2 days), the disease causing products of decaying meat are in constant contact with the digestive organs. The habit of eating meat in its characteristic state of decomposition creates a poisonous state in the colon and wears out the intestinal tract prematurely.
8. Scientists at Harvard have found that the average blood pressure of vegetarians was significantly lower than that of a comparable group of non-vegetarians.
9. Animal flesh contains large amounts of certain fats, such as cholesterol which do not break down well in the human body. They begin to line the walls of the meat eater's blood vessels. As a result high blood pressure, strokes and heart attacks occur.

10. The vegetarian avoids the various drugs, chemicals, pesticides, and dyes commonly found in meat. Meat-eaters consume drugs like penicillin and tetracycline on a regular basis.
11. Animals are shot full of dangerous hormones, drugs, and chemicals. When they are slaughtered they are in fear and pain. These feelings trigger the release of these stored poisons and toxins directly into their systems, which in turn are ingested by the meat eater. The animals slaughtered are often diseased. Meat processors are allowed to use any diseased animals, even cancerous ones, as long as they remove all the parts of the animals that are obviously diseased. The life expectancy of vegetarian groups studied, such as Seventh Day Adventists and Trappist Monks, is longer than meat eaters.

Sources: Parham, Barbara, 1979, What's Wrong With Eating Meat; The Lancet,

Compiled by: **Toronto Vegetarian Association**, 28 Walker Ave., Toronto, Ont. M4V 1G2 Canada.

Food...
the Environment   • World Hunger

1. Meat production is responsible for a high rate of water consumption. Between 2500 and 6000 gallons of water are required to produce one pound of meat, while only 60 gallons are needed for one pound of wheat and 200-250 gallons for one pound of rice.

2. Plant foods yield about 10 times as much protein per acre as meat does.

3. Animal waste in the United States amounts to 2 billion tons annually, equivalent to the waste of 2 billion people, or more than one-half the world's population. The concentration of from 10,000 to 50,000 animals (or up to 250,000 poultry) in a single feedlot results in an abundance of potential fertilizer far exceeding the capacity of the surrounding farmland. As it is not economical to transport this waste, most of it finds its way into our water systems. This leads to the depletion of oxygen, it encourages eutrophication and contaminates the water with pathogens.

4. The production of livestock creates ten times more pollution than residential areas and three times more than industry.

5. Since about 1910, North American agriculture has been using more fossil fuel energy than it produces in food energy. Plant agriculture uses 10 to 1000 times less energy than livestock agriculture. A nationwide switch to a diet emphasizing whole grains, fresh fruits and vegetables, plus limits on the export of non-essential fatty foods, would save enough energy to cut our imported oil requirements by over 60%.

The supply of renewable energy, such as wood and hydroelectric, would increase 120-150%.

6. About 80% of the world's agricultural land is used for feeding animals and about 20% for feeding people directly.

7. Overgrazing and excessive ploughing have caused the rapid erosion of soil. In the U.S. alone, the annual net loss of cropland topsoil is about 2 1/2 billion tons, equivalent to losing 4 million acres of cropland which had 4 inches of topsoil.

8. The conversion of forests to grazing land poses a serious threat to the world's increasing demand for wood and paper products. In the developing world over 80% of people rely on wood for energy. Forests favourably affect regional water resources, improve soil and climate and provide wilderness and recreational areas. If current trends continue, the world is likely to face a major wood shortage by the year 2010. As demands for animal foods and products continue, more deforestation will take place.

9. Calorie for calorie, it takes 11 times as much energy to produce meat and other fatty foods as it does to produce grains and other carbohydrate-rich foods.

Source: The Toronto Vegetarian Association.

1. The food wasted by animal production in the affluent nations would be sufficient, if properly distributed, to end both the hunger and malnutrition throughout the world.
2. In a single year 18 million tons of protein is made inaccessible to humans. This is equivalent to 90% of the annual world protein deficit. It would provide 12 grams of usable protein per day for every person in the world.
3. Imagine yourself sitting down to an eight ounce steak. Then imagine the room filled with 45 to 50 people with empty bowls in front of them. For the "feed cost" of your steak, each of their bowls could be filled with a full cup of cooked cereal grains.
4. About 80% of the world's agricultural land is used for feeding animals and about 20% for feeding people directly.
5. Plant foods yield about ten times as much protein per acre as meat does.
6. As the demand for meat increases, rich nations are buying more and more grain to feed pigs and cattle. Grain supplies, once used to feed people, are sold to the highest bidder, and countless human beings are condemned to starvation. "The wealthy can compete for the poor man's food; the poor cannot compete at all."
7. A cow must be fed 21 pounds of protein to produce 1 pound of protein for human consumption.

8. If Canadians cut their meat consumption by 10% for one year, it would free for human consumption one million tons of grain. This would feed 5 million grain-eating people for a year.

9. We are importing from starving nations large quantities of grain and other foods that are then fed to our animals instead of to the populations who produced them.

10. Factory-farming is producing a population explosion of animals as providers of human food that is outstripping the human population explosion in competition for the basic plant foods.

11. While millions of people all over the world are starving, a few rich people are wasting vast amounts of land, water, and grain in order to eat meat, which is slowly destroying their bodies. North Americans consume over a ton (2,000 lbs.) of grain per person per year (through feed for meat-producing livestock), while the rest of the world averages about 400 pounds of grain.

Sources: Giehl, Kudley, 1979, Vegetarianism, A Way of Life; Moore Lappe, Francis, 1974, Diet for a Small Planet; Tyson, Jon Wynne, 1979, Food For A Future; Toronto Globe and Mail, 1974.

Compiled by: T.V.A.

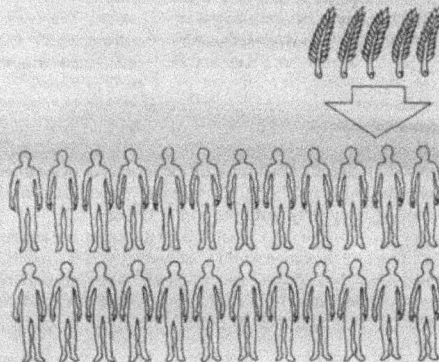

Animals Diary 1986

ANIMAL DEALERS LIST

For your convenience, we compiled a short list of 13 animal dealers. With the exception of one, they are all breeders of animals for the research industry. We simply could not resist including a death train company in this list. Some of these companies have toll-free numbers. Others will gladly accept business via collect calls. Most are located in populous areas, and their real addresses as opposed to their mailing addresses can be found in the phone book.

You may wish to use this list for information gathering purposes, ask for a list of clients and annual reports, or simply to have fun with. Remember that animals are involved, so don't order a bunch to an unknown address unless you are fully equipped to liberate them. Whatever you do, do it to the best of your ability, these exploiters deserve all they can get and more.

Associated Rabbit Industries
1040 Central Street
East Bridgewater, MA 02333
671-378-2309

Animal Express
(overnight animal delivery)
P.O. Box 268
Lansdale, PA 19446
800-624-2232 ext. K-475

Bantin and Kingman, Inc.
"our mice get everywhere"
3403/3421 Yale Way
Fremont, CA 94538
415-490-3036

Buckshire Corp
(primates-wild caught, colony bred, surgical modification)
P.O. Box 155
2025 Ridge Road
Perkasie, PA 18944
215-257-0116 in PA: 800-645-3333

Charles River Breeding Laboratories
251 Ballardvale Street
Wilmington, MA 01887
617-658-6000
Charles River has a real 'cute' number for you to call: 800-LAB-RATS. It has an answering machine after hours - WHAT FUN!
Harlan Sprague Dawley (over 40 different stocks and strains of rats, mice, hamsters and guinea pigs)
P.O. Box 29176
Indianapolis, IN 46229
317-894-7521

Hazelton (beagles, conditioned primates and New Zealand white rabbits)
P.O. Box 7200
Denver, PA 17517
800-345-4114

Hilltop Lab Animals, Inc. (rodents)
Hilltop Drive
Scottdale, PA 15683
412-887-8480 /800-245-6921

Laboratory Research Ent. (beagle specialists)
6321 South 6th Street
Kalamazoo, MI 49009
616-375-0482

Lampire Biological Labs (sheep, horses, goats, donkeys, cows, mice, rabbits, fowl and primates)
P.O. Box 170
Pipersville, PA 18947
215-795-2838

Marshall Farms
(beagles and ferrets)
R.D. 1, Box 91
North Rose, NY 14516
315-587-2295

Thomas D. Morris, Inc. (pigs)
4001 Millender Mill Road
Reistertown, MD 21136

White Eagle (beagles - employs a 'puppy petter' team to pacify their dogs)
2003 Lower State Road
Doylestown, PA 18901

Reprinted from: *The Human/Animal Liberation Front News.*

Sue Real

ACTION REPORTS

Barrie, Ont.
Jan. 17, 1987: Dyck's Meat Market was attacked twice with firebombs, causing over $1,000 damage.

Kitchener, Ont.
May 19, 1987: Kaufman Furs, Kosky Furs, and Brodey-Draimin Furs were spray painted.

London, Ont.
Aug. 30, 1986: Four locks glued at the loading doors of Klyman Furs and Meyer-Epstein Furs.
Oct. 23, 1986: The Fur Boutique was fire-bombed with $1200 damage. Other fur stores in the area have been targetted with rubber cement in their locks and paint on their walls.

Montreal, Quebec
Feb. 26, & March 8, 1987: Delicatessans and butcher shops on Boul. St. Laurent were spraypainted.
March 16, 1987: These shops again attacked with super glue in the locks and posters saying 'La viande est le meurtre - meat is murder' were put on the windows.
April 2, 1987: Brick through the window of one of the most 'visually horrifying' of these shops.

Toronto, Ont.
1986
April - July: The windows of the following fur stores were broken: Furs by Finn on Eglinton Ave., Four Seasons Fur Co. Ltd.; Gimpex Ltd. on Spadina Ave.; East York Furs on Pape Ave. (twice); Golden Diamond Furs on Danforth Ave. (twice); and Barrington's Fur on Lakeshore Rd. East, (Mississauga).
July: Six furs slashed in Eaton's, Toronto Eaton Centre.
Aug.: Three pigeons freed in Kensington Market.
Oct. 16: This day is recognized as World Food Day, and every year it's declared by **Greenpeace London** as a Day of Action against McDonald's. The following McDonald's were disrupted: 584 Bloor St.W. - fire alarm pulled; Queen and Ashdale St. - stink-bombed; 239 Yonge St. - stink-bombed; Yonge and College St. - stink-bombed; Yonge and Dundas St. - fire alarm pulled; 970 Gerrard St. E. - spray painted; 3301 Kingston Rd. - spray painted; 2870 Eglinton St. E. - spray painted; 1925 Victoria Park - spray painted. A bomb threat was also made to McDonald's headquarters in Don Mills (results unknown). The following communique was received:

McMURDER
McDonald's is directly responsible for the destruction of the tropical rainforests upon which we depend for the air we breathe. Rainforests are cleared at the rate of 75,000 acres per day causing the extinction of one species per day. At this rate, rainforests and all the life within them will be completely destroyed within 15 years.
McDonald's is also directly responsible for the torture and murder of untold millions of animals for mass consumption. The results of their production cause starvation world-wide for millions of humans. Not to mention the non-existent nutritional value of their food, and the alarming rate of heart disease and cancer in direct relation to the consumption of meat and high sodium intake.
We are disrupting business as usual today, 'WORLD FOOD DAY', because the urgency of the situation requires an immediate solution.
WE WON'T STOP UNTIL YOU DO!!
Taking responsibility,
DIRECT McACTION

November: The following communique was received:
ALF TORONTO PRESS RELEASE
Sometime in September a small group of friends who have been active in animal liberation have joined together in Toronto as an ALF cell. We carry out actions against McDonald's, Burger King, Wendy's, Harvey's, Kentucky Fried Chicken, as well as various butchers, furriers, and slaughterhouses.
The actions are either spraypainting the buildings and property or smashing windows or both. We try to get together at least once a week and we have averaged lately anywhere from five to twelve targets in one night. Compared to England's average of 40 actions per week, we feel pretty good about our efforts. We will try to keep the various media updated on our actions.
In the early morning of November 5th we attacked 2 McDonald's, a Burgerking, a Kentucky Fried Chicken and a butcher. The week prior we hit a total of 12 targets - our largest yet in a single night! Most of these included window smashing with either the use of rocks or a slingshot.
We don't plan to stop with these small actions (or what some would consider as small), but plan to increase and broaden our range of both targets and tactics. Patience, time and practice are all it takes!
-(Another) ALF Toronto Cell

Dec. 1: The property of the following were attacked: Caledonia Meats had its windows smashed, four tires slashed, and trucks spraypainted; Gross Slaughterhouse had 16 tires slashed on four trucks and a smashed windshield and had to shut down for half a day; Royce Dupont Chicken killers had their windows smashed and walls spraypainted; Gallery Furs had their window smashed and walls spraypainted; McDonald's and Kentucky Fried Chicken were also attacked. $20,000 damage in total.
Dec. 8: Puddy Meats was spraypainted, and an attempt was made to destroy the delivery trucks, but only the tires were slashed.

1987
Jan. 11: Property of Carne Equina horse killers, on St. Claren's Rd. was attacked with spray paint and bricks through the windows, causing $3,000 damage.
Jan. 16: Carne horse killers attacked again, causing $3,000 damage. Kentucky Fried Chicken on Mt. Pleasant Rd. given the same treatment, $1,000 damage.
Jan. 18: The following properties were attacked: Cross Town Foods spraypainted and had windows smashed; A. Stork and Sons had trucks painted and tires slashed; Gross Slaughterhouse painted and tires slashed; Kentucky Fried Chicken spraypainted (Mt. Pleasant Rd.). Total damage $6,000 approx. It was outside this KFC on this date that the five activists were arrested.

Equina Horse butcher, Jan. 16/87

Continued on page 28

ACTION REPORTS

U S A

1986

Oct. 26, Oregon: At the University of Oregon, two science laboratories in seperate buildings had their walls and equipment spraypainted with the initials ALF, 144 animals were liberated and equipment was smashed. Damage to the equipment was estimated at $100,000. Appox. 18 cats, 24 rabbits, 12 hamsters and 100 rats were among the freed animals. (*Please note*: see article "Activist Arrested for Lab Raid.")

Nov. 30, Arizona: Several fur stores were targetted: Cele Peterson, which had 6 fur coats slashed with a razor; Goldwater's, which had manure placed in the pocket of one of the coats, Russek's, which had red paint splashed on the front door; and Mr. Brett Furs & Fashions, which had stickers saying 'Closed due to animal cruelty' put on the windows. 5 other fur stores were also hit.
Nov. 24, California: 127 turkeys were liberated from two farms, equipment was damaged, including sugar poured into farm machinery gas tanks, slashed tires, damage to blinds over the turkey prisons, glue in time-clocks of animal-area ventilating, and slogans were painted on the walls. About $12,000 damage was caused. All of the turkeys were placed in safe, permanent, and caring homes where they will be allowed to live out the remainder of their lives in peace and freedom.

Dec. 7, Rockville, MD: 4 baby chimpanzees were liberated from the laboratories of SEMA Inc., by **True Friends**. They were destined for research on such diseases as hepatitis and AIDS. (*Please note*: see article "Chimps Stolen by Animal Liberationists".)

1987

Jan. 19, Williamsburg, VA: 6 mice were liberated from the psychology labs at William & Mary College.

April 16, Davis, CA: $3.5 million fire set in a veterinary diagnostic laboratory under construction at the University of California at Davis. 18 cars at the University were spraypainted and had their tires slashed, as well as walls being painted. The **Animal Rights Militia** claimed responsiblity for the action, saying the action was retaliation in the name of thousands of animals tortured each year in campus labs.
April 17, Delaware: 40 laying hens from a battery egg facility were liberated by the Farm Freedom Fighters and the Easter Bunny. The hens were adopted into caring, loving homes.
April 18, Riverside, CA: 50 rabbits liberated from a breeding farm by the ALF.
April 19, Bloomington, LA: 115 rabbits were liberated from a rabbit breeding station.

June 13, Davis, CA: Five turkey vultures liberated by the ALF from the Raptor Centre at the University of California Davis campus.

Aug. 13, Las Vegas, NV: Three goats from the biology department of the University of Nevada were liberated by the ALF. The goats were to be used for dehydration experiments, to study how their bodies store water over long periods of time.
Aug. 25, Maryland: 28 cats and 7 African minature pigs were liberated from the Beltsville Agricultural Research Centre. The liberators, the **Band of Mercy**, left behind slogans, pamphlets, a poem and vegetarian recipes. The cats were being used in parasite experiments.

Sept. 1, Santa Clara, CA: A fire at the San Jose Veal Company caused $7000 damage, and was claimed by the **Animal Rights Militia**.

Nov. 25, San Jose, CA: An empty cattle feed barn owned by Ferrara Meat Company was burned down for Thanksgiving, claimed by the **Animal Rights Militia**.
Nov. 27, Washington, DC: Windows smashed at the following fur stores: Miller's Furs and Rosendorf-Evans.
Nov. 27, Bethesda, MD: Windows smashed and red paint thrown at the following fur stores: Gartenhaus, Furs by Yianni, and Saks-Jandel, and Fred's Fur Vault. (*Please note*: see article "Direct Action Against Fur".)
Nov. 28, Santa Clara, CA: A fire destroyed a poultry warehouse owned by V. Melani, Inc., claimed by the ALF, causing $200,000 damage. "ALF" and "murderers" were spraypainted on the walls.

Dec. 5, Bethesda, MD: Fred's Fur Vault attacked again, windows smashed. $50,000 in damages over a period of a year and a half.

1988

Jan. 29, Irvine, CA: 13 beagles liberated from the University of California by the ALF. 12 were used in pollution experiments and one in windpipe experiments (this one had a diode in its skull for brain experiments). (*Please note*: see article "Dogs Liberated form Califorinia Lab.")

Rabbits and their rescuers

Animals' Agenda, July/Aug. '87

DIRECT ACTION AGAINST FUR

Washington, DC - Direct action against fur retailers is in full swing here and in neighbouring Maryland. In the early hours of November 27, 1987, five fur stores had their windows shot out, probably with the use of a slingshot. Later that same day, in broad daylight, Fred's Fur Vault in Bethesda, MD, had its window smashed, and was hit again on December 5, again in broad daylight. No one has been injured and no arrests have been made in any of the incidents.

Representatives of the Fur Vault, which is a national chain, told the Justice Department that they have paid $50,000 for repairs from direct action in the past year and a half. Thomas Riley, a public relations spokesperson for the $2 billion-a-year U.S. fur industry, has been hired by the Fur Retailers Information Council, a group set up by furriers to combat anti-fur sentiment. Riley said that Council members account for 80% of the industry, and have sought the help of federal authorities to stop the activists. They have also pressured outdoor advertising companies and threatened lawsuits over anti-fur ads.

Ecomedia Toronto -*Source*: Washington Post, Dec. 15, 1987

Tucson, AZ - Al Russek, owner of Russek's, an exclusive boutique, says "It's constant harrassment" which has forced him to stop selling furs, and he's tired of the activists' pressure. Since September 1984, activists have thrown red paint on the store, put nails in the customer parking lot, and glue in the locks, among other tactics. Russek claims to have received a bomb threat in November 1987, and he finally decided to board up his windows and get rid of the furs.

Ecomedia Toronto -*Source*: Arizona Daily Star, Dec. 29, 1987

DOGS LIBERATED FROM CALIFORNIA LAB

The **Animal Liberation Front** in California raided the University of California's Irvine campus on January 29, 1988, where they liberated 13 beagles, 12 of whom were being used to study the effects of air pollution on the lungs and on exercise. The 13th was being used for windpipe experiments - and had a diode protruding from his skull, used to attach electrodes for brain experiments. They had apparently backed up their van to the campus kennel, cut the fence, loaded the dogs in and drove away.

The head vivisector for the research group, Dr. Robert Phalen, attempted to justify the experiments in an interview with the *Los Angeles Times* (Jan. 31, 1988), by saying in typical research doublespeak, that the dogs were happy. "These are happy animals. I saw that animal with the diode just the other day and it was up and happy and wagging its tail." Vivisectors not only say that the animals are happy but that they don't feel any pain. What bullshit! Dr. Phalen also said, "(The dogs) breathe pollutants at levels similar to what we have in Los Angeles. These are non-destructive studies." How can anyone tell us with all seriousness that breathing pollution is non-destructive? He further states, "We work in levels that the animals can't even sense is destructive." Great! What the animal doesn't know won't hurt him!

We, in our great glorious industrial world, pollute the hell out of our environment, force animals to breathe the crap, and then tell us the dogs are happy because their tails are wagging, but it's okay because they don't know what's going on! Animal researchers are so far removed from humanity and compassion, and so far involved in the pseudo-science of multi-national drug corporations, that they can't see the forset for the trees. Dr. Phalen proves this when he said, in the same interview, referring to a dog in the same pollution study, "I took one home and she lived six more years ... *before dying of cancer.*"

The ALF said in a communique to the *L.A. Times*, "This liberation was to protest U.C.I.'s growing use of animals in fraudulent medical research, research nothing will come of except pain and misery to humans and non-humans alike." University officials said that there are more than 25,000 animals involved in experiments at U.C.I.

Source: Los Angeles Times, Jan. 31, 1988

ACTION REPORTS

AUSTRALIA

1986

Early Sept., Brisbane: A lamb was rescued from Queensland University Labs.

Sept. 18, Springvale: 3 dogs were rescued from the Springvale Dog Pound by the ALF. The dogs were to be sent to the Prahran Baker Institute for heart disease experiments.

Oct. 9, Melbourne: 14 stores that sell furs had their windows damaged with etching fluid, their locks glued, and their walls spraypainted. One store, Myers, was attacked previously in April, 1986, when they had $250,000 - $500,000 damage done to their windows. The April action was claimed by the **ALF** and this night of action was claimed by **Action For Animals** (AFA).

Dec. 15, Melbourne: A Balaclava fur store had $2,000 worth of stock damaged by **AFA** when red paint was squirted onto coats through a hole in the window made by a sling shot and a marble. The paint attack happened four days after the hole was made.

1987

Jan. 11, Melbourne: 52 mice and 2 rabbits were rescued from the Melbourne University's Microbiology building, by **AFA**. The mice were being used in 'eye bleeding' experiments. $2,000 damage was also caused to lab equipment.

March 18, Melbourne: 16 chickens were liberated from the Kambouris Poultry Farm by Action For Animals. 200 eggs were smashed and walls spraypainted. Three activists were arrested in connection to this raid. (*Please note*: see article "Three Activists Arrested in Australia".)

Mid-May, Tasmania: 2 fur and leather shop windows spray painted with "Animals Suffer for Human Vanity" and "Animals Suffer for Human Greed".

June 15, Melbourne: Montreal Furs had a window smashed, and a butcher next door had its locks glued.
June 17, Tasmania: Spray paint campaign with slogans on blank walls in busy areas, on a fur store, and on a perfume and cosmetic store.

July 16, Melbourne: 2 fur stores had "scum" daubed on their windows with etching cream, as well as a meat shop. All had locks glued.
July 26, Melbourne: 2 fur stores, a butcher, and a Kentucky Fried Chicken shop had their windows damaged with etching cream, and all locks were glued.

Aug. 5, Melbourne: A 6-tonne truck that delivers slaughtered chickens had its locks glued, sand put into the gas tank and cooling system, wind shield screen etched, a front tire slashed, and "death truck" spray painted.
Late Aug., Melbourne: 2 battery hens were liberated from a factory farm by **Action For Animals**, and are now in safe homes.

NEW ZEALAND

1986

Dec. 3, Lower Hutt: $60,000 damage was done to 2 meat trucks that were set alight, claimed by the ALF.
Dec. 12: A fire was set at a Hopuhopu piggery, and the building was gutted.
Dec. 26, Greenlane: A suspected bomb was discovered near an animal laboratory in Auckland's Greenlane Hospital, claimed by the ALF. It was blown up by explosives experts.

1987

May 3, Greenlane: Greenlane Hospital's animal laboratories were firebombed, claimed by the **ALF**. "ALF" was spray painted on a wall, and this action followed a raid a week earlier.
May 5: Windows were smashed at the Karori Park Butchery Deli and Wadestown Butchery.

1988

Feb. 21, Miramar: 4 butcher shop windows were smashed including one in Kilbirnie and one in Newlands.

Wadestown Butchery
-Evening Post 5/5/87

THREE ACTIVISTS ARRESTED IN AUSTRALIA

On the 20th March, 1987, Gary Rowson, Iain Banfield and Matthew Layton were arrested in their homes in connection with an **Action For Animal's** raid on the Kambouris Poultry Farm, when 16 battery hens were rescued and 200 eggs were smashed. The three men face over 40 charges, including: trespassing, theft (stealing 16 laying hens), criminal damage, and having in possession items for the purpose of damaging property. Gary and Iain were also charged with $6,000 damage done to Stephen Dattners Furs earlier in the year, and Iain was charged with having in his possession "items known to be compounds of an improvised explosive device".

The police anti-terrorist squad conducted a raid on the houses where the three men live, arresting them and ransacking their rooms. The filth seized anything relating to animal rights, as well as numerous other things. Each of the men were given bail on a $10,000 surety each, and they had to surrender their passports and report 3 times a week to a police station. Needless to say, they were not supplied with vegan food during their pre-bail incarceration.

Their pre-trial was initially scheduled to start on Oct. 12, 1987, but because of the huge number of exhibits (540!) it was reset for March 21, 1988!! Fortunately, they have

been able to obtain legal aid, but it will still end up costing them quite a lot of money (about $600 each). They have managed to get their reporting conditions dropped, and Gary has been allowed to go to England, although he has to hand over his passport when he returns to Australia. A conspiracy charge has also been added.

At their court hearings, police say that there has been over $1 million worth of damage caused by militant animal liberation activists over the past two years.

In response to the arrests, a support group was formed to help with their defence. The

Supporters' Group for Animal Activists have several aims: They will provide legal assistance to those involved in direct action for the benefit of animals; provide financial assistance to those fined or imprisoned as a result of direct action; provide financial assistance to the families of those imprisoned following direct action; and distribute a newsletter concerning direct actions throughout Australia and elsewhere (check out *FLN*'s Distribution list). The group's main priority currently is raising funds for Iain, Gary, and Matthew. Donations can be sent to: **Supporters' Group for Animal Activists**, P.O.Box 519, Eltham, 3095 Victoria, Australia.

ACTION REPORTS

INTERNATIONAL

Italy
1987
Butchers' and fur shop windows were smashed and circus marquees were slashed.
Jan. 2: 200 pigeons destined for a pigeon-shooting competition were liberated at Sestri Lavante.

Netherlands
1986
April 24: The **Animal Liberation Front** liberated 100 rats and mice for World Day for Lab Animals, from a breeding farm belonging to Central Animals Lab of the Catholic University.
July 8, Scherpenzeel: The ALF freed 30 pigs from a breeding facility. This particular breeding station was an experimental one, so pigs there were to be experimented on as well as sent to the slaugterhouses. The company that was hit - Esvoor - markets the battery cages the pigs were in.
Nov. 8, Arnhem: The ALF freed about 65 deer from the wild-concentration camp of the Van der Valk concern. The deer were driven to another estate. In a letter to the counsellors, the ALF requested asylum for the deer.

Sweden
1986
Nov. 18, Forsheda: Hundreds of foxes (silver and blue) were released into the forests from a fur farm.
Nov. 19, Malmo: 54 guinea pigs were rescued from a train at Malmo Central Stn.

1987
Feb. 26, Helsingborg: 15 dogs were rescued from a lab breeding farm.
April 22, Veberod: 16 crows and 4 rooks were released from a crowtrap in S. Sweden.
June 16, Stockholm: Windows were smashed at McDonald's and paint thrown in.
Sept. 10, Malmo: 39 guinea pigs were liberated from a goods train at Malmo Central Stn., on their way to a lab in Stockholm.

Sept. 22, Stockholm: 8 rabbits were rescued from the Institute of Zoology.
Sept. 26, Malmo/Lund: Swedish ALF raided a vivisection lab in Malmo, and while they were using a welding unit to get through a fire-proof door, a fire alarm went off and they had to leave. They then went to the University of Lund and rescued 8 rabbits from a lab there.
Oct. 6, Lund: A monkey (Saimiri Sciureus) was liberated from the Institute of Hygene and is now in a good home.

West Germany
1986
Sept. 19, Frankfurt: 2000 mink and some polecats were released from a fur farm in the village of Aurigen.
Sept. 21, Bavaria: 300 coypu were released from a fur farm.

1987
March 14, Karlsruhe: 25 cats and 2 dogs were liberated from a research lab at Karlsruhe University.
April 4, Bochum: 16 rabbits, 70 guinea pigs, 1 pregnant cat, 1 pregnant beagle and 3 beagle puppies were rescued from an animal dealer.
May 6, Dusseldorf: 70 beagles and 400 rats were rescued from Dusseldorf University. Files of information on the animal experiments carried out at the University were also taken, along with corpses of animals that had been experimented on and were found in a fridge. The corpses were displayed to the public in front of the Cologne Cathedral on May 7th.
June 11, Heidleberg: 3 beagles were liberated from a lab at Heidleberg University.
June 13, Bonn: Members of **Animal Peace** raided the Pathological Institute at Bonn University, liberating 180 rats.
June 21-28: A number of shooting stands were sawn down.
Aug. 22, Bochum: 120 guinea pigs, 60 rats and 6 rabbits were liberated from Bochum University. The rabbits were reported to be valued at $50,000 each(!).

(Please note: see "Light Sentences for German Liberators pg. 15)

Denmark
March 11, 1987, Copenhagen: Fur shops damaged.

France
1986
April: A pig slaughterhouse was set on fire. An inflammable mixture was put into the anaesthesia machine and put in an electric igniting system, attached to a roll of electrical wire which was rolled outside. The French press totally suppressed news of the action, apparently due to the desires of the slaughterhouse owner.
Oct., Toulouse: A car belonging to a bullfight fanatic was totally destroyed by fire.

1987
March 13, Toulouse: A slaughterhouse was attacked, and two truck front windows were smashed.
March 14, Toulouse: Two more trucks damaged at Toulouse's slaughterhouse. 4 butchers had their windows smashed in the town centre.
April 8, Paris: The front window to a meat van was smashed in a southern suburb.

Direct action in Spain
-ALFSG (France) Bulletin

ACTION REPORTS

UNITED KINGDOM

The following reports are by no means complete. We listed all the animal liberation reports, most of the major damage reports, including most attacks with fire, and any tactics we thought were new and innovative in style. Actions by the ALF happen literally every day in the U.K. and it would be impossible to list them all. A more complete listing in the ALFSG (UK) *Diary of Actions* is available from us.

1986
Sept., Cheshire: Over 100 rabbits were rescued from Hylyne rabbit farm.
Sept., Sussex: 50 hens were rescued from a battery farm, slogans were painted on the walls of the building and a feeding trough was damaged.
Sept. 20, Hampshire: The entire refrigeration unit at a meat processing plant was destroyed. $500,000 damage was caused.

Oct., Hertfordshire: 22 hens were rescued from a battery farm.
Oct., Worcestershire: Over 50 chickens were rescued from broiler units and extensive damage was caused to the building.
Oct. 11, Oxfordshire: $200,000 damage was caused to 3 trucks belonging to Faccenda Chickens by incendiary devices.

Nov. 26, Lancashire: 100 mink were freed from a farm, and property was also damaged.
Nov. 27, Essex: 110 guinea pigs were rescued from Tucks Animal Breeding Centre.

Dec., Cambridgeshire: Fire set at the Monks Wood experimental station, causing $500,000 damage. The station carries out animal and mineral research for the government.

1987
Feb.: 90 rabbits were rescued from a factory farm and the remaining rabbits were sprayed with a harmless blue dye to make their skins valueless.
Feb. 1, Buckinghamshire: 10 incendiary devices were planted in a slaughterhouse and two meat processing plants. They were planted under a diesel storage tank and in refrigeration equipment, but only 3 ignited, burning the slaughterhouse and adjoining meat warehouses, causing $40,000 damage.
Feb. 6, Cheshire: 4 piglets and 52 broiler hens were rescued from Bibby's Research Station. Extensive damage was caused to conveyor belts, wiring, cages, etc. An ALF statement claimed the action in support of the 9 people convicted of various "crimes".

March, Kent: A horse and donkey were rescued from Welcome Lab in Frant. Both needed vet treatment and are now in good homes.
March, Yorkshire: McDonald's of Dewsbury (not yet opened) was damaged by fire. Rent-a-Kill stock/factory/offices in Morley were badly damaged by fire.

April, Wales: Incendiary devices were left in the fur depts. at Deberhams in Cardiff and Swansea, and at Howells of Cardiff.
April 5, Essex: 10 beagles were rescued from the Beechams Essex lab.
Easter Sunday, Oxford: 20 birds were rescued from Jenning's Poultry Farm at Garsington. The liberators' press release said "The hens were in a dreadful state with blistered skin on their necks and chests, featherless wings, and extensive bald patches."
April 26, Hertshire: 12 dogs were rescued from breeding kennels at Bayford, near Broxbourne. The dogs, including 5 old English sheepdogs, were in extremely poor condition and are now in good homes.

May 7, Yorkshire: 24 windows and 2 glass doors of animal abuse shops were damaged with etching fluid in Leeds city centre.
May 8, London: $5,000 damage caused to fur coats in Portabello Rd. Market when battery acid was sprayed on them.
May 11, Norfolk: 19 chickens were liberated from R. Winch & Sons at Upgate, near Norwich.
May 20, Yorkshire: 3 incendiary devices were left in trucks at the Goldenlay Egg Packing Plant. One ignited damaging the back of one truck.
May 27, Avon: 77 hens were rescued from a poultry farm at Lower Claverham, near Bristol. "Concentration camp" was spray painted on a wall.

June 2: 2 fox cubs and 2 rabbits were rescued from the garden shed of a fanatical hunt supporter.
June 2, West Midlands: A cattle market had its P.A. system and lighting damaged and slogans were painted.
June 23, Kent: 9 young male goats were rescued from Hadlow College of Agriculture, near Tonbridge.

July 12, Luton: $18 million damage caused to a Debenhams store where an incendiary device was planted in the fur dept. and the sprinkler system failed. Two other Debenhams stores were damaged similarly in Harrow and Romford.
Late July, Avon: 27 shops in the Bristol area were either super-glued or had slogans painted on them.
July 24, Sussex: Over 300 breeding rats were rescued from Sussex University's Laboratory of Experimental Psychology. All the rats were placed in good homes.

Aug. 1, Surrey: 30 chickens were rescued from a battery farm at Newgate.
Aug. 12, Yorkshire: A stone monument, celebrating the shooting of 2,070 grouse in 1 day in 1872, was painted with slogans, removed from Wemmergill Moor and deposited at the front gate of the British Association for Shooting and Conservation.
Aug. 21, Kent: 2 rabbits and a guinea pig were rescued from cruel conditions in Herne Bay.
Aug. 24, Kent: 1000 eggs were smashed and cars damaged with paint stripper at a hen battery farm in West Kingsdown.

Sept. 1, Sussex: Letters were sent to shops in Brighton displaying circus posters, warning them that their windows would be bricked if the posters were not taken down. Most took them down.
Sept. 12, Yorkshire: A slaughterhouse in Leeds had its roof damaged by fire.
Sept. 26, Dorset: A window at the Hotel Piccadily in Bournemouth was smashed because they were holding a fur sale.

Hamshire ALF action, Jan.1,'88
Diary of Actions #4

Oct. 8, London: Two directors of Unilever, the cosmetics and chemical giant, had their homes paint-bombed and corrosive liquid poured over their cars.
Oct. 11, Sussex: Five incendiary devices were placed under trucks belonging to RP Meats and Quickburger in Fishergate. All ignited and the total damage was over $500,000.
Oct. 16: Actions against McDonald's all over the country (Int. Day of Action). Continued on page 28

ALF ACTION IN VANCOUVER

On Sunday September 20, 1987, three activists were arrested in Vancouver, B.C. for actions against fur stores. Rod Coronado, David Howitt, and Linda May, activists with the **Sea Shepherd**, were stopped in their van around 2 a.m. after an eyewitness to a fur store action gave a description of the vehicle to the police. Shortly after, the Sea Shepherd vessel, Divine Wind, was raided by police and customs officials. Nothing was seized. Although all three are crew members of the Divine Wind and were driving a Sea Shepherd vehicle, a Sea Shepherd spokesperson says that there is no connection to their group. "A.L.F." was spraypainted on Pappas Fur Designers Ltd., Grandview Furs, and Avenue Furs. The stores also had their windows smashed and red paint thrown inside.

The three are charged with a total of 10 mischiefs and 2 break and enter charges. They spent about one week in jail before being released on $10,000 cash bail each. They originally had to maintain an 11p.m. to 7 a.m. curfew, report to the police, stay at a specific house (as opposed to the Divine Wind where they lived), and surrender their passports. A November bail review hearing allowed them to leave the country to continue their normal lives until their Preliminary hearing, which was scheduled for Febuary, 1988. Rod and Linda are from California and David is from England, but they all returned with the Divine Wind to California. Rod and David are the people who sank the two whaling ships in Iceland in November, 1986.

Reaction to the arrests from police and the fur industry has been swift. The police are trying to reconstruct a smashed lightbulb (which was filled with paint and thrown) in order to get fingerprints. The $10,000 cash each person had to put up to get out of jail is viewed as rather harsh for mischief charges. The fur industry flew in public relations spokespeople from across the country to apply pressure on the police and courts and get media attention. They want to use the three as scapegoats.

Animal Liberation Front activity has increased significantly in Vancouver since August 1987. Two fur stores are reportedly closing directly because of direct actions against them. The owner of Grandview Furs says "It's ruining my business because customers are frightened to bring in their own coats for repair." But it's more likely that insurance doesn't completely cover the damage, and Avenue Furs has been hit about a dozen times in the past two years. At $7,000-$15,000 a shot it's not hard to see how easy it is to close down a shop.

Another small victory was realized by activists in Vancouver at the recent Commonwealth Conference. The organizers decided to cancel a fur show because of concern over offending some international delegates and, as well, they felt the pressure from activists. One B.C. government spokesperson says "...the last thing we wanted to do was pose additional security problems. You don't know to what end some of the anti-fur group (sic) will go to disrupt an event." As the saying goes: *"Increase the pressure!"*

The three arrested activists have issued a plea for money to help defray legal costs. "For the first time, not just here, but all across America, and Britain as well, the fur industry has met an opponent it cannot stop. Not only will the furriers have to deal with a campaign of education, and public awareness, but one that strikes at the only place they have shown sensitivity, their pocketbooks. A campaign on behalf of fur-bearing animals is already underway, and it is our duty to see that no aspect of it is halted. It is only a matter of time before the real criminals are behind bars, but until that day, we must continue to fight for the freedom of fur-bearing animals." Donations can be sent to the **Sea Shepherd Legal Defense Fund**, 207 W. Hastings Ave., Suite 301, Vancouver, B.C., V6B 1H7, Canada.

Update

On February 9, the day set for the Preliminary hearing, Rod and David did not show up for court. Linda did though, and had her break and enter charge withdrawn, leaving only her mischief charges. The fact that David and Rod did not show up should not be a difficult problem for us to deal with. The fur industry, who rallied around the arrests last year, seems to have had the wind taken out of them since they now have no one to really focus on. Although Linda did show up, the men were the ones the prosecution and the industry really wanted, following their traditional sexist attitudes. As well, they only have to fundraise for $20,000 (to pay back the money lost to the courts for bail) and whatever Linda's legal fees are instead of fundraising for legal fees for all three, which were likely to be much higher. Not being Canadian citizens, Rod and David will not have to worry about these charges, unless of course they are in Canada and picked up by the police. Linda will have her trial in the near future and we'll report on that in the next issue of *Front Line News*.

F.B.I.

In response to an increase in militant direct action carried out by animal liberation activists in the United States, the Federal Bureau of Investigation (F.B.I.) have begun investigations under anti-terrorism laws - *N.Y.Times, 19/1/88*. The F.B.I. are looking into several cases of arson, including the $3.5 million fire that destroyed a new University of California animal lab last year, which was claimed by the **Animal Rights Militia** (ARM). Other actions under investigation are the Sept. 1, 1987 fire at a veal company in Santa Clara, CA, which was claimed by the same group, and a fire on Thanksgiving at a cattle feed barn. Damage to the meat companies is in the tens of thousands of dollars. A.R.M. are an extreme offshoot of the **A.L.F.** who, in communiques released in England, claim they will not stop short of killing or hurting humans who are involved in the exploitation and murder of animals.

Confidential sources have also confirmed that the F.B.I. have been visiting Toronto in recent months investigating people and campaigns within the **Toronto Humane Society**. The T.H.S. has been the target of many anti-animal people and the media ever since animal rights activists took control through an elected majority on the Board of Directors in 1986. But the T.H.S. is still a pretty 'tame' organization which certainly does not get involved with illegal activities, so one must assume that the F.B.I. are being the reactionary scum that they usually show themselves to be.

Also on the F.B.I. hit list have been the offices of **People for the Ethical Treatment of Animals** (PETA) in Washington, DC. They were raided this past winter by the F.B.I. and the Office of the U.S. Inspector General who were looking for information regarding the whereabouts of the cats and pigs liberated from the U.S. Dept. of Agriculture in Beltsville, MD, and the chimps liberated from the SEMA labs, also in Maryland. Recordings, videos, and documents were seized and are being examined by a Baltimore Grand Jury.

Activist Arrested For Lab Raid

In connection with the Oct. 86 University of Oregon laboratory break-in, three people appeared before a Grand Jury after police raided an Oregon animal sanctuary in Nov. 86 and recovered seven rabbits bearing identifying tattoos. During the break-in, 144 animals were liberated, and an estimated $100,000 in damage was caused to the facility.

Long time animal activist Peter Troen, his aunt, and **PETA** member Sharon Nettles were called to testify. On July 10, 1987, police arrested Peter and charged him with burglary, conspiracy, and theft. He was released after posting $2000 bail on $20,000 security. The police had prepared an affidavit which stated that Benson told them that she had obtained the rabbits from Roger Troen.

Represented by Portland attorney Stephen Houze Troen will be tried on December 1, 1987, in Lane County. Houze says that Troen will plead not guilty, and that their case will be based on the "choice of evils" defence - that committing an illegal act is justifiable if it prevents a greater crime from being committed. The arrest followed nine months of investigation (still ongoing) into animal rights activists and groups in the effort to dig up suspects in the case. Eugene police Sgt. Charles Tilby told reporters that local police are working with California authorities in an attempt to link the Oregon break-in with recent **ALF** action in California.

Source: Animals' Agenda, PETA News

Roger Troen and friend.   Animals' Agenda -May '88

LIGHT SENTENCES FOR GERMAN LIBERATORS

The trial of 10 German animal liberation activists, accused of forming a criminal association, attempted arson and of various animal liberation raids, ended with light sentences at the court in Flensburg on May 14, 1987. The accused, aged between 20 and 60, pleaded guilty to liberating a total of 485 animals from various labs. They were allowed to show the film "Pennsylvania Primates" in the open court, and the judge later referred to the "terrible experiments" in the film which "get under the skin of any person and compel him to give thought to these things."

In his summing-up, the judge stated that he had been impressed by the high motives of the animal liberators, who "had been driven by animal experiments into taking illegal action" and "had wanted to help the animals and free them from their tormentors." After announcing sentences varying from small fines to probationary periods of between 7 and 12 months, the judge ended the trial by urging the accused to "continue fighting for tortured animals, but by legal means."

Dogs rescued from a German vivisection lab. -Action Reports (UK)

Interview With An Activist

This interview was conducted with a person who took part in an ALF raid on the Faculty of Dentistry at the University of Toronto in Feb. 1986, where experiments take place involving the use of pain, and the measuring of facial reactions to pain. A failed attempt was made to liberate animals, but equipment was destroyed and damage exceeded $15,000.

Q What were your feelings when you failed to liberate any of the animals there?

A I'm not sure it is possible to describe the feelings of overwhelming frustration I, and all the others involved, felt at being so close to the animals yet unable to reach them. We were separated by just a wall and even managed to get through part of that, but we just ran out of time. The feeling of frustration has not gone away, it has merely been diverted into an energetic determination to succeed next time.

Q Would you use violence (on people as well as researchers' machines and torture devices) if it was absolutely necessary in order to free an abused animal?

A Violence is a relative term. I do not recognize the destruction of researchers' torture chambers or instruments of torture as violence, merely as economic sabotage. I feel that violence against people turns off the public and it is not something I am personally comfortable with. As the ALF group to which I belong operates by complete consensus, it is therefore extremely unlikely, believing as I do, that I would find myself in a violent situation. Also, in order to reduce the chance of confrontation with a guard, etc., we investigate our targets very carefully over a long period of time.

Q Many "scientists" have commented that the ALF is nothing but a terrorist group akin to such organizations as the IRA and that the ALF's raids in the future are certain to lead to violence. What's your opinion on this viewpoint?

A Terrorism is defined in the dictionary as "mass organized ruthlessness" or "state of terror"; terrorist is defined as "to oppress by fear". There can be no greater terrorism than the violent research going on behind the locked doors of laboratories and no greater terrorist group than vivisectors doing that which they do best - torturing animals. Accusing the ALF of 'perhaps' committing violence at some unknown and unspecified time in the future is not only ridiculous but will not serve to divert our attention from reality, which is that the research community is already committing violence now, everyday, against its helpless animal victims.

Q How do you keep infiltrators out of ALF? Also, how can you be sure that people volunteering homes for abused or liberated animals aren't cops, etc.?

A Infiltration is a serious problem but I believe we take every possible precaution against it. I prefer not to discuss the exceptional security measures taken to ensure people are not 'infiltrators'. Also, I prefer not to discuss the safeguards used where homes for the animals are concerned. Need-

-Lomakatsi

less to say, they are extensive - carelessness that would result in turning an animal over to someone who would return him/her back to a laboratory is not to be tolerated. Everyone involved considers this even more important than being caught and going to jail; we know the risk we are taking, terrifying though it may be, and we made the choice. However, the animal is helpless and once liberated must remain liberated, whatever the cost.

Q Dr. Thomas Salarno, a member of the U of T's Faculty of Medicine and a heart surgeon at St. Michael's Hospital has refused to give me an interview because "it's not a good time to discuss the research" being done at the U of T! What types of research do you know, or do you suspect are going on there? What's he trying to hide?

A I don't wish to answer this question because of security and the safety of others. I cannot explain further. Suffice it to say that all kinds of research are going on at the U of T and we are aware of every detail of that research. In terms of Salarno trying to hide information - it constantly amazes me as to how secretive researchers are about their work. Are they not proud of what they are doing in the 'name of mankind' as they like

to put it? Could it be that they fear their research methods would not stand up in the light of public scrutiny?

Q Dr. William Rapley, director of animal care veterinary services at the University of Western Ontario in London, Ont. was very "nice" when I interviewed him. However, in his efforts at being so polite and "helpful",

he evaded telling me what experiments the animals at UWO are being subjected to. Do you have information on what is *really* going on there now?

A Once again - same answer as above.

Q I know your commitment to the Animal Liberation Front is great and that you are willing to go to jail for your actions. Are there any particular incidents that led you to these beliefs? (Why did you join the ALF?)

A I am passionately committed to creating social change which will make this world a better place for all species, not just for humans. As an animal rights activist, once I had dealt with the fear of realizing that I could go to jail if caught, it seemed the logical step to become a liberator. I want to look back on my life and know I did absolutely *everything* I could to help stop these atrocities, even giving up my freedom, which is the greatest sacrifice one can make. It is important to realize that when liberators

make this decision they do not do so out of any sense of martyrdom, but out of a sense of necessity. Believe me, the last thing we want is to be a 'sacrifice'; the animals need all of us on the 'outside', rather than in prison.

Q Do you think that ALF raids will do

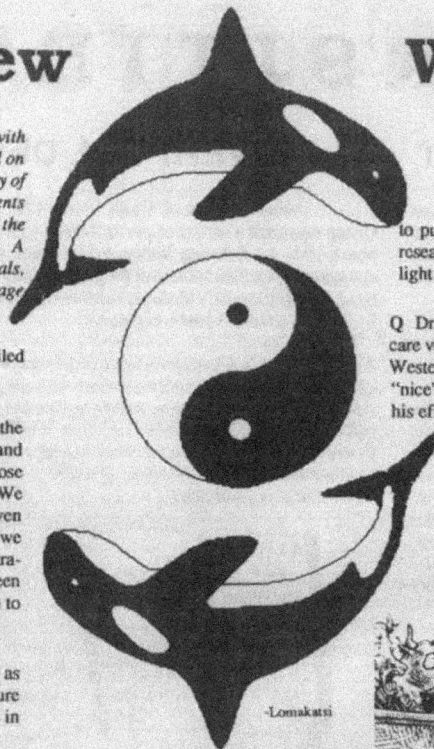

PERHAPS *THIS* WILL REFRESH YOUR MEMORY!!

PIRARO

anything to abolish animal research in the future? What will it take to end the torment once and for all?

A I believe ALF raids are invaluable because, thus far, they have been responsible for bringing to light atrocities in research facilities - e.g., City of Hope Medical Centre, the Head Injury Tapes, etc. It is essential that not only animals be liberated - though that has first priority - but also damning documentation against the research facility. We have to present factual evidence to the public because ultimately, they are the ones who will have to apply pressure to create changes in the system, in legislation, etc. They have to know what is going on in laboratories, indeed in every arena where animal abuse is taking place. Only by knowing the truth can the general public raise an outcry to stop this horror. And of course, in terms of the animals, the ALF is the only hope for an end to the suffering of laboratory animals. If they are not liberated, the only way a lab animal leaves the lab is when it is dead.

UNIVERSITIES

CANADIAN UNIVERSITY FREAKS OUT

The following is an internal memo released to all departments at Dalhousie University in Nova Scotia by Howard Dickson, the Assoc. Dean of Research at the Dept. of Anatomy. Dated Dec. 12, 1986, the subject is "Animal Rights Activists" and is probably typical of the seige mentality at many laboratories in universities across North America.

TO: All Department Heads
FROM: Howard Dickson, Assoc. Dean Research
SUBJECT: Animal Rights Activists

Vice President Sinclair and Dean Murray have requested that I provide all faculty, staff and students with the following information.

As many of you may know, we have recently received word from a reliable source that a very powerful and potentially dangerous animal rights group is organizing locally and plans to raid the animal quarters in the Psychology Department over the Christmas break.

More recent information suggests that the planned action could involve a larger area, and that any animal holding facilities on campus are at risk, including the Tupper, which I feel is a high risk target. Further, we hear now that this group plans to do extensive property damage to gain media attention, and will likely attempt to destroy laboratory equipment and research data, and as they have done elsewhere, will try to free animals.

We are considering this threat to be extremely serious and have taken today a number of steps to add additional security here in the Tupper Building. We have:
1) installed bars on the inside of the A/C windows at ground level.
2) added additional TV surveillance and motion detectors in the A/C area.
3) secured the back door to the A/C so that off hours, access to the A/C will only be possible through the card access door in the basement of the Tupper; access through the CRC will not be possible in the evening.
4) reduced access to the Tupper Building from 5pm to 8am weekdays and from 5pm Friday to 8am Monday; the only access will be through the front doors of the Tupper. A sign-in procedure will be instituted; ID will be required and you will be required to sign out. Additional security will be on duty to patrol the complex and a guard will be stationed at the sign-in station to moniter activity.
5) the RCMP and the Halifax Police Dept. have been informed and they will assist us in assessing our security needs.

It is not my intention to initiate a hysterical response, but we feel that it is only prudent to provide you with the relevant information and to point out to you the seriousness of this threat.

Some simple rules to follow that will help us to enhance our security:
1) Do not allow anyone to get into the A/C area when you enter using your pass card.
2) Do not leave your access card lying around the lab where it could possibly be picked up and used later. If you lose your A/C card please report the loss immediately so that your code can be changed.
3) Keep an eye out for strangers (young or old) in the Tupper Tower in particular, and especially in the evenings and on weekends. If you encounter someone that you do not know, simply ask if you can be of assistance; if you do not get a reassuring response call security at 6400 immediately. Do not attempt to remove anyone by force. If you encounter a group of strangers in the off hours, call security immediately; DO NOT make contact.
4) Finally, it may be prudent to remove from the Tupper Bldg. any laboratory notes and drafts of theses. These items are easy targets and often, if backup copies are not available, are irreplaceable.

If you have any questions, please contact the Dean's office; I will provide all departments with a hard copy of this announcement later this morning.

Howard Dickson

Ed. Note: Shortly after receiving this memo, the animal rights organization **ARK II** in Toronto began receiving phone calls from the media in Halifax demanding to know when they were planning to raid the university, and being irate at having to wait so long for them to show up!! If anyone working or attending a university happens to come across memos and letters such as this one, we would appreciate a copy sent to us if possible. One must begin to wonder (if one hasn't already) at the practice of animal experimentation when the fear of someone freeing animals creates the situation where it must be carried out in a fortress, prison-like atmosphere.

LIVERPOOL DEBATE WON

During the week of March 10th to 17th, **Liverpool University Animal Rights Group** organised a variety of events including films and talks from invited speakers. On March 10th, the Debating Society held a debate on the motion : "This house believes vivisection is justified because of the great benefits it brings to others." Professor Edwards, Head of the University's Medical Department, proposed the motion and Philip Churchward, BUAV's Scientific Adviser, opposed it.

Following a lively debate, with many people speaking from the floor both in favour of and against vivisection, the students overwhelmingly rejected animal experiments. Only 16 voted in support of the motion, with 49 against and 14 abstentions. This verdict, along with other encouraging developments such as the adoption of a "Violence-Free Science Charter" by many universities, clearly demonstrates that animal rights has become an important issue among students who are no longer prepared to accept the cruel practices of their lecturers as necessary, or justifiable.

ANIMAL RIGHTS AT MICHIGAN STATE U.

Students Concerned About Animal Welfare is an animal rights organization on the campus of Michigan State University. Founded by vegetarian student Scott Harris, the group will attempt to educate both students and faculty on issues such as vegetarianism, animals in laboratory research, factory farming, trapping and the fur industry, animals in sports, the philosophies of animal welfare and animal rights, and federal and state laws concerning animals. Harris, a nine-year member of the **American Anti-Vivisection Society** and a board member of the local humane society, reports that the group is doing "surprisingly well. About 25 people attend our meetings regularly, and we've been invited to speak to the Toxicology and Pharmacology Department and the Lab Animal Care Service," Harris said. "Some people are calling us radical, but we're just trying to disseminate information. We try not to be dogmatic - pardon the pun." For more information, write Scott Harris at: 550 Hagadorn, East Lansing, MI 48823 USA.

U.C. BERKELEY TO BUILD TORTURE CHAMBER

The University of California at Berkeley is requesting a whopping $14 million of public money to build an "Animal Care Facility" on the Oxford part of the campus. The title is a filthy, blatant deception, since the only "care" an animal will receive there will be psychological and physical research (a nice name for cruel, savage torture). Although a local animal rights veterinarian is trying to halt construction of the dungeon, it is questionable if he will suceed - the only thing this government is good for anymore is throwing away public money on things like war, cruelty, and destruction of the environment. What you can do to help: Write letters expressing your opinion to Senator Alan Cranston, U.S. Senate, Senate Office building, Washington, DC 20510 USA, and Congressperson Ronald V. Dellums, 1720 Oregon St., Berkeley, CA, USA.

Source: Polly S. and the Green Panther

ANIMAL RIGHTS SCHOLARSHIP

A $1,000-per-year scholarship at North Carolina State University is available to students who have demonstrated an interest in animal rights. The Claire Simmons Alan-Samson Memorial Scholarship in Moral Philosophy was made possible by a $50,000 grant to the university by Claire Simmons Alan, a Charlotte, N.C., woman, who made the gift in memory of her dog, said Dr. Robert S. Bryan. Bryan, an NCSU philosophy professor, explained that the original gift yields $4,000 in interest annually - enough for four separate scholarships. Though it isn't the case now, Bryan said that, ideally, one scholarship each would go to a freshman, a sophomore, a junior and a senior student. If they are interested in the scholarship and they must "present evidence of their interest in animal rights." Also, students who obtain the scholarship must agree to "write a sustained piece of work on the topic of animal rights." Candidates should apply by seeking admission to the university through the school's admission office and by writing: Professor Robert S. Bryan, Dept. of Philosophy and Religion, Box 8103, North Carolina State University, Raleigh, NC 27695 USA. UNIVERSITIES continued on page 27

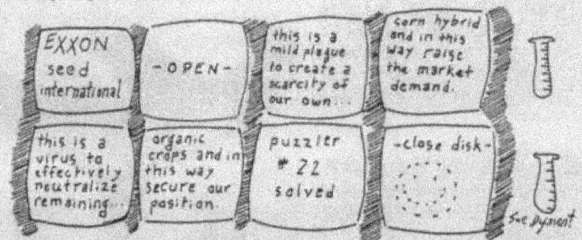

WHY VEGAN?

- A Book Review by Kenn Quayle (re-printed from *Epicene*)

"Vegan," Kath Clements explains, is a word used to describe "those who avoid animal products for food, clothing and other consumer goods."

"Veganism is not about cats' homes and being kind to furry animals, about living in cloud cuckoo-land where nature's cycle of destruction and creation can somehow be avoided. Veganism is about having a consistent approach to human rights and animal rights, ecology, and world food problems."

Clements goes on to say that "It is the over-consumption of meat, eggs and dairy products in the West that underlies the inequitable distribution of the world's food resources," explaining that fertile lands in "third world" countries are used to grow grains for export or for grazing cattle, and that about five times as much land is needed to feed a meat-eater as is needed to feed a vegetarian.

Clements reveals the horrors of mass egg production and "factory" fishing and farming in an indictment of the procedures used in animal-based food industries. She also points out that, "Reliance on drugs and additives (including hormones) to combat infection and enhance profitability increases artificial residues in the products and heightens the risk to the consumer."

"Animals ... have a perfectly developed nervous system and, faced with the prospect of slaughter, reactions similar to our own. Possibly plants, too ... in some way 'feel' and 'suffer' ... but if you eat animals instead (of plants) you are of course responsible for the destruction of many more plants than if you ate plants alone." (Ten pounds of plant protein make about one pound of animal protein.)

Clements suggests growing nut trees as an alternative to grazing animals. This would maintain the water table, and give "a superior quality protein ... 20 times the amount that the same acre would yield in beef."

She also points out that "we are not like the herbivores ... we can't live on grass ... our bodies seem to be 'designed' ... to absorb a diet of fruits, nuts and shoots ... (as do) chimpanzees and gorillas." The bowel of a truly carnivorous animal, unlike that of a human being, is "short and smooth ... for quick release of toxic wastes." She goes on to explain that, "As soon as an animal's death occurs putrefaction begins, and meat is ... in some stage of (arrested) decay. Therefore meat as such is more akin to the carrion that nature's scavengers eat than to the fresh food of the hunting animals."

"'Degenerative diseases' (are) caused by accumulations of wastes our bodies can't deal with, reaching epidemic proportions. The greater bulk and fibrous nature of a vegan diet mean that the diseases associated with the lack of fibre in an animal-based diet, from constipation to cancer of the bowel, can be avoided."

Clements posits that meat-eating and the general acceptance of animals' deaths could be a cause of war, and says, "It is a mark of our insensitivity that such questions are matters merely of speculation or academic study." Mincing no words, she adds that, "People who think they are working for peace whilst still eating animal products, or who think they can forget the issue of animal rights and concentrate on human rights, have not got down to the roots of the problem."

"No one can be quite free from the cycle of exploitation which keeps the economic system turning over, but by refusing animal products wherever possible ... we can take a huge step forward. We can (end) the double

standard, where we ... claim affection for certain fluffy or feathered creatures whilst ... enjoying the results of animal agony."

She begins a limited discussion of animal abuses outside the food industries, dealing with zoos and pets, but does not deal with fur farming and trapping. Another "part of our assumption that we may use animals as we wish" that is barely touched on is that of vivisection: the use of animals in medical experiments and product testing.

In a section called "Why (Strictly) Vegan," Clements tells us that, "As a vegan, you won't be 'making do' without animal products, but rather you will no longer regard them as food at all." For herself, she says, "the decision to do without animal food ... was very life-enhancing ... more like a liberation than an act of self-discipline. The reason vegans are careful where possible to see that they never take animal products is not a sanctimonious attitude of wishing to keep their moral integrity untainted ... but ... is usually because we think it important to illustrate to others that good health can be maintained entirely without animal products."

Clements gives sound advice to nursing and weaning mothers, suggesting that, "You should spend as much time as possible enjoying your baby, and as little as possible preparing food and reading about it."

Why Vegan ends with helpful advice on how to make the switch to a vegan diet, laying to rest fears about possible deficiencies in proteins or vitamins such as B12 (available in yeasts, miso, and tempeh), and D (the best source of which is sunlight). Iron is easily obtained from green leaves - the darker the better. We are left with a selection of yummy recipes, as well as an excellent book with many well-reasoned arguments for ceasing to consume animal products and adopting a vegan diet.

Why Vegan
The Ethics of Eating and the Need for Change
by Kath Clements
GMP Publishers Ltd.
A Heretic Book,
London, UK, 1985

POLICE UNCOVER ANOTHER ILLEGAL TOFU DEN...

AIDS ANIMAL RESEARCH A HOAX

"To date chimpanzees and other animals have contributed nothing to progress in AIDS research that could not have been gained in other ways."

Since AIDS was first recognized in 1981, there have been massive efforts in a variety of directions to bring the virus under control. Therapies such as herbalism and acupuncture need to be more fully and sympathetically explored by the medical profession.

So far the important advances in AIDS research, enabling preventative action to be taken and new drugs to be tested, have all come from investigation of patients or test tube experiments in vitro. Scientists add the new drug to test tube cultures of the T-cells to see if it protects against damage caused by the virus. The use of human cells in this way means that results are directly applicable to patients. Already drugs active in the test tube are being subjected to clinical trials, with promising results.

Animal experiments are not necessary nor particularly helpful in showing human transmissibility of AIDS. Two other lines of research are much more important. First, epidemiologic examination of trends in the incidence of AIDS showed that the disease was transmissible and the likely modes of transmission. Second, the virus had already been successfully isolated consistently from human patients. Clinical studies of patients in hospitals demonstrated the course of the disease and led to the continuing search for means to combat the viral damage. They showed much about how the virus invades the body and weakens its defences.

The obsession with animal experimentation (vivisection) has led scientists to work hard to reproduce the disease in animals. In June 1984, American researchers reported their goal, "to transmit a severe, lasting immunodeficiency or clinical disease to chimpanzees and monkeys..." They injected pure HTLV-III virus or infected samples of spleen, lymph node, bone marrow, brain,

and plasma from AIDS patients into chimpanzees, rhesus monkeys, cynomolgus monkeys, stumptail macaques, a capuchin monkeys, stumptail macaques, a capuchin monkey and a squirrel monkey. The injections were done into the skin, muscle, abdomen and even brain of the animals. To the disappointment of the researchers, all animals remained well up to a year after injection.

In a 1984 study, plasma from AIDS patients was infused into three chimps, none of whom developed AIDS, although two developed antibodies to the virus. In another study the same year, two juvenile chimps were injected with the virus, both of whom remained healthy. A 1986 report observed those chimps and four more injected with the virus. No chimp developed AIDS, although the virus could be recovered from five of the six into whom it had been injected. A 1985 study reported on 25 chimps as well as several monkeys inoculated with various body tissues or fluids from AIDS patients. None of these animals has developed AIDS. The surviving animals remain under surveillance.

No animal other than the human has developed AIDS. Only humans have developed the malignancies and opportunistic infections that are characteristic of the disease. As a result, animal experiments have been directed at developing a "model" for the disease with little success.

In 1986, the *Journal of Virology* reported further attempts to induce AIDS in chimpanzees. The virus was administered to eight chimps, 2-5 years old, and they were reared in a colony at the Yerkes Regional Primate Center at Emory University in Atlanta. Observation continued for up to 18 months but once again there were no signs of AIDS. In a review of the evidence, the Washington-based Physicians Committee for Responsible Medicine concluded that AIDS is a uniquely human disease, proved by scientists having failed to reproduce AIDS in laboratory animals.

Continued next page

AIDS...

Different Systems

For all our similarities with the chimpanzee, the chimp's immune system has significant differences. They naturally have lower numbers of a certain cell, the T4 lymphocyte, the cell which is the principal target of the AIDS virus. They have higher numbers of another blood cell commonly measured in AIDS patients, the T8 lymphocyte. Chimps show a different ratio of T4 cells to T8 cells. This ratio is one of the principal blood tests for the AIDS syndrome. In response to the virus, some researchers have found that chimps have no change in the T4:T8 ratio, while in humans a change in this ratio is the signal that AIDS is underway. In humans, the AIDS virus can be found in blood plasma. In chimps, little or no free virus is found in plasma. The virus is found only in blood cells.

An additional problem is that infant and toddler chimps are often used in AIDS research. The time frame for maturation of a chimp is roughly similar to that of the human. A two-year-old chimp is physiologically and sexually immature. Yet chimps are often used with little regard for their age. Some studies have used a peculiar mixture of older and younger chimps. Infants and juveniles are not ready to live apart from their mothers let alone in the isolation mandated by viral research. Chimps normally live in social groups but for AIDS research they will be kept in solitary confinement for years to see if any clinical signs of the disease develop. The psychological effects are of concern in and of themselves, but also have important secondary effects in the immune function of the animals. It has been shown that the immune system, which is of principal interest in AIDS research, is significantly affected by stresses such as separation and the laboratory environment.

Psychosocial factors, in fact, can modify resistance in infectious diseases, including viruses. This has been documented for the herpes simplex virus, poliomyelitis virus, coxsackie virus, and polyoma virus. In addition, stress and manipulation can effect susceptibility to malignancies, of obvious concern to research on AIDS. Part of the syndrome of AIDS is a susceptibility to unusual malignancies. No primate can be considered physiologically normal if deprived of movement and socialization. This has been clearly shown in chimps, for whom companionship and socialization through mutual grooming are important.

Life Sentences

Animals involved in AIDS research are at a particular risk for long-term suffering. Not only is there prolonged and strict isolation from their peers, there is also a lack of contact with caretakers due to fear of contamination. The animals are never considered free of disease. They may live in confined isolation for decades while observers watch for manifestations of illness. Their "service" and their isolation may never be finished.

Given the limitations of the "chimpanzee model" and the prohibitively small number

of chimps, it is important that better methods of testing be investigated. Production and batch testing for safety of some vaccines can now be done with in vitro techniques. These should be expanded and exploited to streamline research on AIDS.

A special report on AIDS from the National Academy of Sciences (N.A.S.) and Institute of Medicine issued concerns about the ways chimpanzees might be used: "The committee is gravely concerned that chimpanzees have been and might be used for experiments for which the rationale is not compelling in light of the scarcity and irreplaceable nature of these animals."

It will come as no surprise that medical scientists are working to develop a vaccine against AIDS, but there could be major problems. Vaccines against other viruses mobilize the body's immune system. No vaccine has ever been developed against a virus which actually attacks the body's natural defences. The National Academy of Sciences report states: "Developing a vaccine to prevent HIV infection and AIDS presents a number of scientific challenges that have never before been responded to successfully. As a result, an effective vaccine may be very difficult, if not impossible to produce. Should an effective vaccine candidate become available, there are significant social concerns that may limit or prevent its testing and use. Even for the next 5-10 years, the committee generally believes that the probability of a vaccine becoming available is low."

Testing vaccines on chimps will carry a significant problem in interpretation, as neither safety nor efficiency in chimps is any guarantee of the behaviour of a potential vaccine in humans. This problem will be more grave with an AIDS vaccine because of the fatality of the disease. There will be no permissible mistakes. Because animals do not develop human AIDS, any vaccine must ultimately be tested on volunteers to see if it works. But no one can afford to wait years for a vaccine even if it does prove safe and effective. Vigorous and explicit health education campaigns need to be initiated now to stop the disease spreading. Like other sexually transmitted diseases, AIDS can only be effectively controlled by prevention, through voluntary changes in behaviour, and no amount of animal experimentation can achieve that.

Sources: The "Animal Model" in AIDS Research, by Physicians Committee for Responsible Medicine; PETA News Vol. 2, No. 1.

Speaking Out!

Statement of Frank Branchini on behalf of the Gay and Lesbian Caucus, PETA.

As Gay and Lesbian people we condemn the use of primates and other animals in AIDS research at SEMA laboratories....

The infliction of suffering on baby chimpanzees at SEMA is not likely to ease the pain or comfort those who already have AIDS. The money being spent to inflict suffering on intelligent, sentient creatures at SEMA could be more effectively spent on education campaigns to prevent the spread of AIDS and on providing care for those already suffering from the disease.

Assertions of the medical research industry that no medical progress is possible without animal research are ridiculous... With so many people incurably and desperately ill with this terrible disease it is incongruous that medical experimenters are obsessed with the idea of spreading the disease to animals.

Chimpanzees are highly intelligent, highly social animals. Recent research has demonstrated their capability to use tools, use plants for medicinal purposes, and learn and use language. Those who argue that people have a right to inflict suffering on chimpanzees because they are "inferior" fall back on the same arguments which at other times and places have been used to justify genocide against gay and lesbian people (among many others). Those who think this is an unfair or extreme comparison should consider the research conducted by Jane Goodall, Francine Patterson, Dian Fossey, Roger Fouts, and Allan and Beatrice Gardner and then examine the videotapes made at SEMA. These tapes show the filthy conditions which animals are subjected to at SEMA. They show the complete social isolation of primates who are highly socially oriented. They show primates screaming and exhibiting other signs of extreme emotional distress and need.

We call on gay and lesbian people and all people of goodwill to reject the notion that just because people are suffering we have a right to inflict suffering on other sentient

creatures.

The assumption that everyone is naturally heterosexual is heterocentric and ignorant. In acute cases of homophobia (fear of homosexuality), the victim is driven to wild acts of violence against strangers, often those of a different sexual orientation. Institutionalized homophobia runs rabid in the schools and churches, as unquestioning little cogs are churned out regularly by the family to fit nicely into society's machine. Individuality is punishable by electroshock and chemical lobotomies. Taking what is needed for survival is rewarded by prison. In both cases, violent, armed agents enforcing the dictates of the wealthy elite are present to make us conform and follow along nicely with all the other sheep...

The assumption that animals are for humans to use as they may see fit is called speciesism. Wild cases of speciesism lead the one suffering to desperate acts, such as consuming rotting flesh (sometimes even on a daily basis!), or the wearing of skins and furs to satisfy a fashion-tormented ego. Acute cases of speciesism lead one to seek employment in the name of science torturing animals in laboratories, confining them to a life of torture on factory farms, or selling them as pleasure units for family consumption.

The attitude that one may proceed as one wishes, even in such a case where consent may be lacking is a violent attitude. In a case where consent may be obtainable (in the case of humans' inability to communicate with animals in most cases), any further relations must be halted. This 'dominion over everything' attitude is the cause for massive environmental destruction, the macho nuclear arms shit, and sexism, and homophobia.

Some PETA members have formed a Gay caucus to specifically work on issues of animal liberation and AIDS testing on animals, within the Lesbian and Gay community. Some Toronto ALFSG members have taken on similar projects, and the following information is taken from a pamphlet compiled by "Homo Humans for Animal Liberation" entitled Animal Liberation is a Gay and Lesbian Issue.

ANIMAL RESEARCH AND AIDS; ETHICS AND EFFECTIVENESS

Many of us, I dare say most particularly women, have over the centuries increasingly mistrusted the foundations of western medical practice. We have wondered about its obsessive drive to rid humankind of death and "imperfection" at any cost. We have questioned its human chauvinism, its invasive techniques, its disregard for process, and its often arrogant disrespect for the intelligence and dignity of the individual patient.

Because we are now making large and justified demands upon medical and pharmaceutical institutions and because we are a gentle, but angry people, lesbians, gay men and feminists can have a tremendous influence in the changing of current scientific practices, particularly those that encourage useless, redundant and inhumane animal protocols. Even as we fight for our own lives and the lives of those we love, we can teach medicine and industry that the methods by which they accomplish their goals have values in themselves, that there is an ethic to the "how" of science as well as to its "what."

The California AIDS initiative *(The AIDS Research Act of 1988)* raises a serious question of conscience for many of us who fight for both lesbian/gay causes and the liberation of animals. My first reaction was delight that we had finally formulated an initiative that would allow Californians to vote FOR an AIDS bill; my second reaction was dismay that the initiative was for AIDS research instead of for AIDS education and the care of people with AIDS.

The problem I have is that our bill could *increase* the imprisonment, suffering and death of non-human animals. AIDS research is of two kinds: 1) that which seeks a CURE for or an arrest of the disease in people with AIDS or in those who are antibody positive, and 2) that which seeks PREVENTION, specifically research to discover a vaccine or other barriers to the disease. Even most researchers will admit that animals are not necessary in the first area when so many human volunteers are eager to participate in clinical trials for newly-developed drugs and therapies.

It is the second area that many would argue requires animal experimentation, for before a vaccine is tested on human subjects it is ordinarily tested on animal models. The likelihood is not great that healthy human volunteers will elect to take the vaccine before it has been "proved" to work on chimpanzees or other animals (though some people have suggested that the researchers who are convinced that HIV is harmless and not the cause of AIDS could themselves volunteer to be subjects for the testing of HIV vaccines).

I want research, yes, but not at the expense of animals. I want researchers - and lesbians, gay men and feminists - to abandon their efforts to find an animal model for vaccine testing and shift the money presently underwriting that highly questionable research into an area that we know is effective, i.e., into prevention through education.

I take this position because it is becoming clear that AIDS is not a part of non-human life experience. First, *empirically speaking*: seven years of frantic testing, millions of

dollars, and thousands of animal lives have failed to give any animal the disease, not even the chimpanzee, the most promising non-human subject. Second, *scientifically speaking*: HIV infects humans via the T-cells; the fact that the non-human T-cell structure (even that of primates) is so very different from that of humans casts serious doubt on the suitability of non-human animals as models for HIV infection. Finally, *behaviorally speaking*: non-human animals do not ordinarily participate in the activities that most frequently transmit the virus, i.e., they do not exchange it through anal intercourse, intravenous drug use, or the receiving of blood products.

In other words, we have to face the possibility that AIDS is a UNIQUELY human disease and that if we want a vaccine we must test that vaccine only on human subjects who have given their informed consent.

If I understand correctly the initiative's history, we at first attempted to get the State Legislature to place it before the voters on the Nov. 1988 ballot. That body resisted doing so because legislators felt that the Governor would certainly veto the action. Thus we are left with the task of getting the signatures ourselves for its inclusion on the ballot.

Originally the measure had proposed the use of laboratory animals in three specific parts of its detail. When the statewide committee set to work to ready the initiative for the signature-gathering campaign, some animal rights activists from the lesbian and gay community challenged those recommendations. The committee responded immediately; it deleted those three references and sent the entire initiative back yet again through all the red tape of the Office of the Secretary of State for a final approval. Thus what is before us is a proposition that has within it No Reference Whatsoever To Animal Use, and even more important, a position from which any such reference has been deliberately and laboriously deleted.

The fact that so much effort went into this changing of the language testifies that we do not by this initiative intend any AIDS research to use animals. Those efforts allow us as voters to expect that the Board administering the funding will steadfastly refuse to fund any such research.

Our task when the initiative passes will be to remind the board and the legislature of the clear intent of the proposition. Between now and Nov. our task is to educate ourselves, medical science, and the pharmaceutical industry about our needs as a community stricken with AIDS and about our desire not to exploit other species in helping ourselves.

As a strong political entity in this state and in the nation, our lesbian and gay community is in an almost unique position. The epidemic has touched our lives more deeply than it has touched any other organized group and as a result we have been and will continue to be forced to deal with medical institutions on a large scale. We have discovered over these years some of the miracles of medical science and some truly sensitive, caring, and intelligent practitioners of it. We also now know how self-aggrandizing and with what

questionable eunics medical science can operate. We have seen that the pharmaceutical industry can be competitive, profiteering, and exploitative to the disadvantages of those they purport to help.

So I call on all of us to join forces with animal rights activists and to make the next decade more than just a battleground for our rights, our dignity, and our health. It can be as well a time for our education of the medical establishment and a time for our expression of concern for all life, whatever its form.

Sally Miller Gearhart is a lesbian and feminist activist and writer from San Francisco. This article was reprinted from the April 10-16, 1988 issue of Gay Community News (GCN), 62 Berkeley St., Boston, MA. 02116 USA.

AIDS and Vegetarians

Aside from the more obvious areas of prevention, such as safe sexual practices, you can also help protect yourself through a strong immune system. 97% of food poisoning and other immune failures annually are related to animal products. While vegetarians are 5 - 8% of the population, they are hardly any of the people with AIDS. The percentage of gays and lesbians who are vegetarian and non-vegetarian is the same. Since the lymph glands and immune systems of vegetarians have not spent years battling animal bacteria present in dead flesh, their systems are stronger in this most essential of battles. For more information write APP E - AIDS Protection League, Box 115. kron, Ohio, USA.

Source: Talk Is Cheap, Vol. 1, No. 6.

Chimpanzees *"Stolen"* by Animal Liberationists

Representatives of People for the Ethical Treatment of Animals (PETA) announced on Sunday December 7, 1986, that earlier the same morning, "the animal liberation group, **True Friends**, removed four baby chimpanzees" (valued at $60,000) from the laboratories of SEMA Inc. in Rockville, Maryland. SEMA, a contractor of the U.S. National Institute of Health (N.I.H.), acquired the Maryland facility in 1986, formerly known as "Meloy Labs". The contract research performed by SEMA is mainly related to carcinogens and infectious diseases such as hepatitis and AIDS. The company houses 600 to 700 non-human primates of a variety of species as well as guinea pigs and woodchucks.

At a PETA press conference held in Washington, DC, on Dec. 8, 1986, a 15 minute videotape narrated by Ingrid Newkirk was shown. The tape, said to be taken as part of True Friends' surveillance activities, consisted of a tour through primate rooms (allegedly SEMA's) conducted by two masked women. The narration focused on the animals' isolation and "expressions of insanity." An exhibit of still photographs, mostly of caged primates, was also shown at the press conference. The exhibit and other written materials were labelled "Breaking the Species Barrier." True Friends are quoted as saying, "We must break the spe-

cies barrier ... these experiments are a horrendous crime that displays human arrogance and irresponsibility in its ugliest form."

The rescued chimps were about a year and a half old. It is important to note that these animals had just been weaned and are highly susceptible to viruses of all kinds as well as other health hazards. PETA said that they were due to be used in AIDS and hepatitis experiments. According to Alex Pacheco of PETA: "The differences between us and chimpanzees do not justify taking these highly intelligent individuals and infecting them with a disease they would never get, sentencing them to up to 50 years alone in a sealed, soundproof chamber. The chimps in the film have gone mad from the desperation of enduring living death."

Newkirk reported that True Friends had stolen many documents in addition to the chimpanzees. She claimed the SEMA facility had a history of accidental primate deaths that were preventable and predicted PETA would be sitting down with the N.I.H. to discuss such charges once the documents were reviewed. Newkirk declined to answer questions concerning True Friends on the advice of legal counsel, saying only that the Federal Bureau of Investigation was involved in the case.

These young chimps were rescued from a lab conducting AIDS and hepatitis research. It was the first chimpanzee liberation ever.

HOMES FOR ANIMALS

One of the most important responsibilities of the **Support Group** is finding homes for the animals. These animals desperately need good homes. The ALF can only rescue as many animals as there are homes, so try to imagine what it must be like to have to leave someone behind.

You might remember the raid that took place at the University of Western Ontario where 3 cats and 1 monkey were liberated by the ALF. There were homes arranged for these animals before this action took place and as soon as it hit the media these people refused to take them. There are probably a number of reasons why this happened. A lot of people don't realize what is really involved in taking an abused animal into your home. People sometimes may think that taking an abused animal, especially one that is liberated by the ALF, is somewhat exciting or adventurous and a lot of serious consideration is not taken into account. There are a great many risks involved not only in liberating these animals but equally in providing loving, stable homes for them.

The first consideration is the fact that it is illegal. You could never tell anyone where the animal came from because you are not only at risk but the animal would go back to the facility. An example is the raid that took place at the City of Hope National Research Centre a few years ago where two people were arrested on burglary and stolen property charges after the police received a tip. They admitted harbouring 12 rabbits taken by the ALF. The judge gave them both probation sentences and ordered one to do 360 hours of community service and the other one to pay a $10,000 fine to the City of Hope Research Centre. They were also not allowed to affiliate with an animal rights organization for 3 years, and the rabbits were taken back to the lab.

This case was pretty harsh but it could happen. You might be the one they want to make an example of. Another consideration is a lot of these animals could require expensive medical attention and certainly a lot of time to heal physically and mentally. A lot of these animals have been through hell and you might be faced with an animal that does not respond to your affections, and possibly never will. There have been reports of liberated animals that cry a lot, stiffen when approached, cower, eat compulsively and may even try to bite. Immediate medical attention is usually done before an animal is placed, and initial costs in most cases would be provided.

One example I'd like to mention is from an article from the **Rescued Animal Sanctuary Fund** in London: Many ALF groups who liberate large numbers of animals have special "Holding Units" where animals are taken after raids. The animals are given time to settle down and the injured ones are treated before they are taken to their permanent homes. The people who run these holding units provide an essential service. Their work is not glamorous and is often painfully sad. There are good times too. The following is just one example of the good and the bad side.

"Vivisection animals - I hate receiving them. I'm used to it now but I always feel ashamed. Sometimes I hold an animal and all I can do is weep and whisper "sorry" to it. I've apologized so many times to animals for my species. The accusations in the animals' eyes are always too much to bear. We had a group of beagles from a lab, and I soon learnt that I couldn't wear a white or dark green dress near them - if I did they would go mad, running around crashing into walls and furniture. God knows what they had gone through - it took them ages to settle down, and even after a few months you could tell that they didn't totally trust you. Mutilated animals are very difficult and very expensive to deal with. Some have to be helped to eat, some just stand and stare or tremble all the time. Sometimes an animal is so bad that nothing can be done and we are forced to have it put to sleep. We always make sure that we are there when it happens - once or twice I've seen the vet gasp as we've opened the animal basket. Yes, I can say that I don't give a damn about being called an extremist - do my job for a month and you'd probably be after blood."

"It can't be all bad? No, that's true - one extreme to another - sometimes I'm crying with happiness. To see an animal come out of its shell and learn to enjoy life is brilliant - to be finally trusted is a wonderful feeling. We are so careful not to break our part of the deal. I can't tell you what it feels like to see a once battered animal have the confidence to play and roll over on the grass. Young animals who have been kept in cages all their lives love to stretch out on the grass - they seem to drink in the fresh air. When animals go to their new homes it is both good and bad - we worry about them because we think

Continued on page 28

BAN ON DRAIZE TESTS

New Jersey is the first state in the U.S. to ban the notorious Draize test. On December 7, 1987, a Senate committee voted unanimously to endorse the bill, which would prohibit the testing of cosmetics and other household products in rabbits' eyes. Michael Petrina, a spokesperson for the Cosmetics, Toiletry, and Fragrance Association claims that the tests are required to establish the safety of all cosmetic products. Animal rights advocates disagree, saying that there are alternatives, but the industry has simply neglected to use them.

During the Senate committee hearing, Senator Raymond Zane (D-Salem) asked Dr. Robert Scala of the cosmetics industry how they "know if they are hurting the rabbit?" Dr. Scala replied, "It howls." Zane asked, "Why are rabbits used instead of rodents or mice?" Scala responded, "Because Senator, they have large eyes." What he neglected to mention here is that rabbits do not have tear ducts, so they can not wash away any chemical put into their eyes. Senator Zane noted that if a spray accidentally got into his eyes, "I'd know what to do ... but if it got into a rabbit's eye and burned, what can a rabbit do? It must be extremely painful."

Dolores Phillips of the New Jersey **Animal Rights Alliance** says, "Experimentation on animals has become a citizen rights issue. The right to demand an end to the torture of animals. The Draize test produces unimaginable suffering now inflicted upon harmless animals and is an unethical treatment ... for a grossly unnecessary purpose."
Source: New Jersey Star-Ledger, Dec. 8, 1987.

The LD50 and Draize eye irritancy tests were recently banned in the Australian state of Victoria. The state is currently formulating a new anti-cruelty act which will incorporate these measures. The Australian organization **Animal Rights** greeted the news of the ban with caution, worried that the government is using the ban to try to make other types of toxicology testing more acceptable to the general public.
Source: Animals' Agenda, Oct. 87

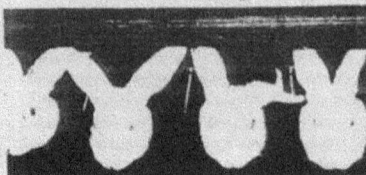

TOXICOL 1984

DRUGS AND POISONS: THE FRAUD CONTINUES

One of the strongest arguments against vivisection is that the whole process, along with the research institutions, are a complete and total fraud. The anti-vivisectionists who take this viewpoint base their arguments many times around the science and drug industries own published reports. Research on animals and the resulting drugs produced by the multi-national pharmaceutical industries have done more to harm human health than they have to better our lives, contrary to what the vivisectors and drug officials claim. The following reports back up the fraud argument:

A 'Business Day' report in the *New York Times* (June 6, 1987) describes in glowing terms how American Cyanamid Corporation developed its highly successful insecticide called "Combat". Apparently what they were really working on at the time was a cure for malaria. Someone in the lab left a beaker of it out overnight and in the morning they found dead cockroaches. The active ingredient, hydramethylnon, a slow metabolic poison, is now used as an insecticide rather than its first intended use, a cure a disease. It would be interesting to know whether any insecticides that fell short of the mark were later recycled as drugs.

A Pickering couple sued for damages when their 3 year old daughter suffered brain damage after taking a cumpulsory vaccine. They sued the following for ten million dollars each: the Durham Regional Health Dept., the Province of Ontario, the Whitby doctor who administered the vaccine, and Connaught Labs who developed the drug. The vaccine is called DPDT, a combination of serums for diphtheria, polio, tetanus, and whooping caugh. Within a year of being given the drugs, the child was diagnosed as physically handicapped and mentally retarded.

And in yet another example of scientific fraud, rats, mice and monkeys are being used to test the effects of "Lasso", a herbicide developed by the Monsanto Company in St. Louis. At an independent inquiry in Alberta, a professor of pharmacy and pharmaceutical science has said that scientists are wrong to experiment on rats merely for convenience when trying to predict how chemicals or drugs will affect people. The inquiry heard how the animals develop different cancers after being fed large doses of "Lasso".

What is important to note here is that a professor of pharmacy, which you and have come to know as meaning drugs for humans, is talking about herbicides, which are undoubtedly poisons. The relationship between the two, drugs and poisons, is becoming more and more clear, and we should begin questioning those research institutions which ask for our money to develop drugs intended to cure all our ills. What they are producing are poisons, all at the untold expense of animal lives and human health.

For excellent reading material on the scientific fraud arguments, suggested reading are two books by **Hans Ruesch** - *Naked Empress* and *Slaughter of the Innocent*. Both are available from **ARK II**, P.O.Box 66, Stn. O, Toronto, Ont. M4A 2M8 Canada.

COSMETIC AND PRODUCT TESTING

I think in order to even attempt to understand why the general public condones the torture of millions of animals in labs each year in order to get a new deodorant, toothpaste, air freshener, diesel oil, whatever, we must first recognize the total absorption of "self" that the mainstream of society has been persuaded by the advertising industry to revel in. We are self-indulgent and are motivated by self-gratification and self-adulation. We want to look more beautiful, more handsome, younger, want life to be easier, "get that new improved oven cleaner - buy that new, double strength garden fertilizer," etc. In other words, give us the maximum of pleasure for the minimum of effort, *AT ANY COST*, and make it last for as many years as possible - "because life's too short, right?"

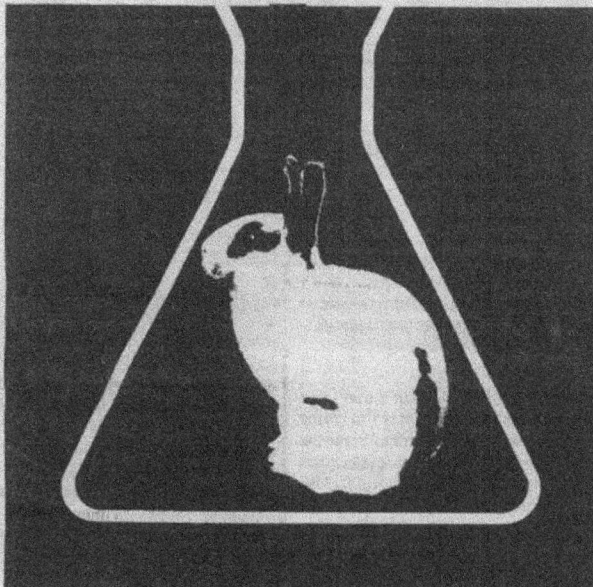

Animals' Agenda - March '86

Well, life is too short, but it's the animals' lives that are being shortened, and it does cost - but it's the animals who are paying the bill. And while someone out there in never-never land is trying to make themselves lose their wrinkles by smearing a cream containing animal guts over their face, the animals are paying in the labs. They are paying with screams, with agony, with convulsions, with burst internal organs, with blindness, and brain damage, and finally, if they aren't liberated, they are paying with death - the *only other escape* from torment they'll ever know.

So what is this testing like? Well, it's simple, basic and crude, out-dated and invalid. It resembles something out of the dark ages where, within the walls of inquisition chambers, you could use any method to get results. The bottom line in this particular kind of testing is that **nowhere** does the law of the land demand these tests be done on animals. The government demands a battery of tests. The *kind* of test is up to the manufacturers - they can use the alternatives available if they wish. We the consumer, by boycotting their products can most definately make them "wish"! The tests themselves have names like the LD50 (devised around 1920) and the Draize, a leftover from the 1940's.

The **LD50** means Lethal Dose 50, and within a group of animals being tested, 50% must die spontaneously before researchers determine what a lethal dose of the tested substance consists of. They are dosed by a stomach tube, capsules or a substance mixed into the food. Toxic symptoms are carefully noted: e.g., choking, paralysis, convulsions, etc. If the animals are dosed orally and can live that long, they are observed for a two-week period. If the substance is given by a stomach tube the animals can sometimes live as long as a week. Often the doses given to the animal are so great (because, after all, the researchers are only *guessing* at amounts in very small animals to determine what the toxic level is for us), that the internal organs burst in the animals and they die before any toxic symptoms can be noted.

The **Draize** test or eye-irritancy test is used mostly on rabbits, who are placed in miniature stocks to immobilize their heads. Their lower lid is pulled away from one eye to form a cup of skin and the test substance is poured in. Often the rabbits scream with agony. They cannot cry, so there are no tears to wash out the substance. It stays to ulcerate and literally burn away the eyeball in many cases. The animals' other eye are left clear, as a control. This torment lasts 3-4 days before they are killed.

Acute Dermal Toxicity testing results from abrasions being made to the animal's body - the test substance is rubbed or poured on the cuts and a tight fitting rubber sleeve or gauze is placed on the animal's body, keeping the test substance against the cuts. That remains for 24 hours, while the degree of suffering, writhing in pain, etc. is noted and then they are observed for another two weeks while the skin cracks and blisters.

Acute Inhalation testing, which is used for all aerosol products - animals are placed in chambers with the head and upper body exposed. That part of them is sprayed with the test solution. They breathe it in for 15 minutes. The procedure is repeated at 30-minute intervals until each animal has been sprayed ten times. After 4-7 more days of observation they are murdered and an autopsy is done to discover what respiratory effects resulted from the spraying.

All of these tests are supposedly done to keep us safe and healthy. We are not mice, nor rabbits, nor dogs. We are, as human animals, like them; a species that is physiologically and biologically unique unto itself. So results of testing tell only how that substance affected that species, nothing more. Some examples of animal tested substances which injured people are as follows:
-Hair ignited 8 hours after using hair spray.
-Underarm deodorant was ignited when a person reached over a stove.
-A woman was blinded by contaminate cosmetics.
-A woman who used cologne, struck a match and her face and neck caught fire.

Interestingly enough, **no injuries** have ever been reported from using cruelty-free products, which use natural ingredients and alternative testing methods. Companies who are so pious about keeping us safe won't pay for child-proof packaging. 10,000 children are taken to a hospital annually after ingesting make-up and household products. An example of the double standard that exists is that of a woman who took a manufacturer to court after being blinded by shampoo. The court found in favour of the manufacturer because the shampoo (which for the sake of the court case was *retested* on rabbits) was found no more toxic than others on the market. Also many researchers now admit results of animal-based testing has no bearing on results when the products are used on humans, which is of course, what animal rights activists have been saying all along.

So, despite the evidence, manufacturers continue to carry out unnecessary testing, thus ensuring the suffering and death of millions of animals each year. Use your power as a consumer - purchase cruelty free products and tell manufacturers why you refuse to buy their animal tested goods. As a consumer, you have a tremendous amount of power that you can use on behalf of the animals. For a complete list of companies which do not test on animals nor use animal ingredients, write to **ARK II**, P.O.Box 66, Stn. O, Toronto, Ont. M4A 2M8 Canada.

CAT DROWNING EXPERIMENTS STOPPED

Animal experimentation on cats used in child resuscitation research was halted in November 1987, at Huntingdon Memorial Hospital, in Pasadena, California, after twelve nurses and one doctor protested and alerted an animal rights group (*Pasadena Star-News*, 24/11/87). To measure changes in the cats' brain biochemistry, the researchers poured salt water into the their windpipes by way of tubes to simulate drowning. Four cats died immediately while two others were killed with Nembutal injections 24 hours later. Two other cats were spared when the experiments were stopped.

One nurse at Huntingdon complained because of the disinformation she was receiving, and says that the doctor in charge told her "... by drowning a cat, you can save a child's life." She replied, "... but a cat is not the same as an infant - you just can't cross over the information." Dr. Kenneth Stoller, a Pasadena pediatrician associated with Huntingdon agrees, saying that when researchers try to apply data from animal experiments to humans, they enter a "scientific grey zone." Another nurse said that the experiments were unethical because the results were useless for people who are brain-damaged after near-drowning. "If you drown and you don't get oxygen to the brain, you're not going to grow new cells. Brain damage is brain damage."

Lucy Shelton, a spokesperson for **People for the Ethical Treatment of Animals**, considers the research "scientifically flawed" on the basis of opinions given to her by the **Physicians' Committee for Responsible Medicine**. Douglas McCreery, who leads the Huntingdon Animal Care and Use Committee, defends the research, but says the experiments were stopped after reaching a point where they could "assess whether the study has produced a useful model for the resuscitation of a nearly drowned child." He later said that he feared that more militant animal liberationists might take direct action against the research, which, in California, would be very likely.

No other product will keep your ears so young and perky-looking AROUND the clock - keep it away from your eyes though, it's still being tested.

The revolution has brought such progress

Sue Real

ANIMAL LIBERATION AND NATIVE RIGHTS

In the debate over animal rights versus Native rights, people on both sides continue to become polarized as tensions mount. Animal rights activists are increasing the pressure on the public and government officials to support a ban on all hunting and trapping, while Native leaders increase their counter-campaign by producing movies and videos on indigenous ways of life, and forging stronger ties with the fur industry. I would like to add my voice and opinions to this controversy, by suggesting alternatives to what I feel are the dogmatic and rigid views expressed by both sides. As both an animal liberation activist and a supporter of Native peoples' rights, I believe that there is much common ground between the two groups that needs to be further explored. Very briefly, here are the basic statements being made:

The animal advocates want a total ban on all hunting and trapping, as this practice is not only cruel and unnecessary, but it supports a multi-million dollar industry that profits from the killing of animals for the vanity of rich people in New York or Paris, among other places. They also state that the fur industry and Native hunting and trapping do not represent indigenous ways of life because the methods and tools used in the hunt are modern devices such as snowmobiles, high powered rifles, and steel leg-hold traps made in New York.

The Native peoples' position is that they have always traded in furs, long before white man and the Hudson's Bay Company invaded Turtle Island. They say that if the campaign to ban hunting and trapping is successful, it will not only force Native people into a life of welfare, resulting in social breakdown of their communities, but it will open up their land to the government and development corporations who will come in and proceed to exploit the earth for minerals and oil, not to mention the military's use for low-level flight testing of

fighter jets. As well, if Native people can't use the land for hunting and trapping, they say that this will make it harder for land claims in the courts.

Given this, albeit a very simple breakdown of the issues, there are many ways in which both groups can reach common ground and perhaps work together.

First of all, I see the alliances made between Native people and the fur industry as being totally unnatural, and that, despite what some Native people claim, the fur industry - the white greedy profiteers - are once again exploiting the Indians for their own interests. I also believe that, whether or not Native people will admit it, this alliance is for purely political reasons that have nothing to do with indigenous ways of life. But, of course, if you're fighting for the survival of your people, you may use different tactics, including siding with your exploiters if the short term gain is worth it. I believe that if there are any natural alliances to be made, it is between the Native people and animal liberation activists. Please note that I specifically mean animal 'liberation' as opposed to animal 'rights'. By far the majority of the animal rights movement is composed of people who are white, middle or upper class, and who have little or no analysis of any other political struggles other than that of saving animals. Quite often animal rights people come across as uncaring towards oppressed people, if not outright racist. This, I believe, is a major obstacle in the struggle to bring the two movements together.

As an animal liberation activist and an anarchist, I see no hypocrisy between my anti-fur position and my pro-Native struggles position. I believe that the earth is a living entity, and that all life on her is connected - whether in a life and death cycle or part of an extremely complicated ecosystem.

My main focus in my anti-fur politics is those who are the exploiters: the multi-na-

tional fur industry, the fur retailers, and the person on the street wearing a fur out of vanity or ignorance. I choose to attack these people in my campaign and not Native people, because I believe that Native peoples' struggle for their land and their lives is much more important than whether they hunt and trap.

In the fur industry in Canada, Native hunting and trapping make up only 8% of the total industry, while the majority of the rest comes from factory farming. And hardly any of the Native people involved in the trade are part of the wholesale and retail parts, where most of the money is made. It simply makes absolutely no sense whatsoever to focus on Native trapping and hunting in the anti-fur campaign.

So where does this leave the animal rights people as they work toward a total ban on hunting and trapping, and are trying to destroy the fur trade? Well, regardless of how successful they are in destroying the fur trade, there will still be a market, however small it may be. If we can get rid of the multinational corporations and the white man's interference, and leave an exemption clause in the campaign against fur for Native hunting and trapping, then I'm sure the 8% market share Native people have now will not decrease at all.

Native leaders who are siding with the fur industry are making a big mistake. The fur industry has no interest in indigenous cultures and will sell them short when the time is right. Animal rights activists who refuse to develop a wider analysis of different people's struggles will always show themselves to be an arrogant group. Clearly the fur industry is the target, and not an 8% market share group.

Native people, animal liberationists and anarchists have much in common. We have a common enemy, if we choose to recognize

it; that being the profit-making, greedy capitalists, who will exploit everything and everyone if there's money to be made. We also have a common desire to save our planet. This entails many ideas, from stopping the military and government interference on the land to combatting destructive practices of the white race.

Many Native people are very opposed to vivisection, factory farming, fur farming, and other animal abuses, because the exploitation and torture of animals is not in balance with our life cycles. And most animal liberation activists are very supportive of Native struggles. In Toronto, animal liberation activists can always be seen at Lubicon support demonstrations, or rallies for Leonard Peltier for example. By the same token, more Native activists are purposely seeking out animal liberation activists and anarchists to form alliances with - because the strong possibility for unity is there.

These groups must find ways to work together, because we do have a common goal - the desire to bring a balance back into our lives on this planet, and to evolve toward a harmonious relationship with our Mother Earth.

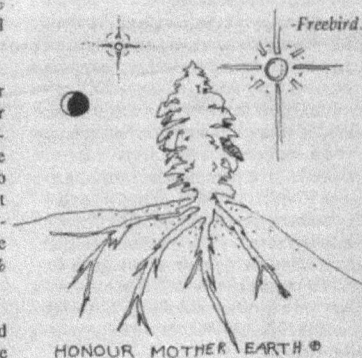

-Freebird.

HONOUR MOTHER EARTH

LETTERS

Lust For Revenge

Dear FLN:

Enclosed is ten dollars for a subscription.

I liked practically everything except for the Ursula Crabtree letter and the "Crush .... Vivisectionists" graphic. The theme that both contained (i.e. "eye for an eye", lust for revenge) only gives our opponents opportunities to call us hypocrites. Such thinking leads to the holocaust of capital punishment as witnessed in many U.S. states today.

Is it possible for the ALFSG to produce, manufacture, or distribute items much like those of PETA? I am referring specifically to the "Meat is Murder" t-shirts and the "Cancelled" stickers. I think the latter could have been quite appropriate for the adverts for the rush of fur sales that have taken place here.

(Ed. Note: Check out our Distribution list for what we are selling.)

M. T.
Winnipeg, Manitoba

☺ ⏚ Ⓔ ⬡ ⚧ ⚥ ☮ ⚭ ⚭
♡ ✡ ?

Extremist Language

Dear FLN:

I received *Front Line News* #3; you got me from a mailing list which is okay. I feel that the newspaper would be vastly improved if the extremist language in the articles was removed; it is not productive to insult people who are, in a sense, on the "other side" of an issue, as such writings do not further the cause and only elevate the ego of the writer. I agree that treatment of animals in labs, etc., is barbaric, inhumane, etc., etc. I contribute to a newsletter that focuses on two-legged homelessness and other issues.

On Aug. 24, 1985, I broke through the fence surrounding Romeo-29, a Minuteman III missile silo in Montana, and acted in a civil disobedient manner. Upon my arrest I tried to find points of commonality between myself and the arresting soldiers from Malmstrom AFB. Other anti-nuclear activists have discovered that it is better to deal with arms making, factory workers, et al, with persistence, love, and creativity. Why can't animal liberationists do the same, in their context?

Thornton Kimes, Dec. 7, 1986
Des Moines, IA

P.S. Has anyone noticed that chickens don't fly? The Alberta students (see *FLN* #3) burned the village to save it - yea team!!!

Anti-Authoritarian Thoughts

Dear FLN:

Recently I read for the first time *Front Line News* and learned of some of the activities of ALF in Canada, as well as that of groups elsewhere. I am writing because I believe that it would be to our mutual benefit to establish contact.

I am presently at the tail end of a ten-year sentence. *(Ed. note:* now released.) Suffice it to say that I am anti-authoritarian, although my convictions are based more upon my personal experiences with the state and other authoritarian systems (family, school, church, etc.) rather than any clear understanding of anarchist philosophies. Much preferring to keep things simple, I equate anarchism with freedom and freedom with the ability to say no. No to any impulses of my own to impose restrictions upon others and no to anyone's attempt to restrict me.

In recent years I have come to be immensely interested in animal rights, but continue to be somewhat divided in my thoughts on the subject, perhaps because of an inability to come to terms with my own desires. Although I have in the past adhered to a strictly vegetarian diet, I now eat some meat. In my own mind I am able to rationalize this by arguing that to deny humans to eat animal flesh we must also deny other species from eating meat, including that of man himself (sic). I prefer to believe, however, that the central issue to the argument should properly be the manner in which animals are raised for slaughter, not to mention the manner in which they are slaughtered. Equally important should be the effect on the world food supply of diverting high-quality grain products toward meat production. As to the use of animals in experiments, I cannot forsee any circumstances under which I could condone such, and believe that we are all probably the worse off for having engaged in such as a species.

As you can see, I am unable in my own mind to reach any hard and fast conclusions, other than to perceive that the status quo is grievously wrong and must be changed. My biggest problem is deciding how much change should be effected and what the end result will be. Possibly such thoughts also plague others involved in the animal rights movement and I would enjoy learning differing views along these lines.

This is one area that I am interested in and which I intend to devote some of my time to upon my release. Believing that people like ourselves can often help each other out in a variety of ways, I have taken it upon myself to write to you and a few selected others. Certainly there are certain advantages to be derived from knowing others that you can trust. Of course, in my present situation I am subjected to a certain amount of mail censorship and must often write for the eyes and simple minds of others who will read my letters before their intended recipient. Thankfully that will all change soon.

Anyway, I would be interested in learning of what you are involved in presently. Perhaps there are ways in which we could assist one another. In any event, I look forward to a synergetic relationship with you.

Yours for a world without chains,
L.T.
Norco, California

Networking

Dear FLN:

I have given your article on networking very serious thought; the mail correspondence. Although the mail system has some very attractive reasons for being used, such as being available worldwide, being the least expensive to participate in, being the most private, is probably the most reliable, and is something anyone so inclined can do, I still think it is a wide open invitation for infiltration. Maybe I don't understand it clearly enough.

How would one "smoke out" an infiltrator in a procedure such as this?

However, if and when in some way networking is put into effect I would like to help if at all possible. Please keep me in mind and in touch with proceedings.

Sincerely,
D.H., Aug. 9, 1986
Mena, Arakansas

Dear FLN:

I am, at present, on a shoestring budget, but when I will be working, I'll support your group primarily. In the meantime, I do my best to find homes for stray cats, and I feed a dozen cats on a farm who otherwise would be near starvation. (I also write protest letters.)

I was going to write to you about contacting me with other members in Brantford as I'm very frustrated lots of times and would like some moral support; my boyfriend isn't enough, mainly because I'm much more conscious of animals' plights.

I already have a Box #. I am very nervous about getting an undercover butcher or a furrier as a contact. One way to make certain that the person is legit is to observe their households, whether they are vegetarians, etc., before you become any chumier with them. Maybe you could outline such strategies in the newsletter. However, I would limit my activities in the beginning to finding homes for strays, etc.

How does one beat the frustration and depression one feels over the animal torture that goes on?? A lot of times I am paralyzed by it, like those restrained animals. I literally want to murder those hunters, vivisectionists and any other animal abusers.

Sincerely,
I.G., July 30, 1986
Brantford, Ontario

Industrial Art Mirrors Society

Dear FLN:

I was very disturbed by your article on the industrial performance art group **Survival Research Laboratories** (not "Science Research Laboratories"), but not in the way you might expect. As an experimental artist and someone involved in industrial culture (mainly through music), I would like to respond to the article.

First of all I would like to make clear that, although I admire much of SRL's work, I do not in any way support or condone their use of animals (until reading that article, I was not aware they were planning to use live animals). However, I feel that the

Continued next page

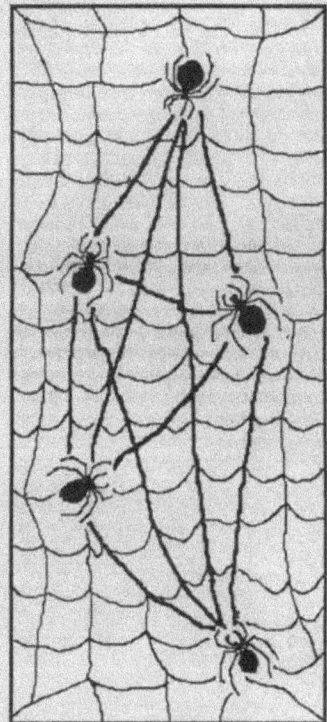

Editors' Notes On Networking

In *Front Line News* #3 we printed an article on networking, noting that there are many people who write to us telling us how frustrated and isolated they are working alone, and who would like to network with other like-minded people in their area. We posed the situation as a problem of dealing with infiltrators and of being security conscious, and we still haven't realized a tight, secure way of networking total strangers. And the problem is, of course, that most of you are total strangers to us, and it would be utterly stupid for us to get people together who we know nothing about. The immediate and safest solution is, as always, to work alone or with your most trusted friends. If anyone has more ideas on this subject, we would be most happy to hear from you.
More letters next page...

Nosy raccoon knocks out nuclear plant near Detroit

Star May 10 '88

MONROE, Mich. (AP) — The Fermi II nuclear power plant south of Detroit, designed to withstand tornadoes and earthquakes, was knocked out by a raccoon.

The curious animal climbed into electrical equipment Saturday at a switchyard outside the Fermi II plant, causing a short circuit, knocking out some power and triggering a shutdown of Detroit Edison Co.'s $6.6 billion plant.

The raccoon died. Company spokesman Dan Vecchioni said backup generators kept the plant's safety systems intact.

LETTERS...

Industrial Art

Continued from previous page

vehemence of Phoenix's article attacking SRL was unwarranted, and that the article was largely based on a total lack of understanding of the nature and purpose of radical/experimental art; particularly that area of it known as "industrial". There were also some very reactionary assumptions made about the role of art in society.

About 75% of the article could have been written by virtually any mainstream art critic: "insanity, horror, and lunacy"; "based in a dingy foundry" (instead of a chic downtown studio like respectable bourgeois artists); "sickos"... And, no, SRL have *not* met with "critical acclaim", except from a few alternative/underground sources. In fact, they have made every effort to distance themselves from the mainstream/trendy "art world". The very extremity of their work precludes the possibility of co-optation.

From my own experience, when I used a found dead bird for an art piece, the general public does not react well to anything that reminds them of the existence of death. Phoenix makes no distinction between the mainstream and underground art scenes when s/he speaks of SRL having been "accepted by the San Francisco art scene" or of receiving "critical acclaim". Considering the use of the terms "exhibits" and "art shows", it is probably safe to assume that s/he is also unaware of an underground art scene.

Most likely, like the majority of people, Phoenix probably thinks that art should be 'nice', decorative, comforting, and never challenging or disturbing. If something disturbs or upsets you, it has transgressed the boundaries of acceptability, and is not art.

The purpose of industrial art/music is to disturb, upset and horrify people, and to force them to confront the fact that we live in a disturbing, upsetting and horrifying society; a "nightmare culture" as **Current 93** and **Coil** (industrial bands) put it. Industrial culture is thus an inherently political movement, though its political dimensions may not be immediately evident to those unfamiliar with it.

SRL's performances succeed admirably in reflecting/caricaturing our hellish, oppressive, technocratic death culture. They spend months preparing for each show, constructing horrifyingly ugly, frightening machines which are then set to destroy each other in performances, mirroring the horrors and destructiveness of the arms race, the military/industrial complex and our own society's ever increasing ghoulish obsession with phallic death technology. The hidden atrocities of our dying culture are thus brought to the surface and thrown in the faces of those who would rather remain blissfully ignorant. Many people react with hostility and violence to this forced confrontation and misdirect their hatred toward the artists instead of the society which makes such art necessary, much like the ancient rulers who executed the bearers of bad news. It is my feeling that these are the reasons underlying the extreme responses to SRL.

──── Animal abuse in art is nothing new. ────

There is no concrete reason why the members of SRL should be considered any more revolting than most other artists, or most people in general for that matter. Animal abuse in art is nothing new. Let's consider "natural (animal) bristle" brushes, paints containing animal ingredients, cat gut strings on musical instruments, leather dance shoes, art materials that are tested on animals ... to name only a few things. Is SRL's use of animals worse because they do it openly instead of hiding behind convention and commodities? ... Because they use them in a way which forces the viewer to confront things they would rather ignore?

I would rather see an SRL performance than a fur fashion show or a McDonald's commercial. The real horror to me is the casual, unacknowledged everyday torture and killing which we are bound by custom and politeness to ignore. I am by no means uncritical of SRL, their work, or their politics. I think that they definately have some questionable ideas and are obviously, whether wittingly or not, engaging in oppressive actions. However, these actions must be seen in the proper context. The way

to deal with radical/underground people who are acting oppressively is not the same way that we would deal with a university, or a multinational corporation. Other means are open to us in this case, such as *communication*.

Phoenix tells us to write to **Target Video** and various animal rights organizations. Why not write directly to Survival Research Laboratories?! They can be reached c/o the industrial music/art magazine *Re/Search* (SRL appears in issue #10). Their address is 20 Romolo #B, San Francisco, CA 94133 USA.

Finally, I would like to point out that many industrial artists are explicitly pro-animal liberation. **Nocturnal Emisions** have used material on vivisection in a video; Toronto's **Violence and the Sacred** have songs about animal liberation and have played at a benefit for the **ALFSG** Canada (Toronto); and **Tibet 93** of the band **Current 93** recently co-ordinated a benefit album for the British **ALFSG** (entitled **Devastate to Liberate**) which features a wide variety of industrial bands.

In Solidarity,
Lycanthia
Toronto, Ontario

Friends Of The ALF

Dear FLN:

It was with interest that I read your first issue of *Front Line News*. I am the editor of your Dutch counter-part *'Dierenbevrijding'*, which first saw light in March this year. I made a translation into English for **ALFSG** (UK). I did not keep an extra copy of it, but the plan is that I send ten copies of an English translation both to UK and to you, together with a copy of the Dutch version. In exchange I would like to receive ten copies of your *Front Line News*.

These ten copies include the copies which you eventually used to send to the address Oude Gracht 36 at Utrecht. No more copies should be sent to this address, as the post is keeping an eye on it. I will pass on the copies to them who need them, and keep one for myself to take over publication in 'Dierenbevrijding' (Dutch for 'Animal Liberation'). Our SG group is called '**Vrienden van het DBF**' = '**Friends of the ALF**'. Second issue of our quarterly will be ready in a few days.

HE DID VERY WELL; NOW WE'LL TRY HIM ON PIPE TOBACCO...

Depression In Saskatoon

Dear FLN:

I would like to inform you that I learned on March 8, 1986, in Brussels, from a conversation about depression, that Dr. J.S. Richardson of Saskatoon, Canada causes depression in animals by causing lesions in rats' brains, giving constant and unavoidable electric shocks to dogs and rats, forcing rats to run until they collapsed (he didn't say how but I assume by administering electric shocks), and forcing rats to swim until exhaustion.
(Translated from a letter by a Belgian psychiatrist to the ALFSG-UK).

Dr. E. V., March 9, 1986
Belgium

Besides the **ALF** we have a group called '**Angels Versus Skinners**' which is mainly involved in psychological warfare against animal abusers. With a boycott action against one of the biggest users of animal testing, Bayer, AVS reached newspapers in Germany and medical press in Austria. In the action 50,000 pamphlets were spread over the country to call for a boycott of Bayer products, especially the anti-flem drops 'Bolfo' (Tugevon). Fur merchandisers over the country were warned to stop their bloody business or else... and a small village having plans to build a new commercial (U.S. funds!) lab (animal) breeding centre was warned that actions would follow which will be harder than the concrete of the building if they start working on it.

Well, that's all for now. The packet will be in the mail to you in a few days after you get this letter. Hope to get yours in return. BEAT THEM HARD!

So long,
Jan,
Holland

RE/SEARCH #6/7
Mark Pauline of S.R.L. with his "Rabot" - a dead rabbit connected to a mechanical device.

LETTERS...

Notes From Chicago

Dear **FLN**:

Thanx alot for Issue #3 of *Front Line News* - it was indeed most refreshing to read something more resembling my personal views of the whole animal experimentation/vivisection controversy, other than the usual staid and smug "welfare societies'" admonitions against "pound seizure", et al... (Which is not to denigrate the anti-pound seizure campaign - our own city of Chicago is merely now beginning to consider it.) Ya gotta start somewhere, right? So, since I've now become the semi-plagued owner of three stray dogs (at least, in a large city apartment), I started by making sure they at least all have collars and don't run around without supervision - tags and collars are essential. Then, a brief part-time graveyard stint at the Flying Tiger organization at Chicago's O'Hare Airport brought me around to the modus operandi of the larger laboratory animal suppliers, the "merchants of misery" if you will, such as Charles River and Co., USA:

Beagles and rabbits shipped by the hundreds every evening to destinations and fates unknown. The monkeys in their tiny, squalid wooden cages were the most pathetic of all; the irradiated, experimental mice left out to drench during rainy nights on the airport tarmac; the zoo-bound freshly-nabbed seals I was instructed to hose down every hour; the strained and irksome barking of a beagle whose vocal cords probably had not been "expertly" cut; the primates reaching through their shipping cages for my lousy day-old fruit and cheese sandwiches; the odium of such an animal slave trade screamed out too loudly to forget...

Onward, to the contact of the three anti-vivisection societies in the USA - remembering from years hence of my mother asking me not to bother looking at their flyers in the morning mail ("can't do anything about it anyway, son"), and the resultant monthly mailings. Yes, indeed, just for my personal edification, the vivisection situation hasn't been resolved yet... Further scrutiny of some extremely irritating items

Beagle with electrode liberated
from U.C. Irvine Jan. 29/88

leads to the *Animals' Agenda* magazine - and then the horrifying facts as presented by **People for the Ethical Treatment of Animals** (PETA), Dr. Katz' *In Defense Of Animals* and various lesser animal mobilization organizations, and finally, to several publications such as Peter Singer's, Richard Ryder's, J.D. Whittal's, and most notably, Hans Ruesch's *Slaughter of the Innocent*...

I have become convinced that Mr. Ruesch's philosophy of attacking the vivisectors on grounds of scientific innacuracy and uselessness (re: his **CIVITAS** group) is the most accurate of all the attacks (all of them justified) against the idiocy of vivisection. Yet, despite government clampdowns in this country against lab break-ins, and the imposed penalties upon "liberators" and "harborers" of liberated animals, I am absolutely convinced that ONLY the activities of sub-groups like the ALF can truly expose the monstrous lunacy of "modern science" nowadays - so, COUNT ME IN.

On to specifics... Ursula Crabtree's letter was just the sort of item I expected from an actual ALF supporter - her invoking of the ancient code of Hammurabi (an eye for an eye, etc.) I found particularly noteworthy; "A Scenic Harvest..." was a most disgusting article written no doubt to awaken us to the sort of individuals who would do most any thing to profit from animals' misery (*Ed. Note*: Read Lycanthia's letter "Industrial Art Mirrors Society"); G.B. Shaw's classic indictment of the vivisector is something I expected of such a great mind...

The most damning of vivisectionist violence I found in the articles about the ALF Toronto dentistry raid. Any fool who has ever found himself in a dentist's chair knows about chronic pain, immediate pain or even mere fear of pain - there can be no possible logic behind "Dr." Sessle's hideous and sadistic "experiments". Why, the photo of him itself depicts an individual who's "lost it" a long time ago - note the strange eyes... The article on the ALF's endeavor to storm Sessle's Citadel of Pain

was a moving and extremely frustrating one. Clearly, he is now aware of our displeasure with his "work", especially after his auto has been vandalised, but he still has his mortgage to pay and bills galore so this is not going to stop him, or his ilk, in their sordid livelihood. So, in the interests of the poor tormented animals suffering under his thumb, what is then the alternative, short of assassination? Or, is indeed the answer to be found in a stray bullet... Enough diatribe.

Do you have any problems with your government interfering with mail deliveries? (*Ed:*-Yes!) I can almost see where they might want to intercept a few of these or other communiques - understandably so, from their distorted viewpoint. As far as I'm concerned, every movement of any credible consequence has had its roots in a reform group of a rather radical nature. Remember John Brown and the anti-slavery, abolitionist movement of the pre-Civil War days in America (and the related Underground Railroad of the same era)? Being primarily an anti-vivisectionist, it is these organizations which remind me of the total righteousness of groups such as yours, and hopefully, despite horrendous odds, indeed, "we shall overcome"!

Sincerely,
A. P., Aug. 13, 1986
Chicago, IL

Drain The Resources

Dear FLN:

Lately there has been a lot of pro-fur disinformation presented in the national media. Two main proponents of the lies have been Alan Herscovici and The Fur Trade. These two are apparently trying and willing to send out information to those who request it. I believe we should be deluging these scum for their material so as to drain their resources as much as possible. Anyone who knows how successful the "Jerry Falwell Game" was will realize that this can be attempted again.

Their addresses are: Alan Herscovici, 856 A Blumefield Ave., Outremont, P.Q. H2V 3S6 Canada; The Fur Trade, 1435 rue St. Alexandre, Suite 1270, Montreal, P.Q. H3A 2G4 Canada.

While we are at it, there is a pro-rodeo organization that deserves the same treatment: COWBOY (Cowboys Outraged With Rumbling Obnoxious Yahoos), P.O.Box 8160, Nashville, TN 37207 USA.

It should go without saying that one should drain as much from these sickies without giving them one cent in return.

(*Ed. Note*: The Jerry Falwell Game was a mass circulation of christian fanatic's toll-free phone numbers which people would call and request info mailed to them. Also each call cost Falwell a couple of dollars. Press reports indicated that Falwell sustained tens of thousands of dollars in bills due to a large participation in the "game".)

Anonymous
Winnipeg, Manitoba

Letters To The Editor...

We are aware of an increase in mail that has been tampered with and letters that have not reached us. We must all assume that any communication is looked at by unfriendly eyes. When writing to us, some basic security procedures should be practiced. As much as we all feel outrage toward animal abuse, please do not write anything which could be incriminating to you or us. This includes telling us what you have done or what you would like to do. We don't want to know! For sending us action reports read what "Zuc Legume Sez" on pg. 28. To help us moniter mail tampering, putting tape across the seal of the envelope leaves a noticeable mark if it's removed. There isn't much we can do about the mail that is confiscated or turned back, so if you've sent us a letter or donation and haven't heard from us, send another letter to see if we've received it.

MAN DEMONSTRATING HIS SUPERIORITY OVER ANIMALS.

R.COBB

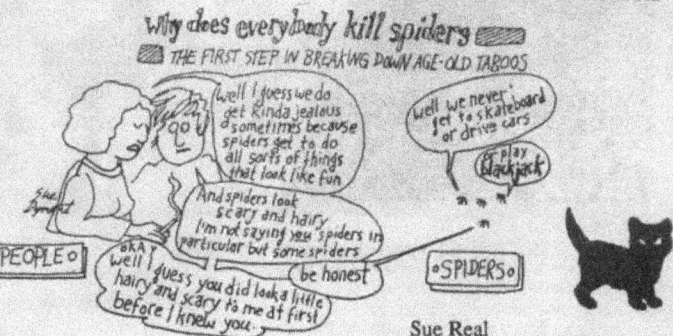

Why does everybody kill spiders
THE FIRST STEP IN BREAKING DOWN AGE-OLD TABOOS

Sue Real

ANALYSING ANIMAL ACTION

ALF claimed responsibility for the $3.5 million fire at U.C. Davis, where new labs were being built.
Animals' Agenda
-Sept. '87

A short while ago, at a meeting for the Support Group, a number of concerns were expressed about certain actions supposedly carried out by the ALF. It was felt that these concerns were important enough to be addressed in the *Front Line News*. Several ALF actions were reported in the media including the attempted fire-bombing of a fur store in London, Ont., to the spray painting of a church, community centre and shopping mall. To the best of our knowledge, only one action has been officially claimed by the ALF during this period - namely, economic sabotage to some meat stores.

As we have stated many times, YOU are the ALF! Everytime you graffiti a fur store, glue one of their locks, smash the window of a meat store, or break into a research facility, YOU then become the ALF and you automatically receive our support. However, when one first begins to take part in such actions, one is bound to make mistakes and it is from those mistakes that one learns. Particularly for those who are just beginning their activist careers, as it were, I would like to mention a couple of issues that came up at our meeting.

First, it is essential that an ALF action be identified as such. Even if you yourself do not feel comfortable sending a press release to the media, at least send the SG your action reports. That way we can write up a raid or action *accurately*, which rarely happens with the regular media, and also, if an ALF action *has* taken place and no one claims it, then it loses its impact. We want and need the public to know the ALF is out there and is growing. Secondly, and of vital importance, on no account should you include anyone's name or address (including your own) in any action reports. Send them to us anonymously, and free of fingerprints. Believe me, this is not a redundant warning, people have actually identified themselves and others to us as taking part in or planning to take part in raids. *Security is of the utmost importance.*

The concerns that arose during the Support Group meeting were about two actions in particular - the fire-bombing and the alleged theft of $800 from a meat store that was raided. The fur store that was hit with the molatov cocktail apparently had a family sleeping above the store and only the fact that the shop was fitted with fire-retardant carpet prevented the flames from taking hold. ALF Canada (Toronto), as we know it, advocates non-violence to ALL beings, and that includes people who choose to live above a fur store. Also, if one steals money during a raid, one *immediately* loses the activist image and gains one of 'petty thief'. All media attention is focused on the theft and the benefits accrued from bringing the attention of any supportive member of the public to the plight of the animals is completely lost! It does not even matter if you believe it to be another form of genuine economic sabotage - to the public at large, it becomes merely theft!

When dealing with fire, molatov cocktails, etc., you are literally playing with life and death. There is simply no excuse for not checking to see if people are on or around the premises, within the vicinity, etc. At no time should any innocent bystander be at risk. (We have seen a perfect example of the

tragedy that can occur in this kind of action with the recent hotel fire in San Juan - set as a mere protest!) If, on the other hand, you really don't give a damn about any innocent bystanders, then perhaps you should begin identifying yourselves as a more radical offshoot of the ALF. Possibly, as in England, the Animal Rights Militia, or some such title. We want the tide of public opinion to swell *for* the ALF not *against* it. *Keep in mind at all times* if the ALF loses support, the animals lose support.

It is abundantly clear to us all that the establishment, the media, the police, want the ALF destroyed or discredited. What better way to do this than through false reporting. For example, the four people who spray painted the church, community centre and

shopping mall were caught. After two days of interrogation, during which time they explained repeatedly that the ALF slogans they spray painted were a few among many signs and slogans they had used, and they themselves had nothing to do with the Animal Liberation Front, the police then informed the media that it was probably an ALF action. What better way to discredit the movement than report they are now defacing churches and community centres - none of which has anything to do with animal liberation. If the media attempts to discredit the ALF by falsely reporting an action in which you have been involved, e.g., stating that money was stolen when you know it was not, put out an immediate denial or let us know and we will put out a press release for you

Finally, in *all* ALF actions there should be only one consideration, the animals! You should always be asking yourself when planning something; how will this impact on the movement and ultimately on the animals? Will this have negative repercussions on the movement and on the animals? Will this benefit the animal liberation movement and so benefit the animals? If you keep these things in mind, you will be on the right track and should not go far wrong. We would be interested in your thoughts on this article and the issues it raised, so please write to us!

- Phoenix.

UNIVERSITIES continued from page 17

PSYCHOLOGY STUDENTS
ORGANIZE

Virtually none of the students who enter into psychology ever intend to have anything to do with animal research in their future career. Ironically, in order for a student to be able to obtain their degree in psychology from the University of Toronto's Scarborough campus, they must successfully complete Psychology B01 (Introductory to Psychology Research). This course charges a lab fee to cover the cost of animals used in experiments. These experiments are designed by, and are under the instruction of professor Beiderman, an animal researcher and instructor at the university.

The Canadian Council on Animal Care, a committee predominantly made up of animal researchers and industries, which was formed to supposedly set the ethical standards for the use of animals in research, stresses that animals should only be used when there are no other alternatives available. In fact, there are many other teaching aids available that are suitable for understanding the same principles being presented with animal experiments in Psychology B01. Several years ago, because of the persistant action of a concerned psychology student, professor Beiderman, who at that time was president of the Scarborough campus Animal Care Committee, was persuaded by a C.C.A.C. member to stop the practice of having students shock rats in his course.

A group of students concerned about the necessity and ethics of requiring students to perform experiments on animals, formed and began a petition requesting that Psychology B01 labs do not involve any animals. The purpose of the petition was to encourage those students who felt pressured to participate in animal experimentation, to express their right to moral choice and insist on having the opportunity to learn what is necessary for the completion of a course in a way that was consistant to their ethical standards. This, of course, is not a privilege, it is a student's right! An overwhelming majority of the students in Psychology B01 signed this petition. Unfortunately, professor Beiderman did not change his course agenda and the requirements for the course were insisted upon.

If you are a psychology student in the Toronto area, and are concerned about being expected to perform experiments on animals as part of filling out your course requirment, you can get some practical advice and help in forming groups or other activities. Write to Charlene Winger, Box 520, Pickering, Ont. L1V 2A1.

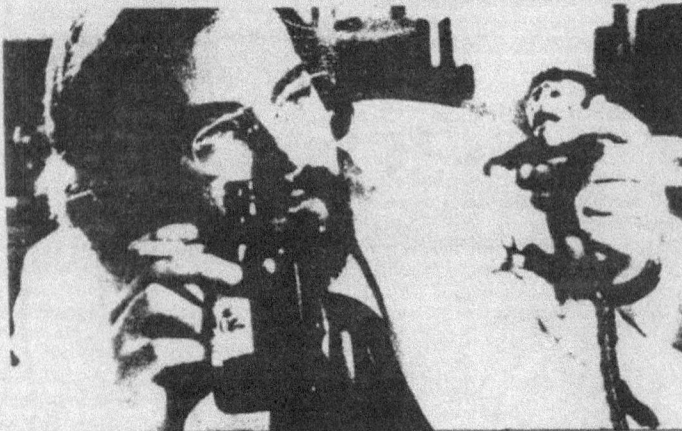

Greg Stickrod, U.O.'s Director of Animal Care, holds a screaming baby monkey aloft in a 'joke photo'.

PETA News, April/May '88

Action Reports Canada

Continued from page 10

Feb. 8: A. Stork & Sons had three trucks spray painted.
Mid-Feb.: Locks glued on the following: Finn Furs (Eglinton Ave.); Laird Meat Market (Eglinton); The Butchers (Yonge St.); Cowiesons Meats (Yonge St.)

Sept.: Victory Furs and Madison Furs (Bloor St. W.) had their windows smashed.

1988
Mid-Jan.: Kentucky Fried Chicken outlet (Bloor St. W.) had windows smashed.

Vancouver, B.C.
1987
June/July: 3 butcher shops, 1 McDonald's and 1 Kentucky Fried Chicken shop had their locks glued. 1 butcher's shop window was smashed.
Aug. 3: 2 fur shops had locks glued.
Aug. 8: Walls, doors, and windows of a sausage plant, a chicken factory and 2 fish export companies were painted with ALF slogans.
Aug. 20: Grandview Furs had windows smashed and red paint thrown inside, damaging mink and red fox furs; $7,000 damage.
Sept. 20: Avenue Furs, Pappas Fur Designers, and Grandview Furs ($5,000 damage) had windows smashed and red paint thrown inside damaging furs. Three people arrested. Avenue Furs and Grandview Furs have since gone out of business due to direct action. (*ed. note:* see "ALF action in Vancouver".)

Zuc Legume sez:

Send Action Reports! Receiving Action Reports in the mail is one of the most exciting things that happens here. To know that people are active in all parts of the world confirms that we are not alone in our beliefs and convictions. We list all actions that we receive based on their alliance with the Animal Liberation Front's principles of non-violence (no injury or death to any animal or person - except in the course of self-defence). Of course, our ability to serve everyone with these listings depends a great deal on your co-operation in sending us reports. Far too often we only hear of actions by chance or from other publications. Please spread the word - if you see or know of a direct action for animal liberation in your area, send us either a news clipping if it was in the media, or an anonymous report. If sending us an anonymous report, please follow these basic security rules: don't use a typewriter that you or anyone else could be found with later in event of police raids. Use a typewriter that many people have access to or cut and paste words from a common paper, then throw the paper out. Do not give us your address or put a return one on the envelope, don't put fingerprints on the page, and don't lick the stamp - wet it with a sponge.   Your security ensures ours!

Action Reports U.K.

Continued from page 14

Ireland
1987
March, Dublin: A fish wholesaler's van was paint stripped and painted with slogans. It was attacked a second time when it was repaired.
March 28, Beaumont: A veterinary research lab had approx. $70,000 damage when the medical supply rooms were destroyed along with their contents. Extensive damage was also done to cars and vans.
May, Dublin: Butchers in Sutton and Lennox Street had their windows smashed.
May 31, Dublin: A meat shop in the Glasnevin area took extensive damage by bricks and paint bombs.
July, Belfast: A pork delivery van was repainted and covered in glue. A Kentucky Fried Chicken shop had its windows and sign smashed.
Aug. 1, Belfast: Fast food shop's window and sign smashed.
Aug. 3, Belfast: Butcher's shop windows all smashed.
Aug. 10, Belfast: A meat delivery van had its windscreen smashed.
Oct. 6, Belfast: Two fires were started in a chemical store of Associated Egg Packers, and damage was confined to the store.

Homes

Continued from page 21

they might think they were being put back in the lab or whatever. You never have much time to dwell on it for long though because there are new animals that need your help. I suppose its like a hospital in some ways."

There are of course a lot of animals that need homes that are not in as serious a shape. It is really hard to imagine what it might be like to live in a laboratory where every hand that reaches for you tortures and mutilates. I don't want to misinterpret the animals feelings and attitudes, but I do know that animals which are continuously subjected to punishment and suffering become as unstable and unhappy as humans would in a similar situation. You can see this in an abused family pet that has been hit too often so you can

imagine how much worse it would be for research animals. One example in particular is Britches - a 5 week old stumptail monkey who was born at the University of California. He was just one of 260 animals liberated by the ALF in 1985. Britches was being kept in isolation with his entire skull and most of his face covered by surgical tape and electrical gadgets as part of a study of combined effects of sight deprivation and isolation.

It takes a lot of courage but the rewards can be endless. Just showing one of these animals that hands can reach out in love and respect for their needs is one way you may be able to help - and with enough people with this kind of strength and courage we can end this needless suffering.

Memoirs of a Third World Kat

SUPPORT GROUP DISTRIBUTION

The following are some of the magazines, booklets, and pamphlets that are available through us, as well as buttons and t-shirts. If you require information about a certain issue, or about ALF or Support Group activities, please send us a letter and we'll do our best to answer it. The following have postage included in the cost, but any extra money you could send would be appreciated. Please note that many of the publications listed are photocopied reprints.

MAGAZINES AND NEWSLETTERS

Front Line News   *Newsletter of the ALFSG Canada(Toronto)*
Issues #1 (Fall 85), 2 (Winter 85/86), and 3 (Fall 86) $1.00 ea.
Issue #4 (Spring 88) $2.00 - 10 copies or more are available for $1.50 ea. Subscription $10/yr.

ALFSG (Montreal) Newsletter
Issue #1 (Fall 87 - McDonald's mini-issue) $1.00

ALFSG Diary of Actions   *Bulletin of the ALFSG (UK)*
Issues #1 (4/87), 2 (7/87), and 3 (11/87)   4/5/88
$1.00 Current issue $1.00

Action Reports   *(Now called Diary of Actions)*
Issues #1 (7/85), 4 (2/86), 5 (5/86), and 6 (8/86) $1.00 ea.

SG Newsletter   *Former newsletter of the ALFSG (UK)*
Issues #2 (12/82), 3 (1/83), 6 (8/83), 9 (12/83), 11 (6/84), and 12 (8/84) Avg. 10 pp. ea. These copies are not in 100% good condition. $1.00 ea.
Issues #14 (11/84), 15 (3/85), 16 (5/85), 17 (8/85), 18 (5/86), and 19 (7/86) Avg. 30 pp. ea. No. 19 "International Rescue" was the last issue printed. $3.00 ea.

Action Report   *Diary of actions from Australia.*
Issue #1 (4/87) $1.00

Action For Animals Newsletter   *Direct action group in Australia.*
Issue #3 (10/86) $2.00

ALFSG (France) Bulletin   *Also known as Combat and Front News.*
Issues #1 (12/85), 2 (4/86), and 3 (4/87) French only. $1.00 ea.

Friends of the ALF (Netherlands)
Issue #2 (7/86) English or Dutch language. $1.00
Issue #6 (11/87) Dutch language only. $1.00

The Agitator   *Newsletter of the Supporters' Group for Animal Activists (Australia)*   Issue #1 (2/88) $1.00

Direct Action Animal Bulletin   *Currently non-existent UK newsletter.*
Issue #5 (Winter 84/85) Special prisoners issue. $1.00

Lomakatsi   *Animal liberation magazine with an anarchist perspective.*
Issues #1 (40 pp.), 2 (32 pp.), 3(32pp.). $2.00 ea.

PAMPHLETS

Single copies are free, up to 49 copies are 15¢ each, and 50 or more copies are 10¢ each.

ALFSG (Toronto)
Introducing the Hunt Saboteurs
It's a Man's Game; Hunt Sabotage and Men
What Happens to the Calf?
What's Wrong With McDonald's?
Meat and Misogyny
Various leaflets from ARK II (Canadian Animal Rights Network)
ALFSG (UK) Factsheets: The Egg Industry, The Fur Industry, The Milk/Dairy Industry, The Pig Meat Industry, Teratogenicity Experiments, Factory Farming, and Psychological and Behavioural Experiments. *(Please note that these pamphlets have some basic factual information but the facts and figures pertain to the United Kingdom only.)*
The Vegan Society Factsheets *(Again, these five pamphlets are from a UK group and have facts and figures from there only.)*

AGITATOR
NEWSLETTER OF THE S.G.A.A.   NUMBER ONE

URGE + ORP!
ARE YOU COMFORTABLE?
FALL 87   #3 $1

LOMAKATSI

BOOKS

ECODEFENSE: A Field Guide to Monkeywrenching
Second Edition (1987); Edited by Dave Foreman and Bill Haywood; Forward! by Edward Abbey (all of *Earth First!*) Detailed and field-tested techniques for ecotage - direct action in defense of our planet - with tips on security and leaving no evidence. Heavily illustrated. (308 pp.) $15.00

BOOKLETS

Interviews With Animal Liberation Front Activists
Compiled in England from interviews with many different ALF cells. Covers most aspects of the ALF. Recommended.   (52 pp.) $5.00

ALF On Trial; Capitalism Under Attack in the 1980's
Excellent account of the arrests, trials, and convictions of 9 activists in England in 1986/87.   (20 pp.) $1.00

Feminism and Animal Rights
Essays and excerpts, compiled by Marjorie Spiegel.   (30 pp.) $1.50

Meat Is Murder
Information on the flesh industry, compiled by Marjorie Spiegel. (22 pp.) $1.50

Animal Liberation is a Gay and Lesbian Issue
Connecting the issues; AIDS research, activism, etc. Compiled by gay and lesbian ALFSG (Canada) members.   (22 pp.) $1.00

BUTTONS - $1.00 ea.

Animal Liberation
ALF Supporters Group
Vivisectors Are Scum
Animal Liberation/Human Liberation
Against Pound Seizure
ARK II

STICKERS - 50 for 50¢

"Your donation will be used to torture animals in useless experiments." These are used on ads for medical research and "charity" organizations.

T-SHIRTS

We have two designs: t-shirt #1 has a picture of "Granny" - the primate liberated from the University of Western Ontario - with the words "I Support The ALF"; t-shirt #2 has on the front a picture of an ALF activist carrying a dog and cat with the words "Support The Animal Liberation Front", and on the back it has the words "Vivisectors Are Scum". Sizes and colours vary at different times, so you may not get exactly what you ask for; please give us options. Sizes are sm., med., lrg., and ex-lrg., and colours are red, grey, white, and, in the near future, yellow and green. The cost is $8 for unemployed and $10 for employed, postage included.

YOUR DONATION WILL BE USED TO TORTURE ANIMALS IN USELESS EXPERIMENTS

Send me stuff!

(Photocopy this form or write your order on a separate piece of paper.)

MERCHANDISE	PRICE $	QUANTITY	TOTAL $

SUB-TOTAL $ _____

SUBSCRIPTION TO *FRONT LINE NEWS* ($10/YEAR) _____

BULK ORDER OF F.L.N. #4 (10 copies or more at $1.50 each) _____

DONATION TO THE *ALF SUPPORT GROUP* _____

DONATION TO THE *TORONTO ANIMAL RIGHTS DEFENCE FUND* _____

TOTAL $ _____

Please send a cheque or money-order payable to the "ALF Support Group" at P.O.Box 915, Stn. F, Toronto, Ont. M4Y 2N9 Canada. Allow 8 weeks for delivery. Donations to T.A.R.D.F. can be sent directly to them, payable to Mary Bartley, Barrister and Solicitor, 11 Prince Arthur Ave., Toronto, Ont. M5R 1B2 Canada. (Please note on your donation, "In Trust, T.A.R.D.F.")

Name _____
Address _____
City Prov./State _____
Code Country _____
Phone No. (optional) _____

If you live in or near the Toronto area and have any skills or services you could offer the Support Group (i.e. anything to do with the production of a magazine, such as writing, printing, etc..), please let us know! Folks writing us should check out "Letters to the Editor..." on page 26.

CONTACT GROUPS

Animal Liberation Front Support Groups:

Action for Animals
P.O. Box 152
Lutwyche
Queensland 4030
Australia

ALFSG (France)
B.C.M. 1160
London WC1M 3XX
England

ALFSG (Montréal)
Box 4007
Montréal, P.Q
H3Z 2X3
Canada

ALFSG (U.K.)
B.C.M. 1160
London WC1M 3XX
England

Friends of the ALF - "Vrienden van het DBF"
Oude Gracht 36
3511 AP Utrecht
The Netherlands

Support Animal Rights Prisoners
B.C.M. 5911
London WC1N 3XX
England

Supporters Group for Animal Activists
P.O. Box 519
Eltham
Victoria 3095
Australia

ALFSG (U.S.A.)
1543 North 'E' St., #44
San Bernardino, CA
92404 USA

ALFSG Canada (Toronto)
P.O.Box 915, Stn. F
Toronto, Ont.
M4Y 2N9
Canada

Direct Action Support Groups:

Animal Legal Defence Fund.
P.O. Box 4066
Rockville, MD.
20850 U.S.A.

Earth First!
P.O. Box 5871
Tucson, AZ.
85703 U.S.A.

Sea Sheppard Society / Earth First!
711 South Riverside Dr. #3
Palm Springs, CA.
92262 U.S.A.

Sea Sheppard Society
P.O. Box 48446
Vancouver, B.C.
V78 1A2
Canada

Toronto Animal Rights Defence Fund
c/o ALFSG-Canada (Toronto)

Farm Sanctuary
P.O. Box 37
Rockland, DE.
19732 U.S.A.

FRONT LINE NEWS ♦ P.O. BOX 915 STATION F ♦ TORONTO ♦ ONTARIO ♦ M4Y 2N9

¢ombat No. 1

MAXIMUM DAMAGE not MINIMUM DESTRUCTION

THE NEWSLETTER OF THE ANIMAL LIBERATION FRONT SUPPORT GROUP (CANADA)

WELCOME TO COMBAT AND THE ANIMAL LIBERATION FRONT SUPPORT GROUP (CANADA)

This newsletter hopes to bring you news of the Animal Liberation Front, and the
ALF Support Group. We also hope to bring you a forum for activists to circulate
their ideas, discuss 'technical problems', and bring you info on animal liberation
in general. We welcome all letters for publication, articles, artwork, comments,
and action reports(see article on mail security). The ALF Support Group is a
seperate organization from the Animal Liberation Front, whose purpose is to support the ALF in all legal means possible. It has been formed for those who wish
to support the ALF without breaking the law.

ANIMAL LIBERATION FRONT GUIDELINES

The Animal Liberation Front carries out direct action against animal abuse in the
form of rescuing animals and causing financial loss to animal abusers, usually
through the damage and destruction of property. Their short term aim is to save
as many animals as possible and directly disrupt the practice of animal abuse -
their long term aim is to end all animal suffering by forcing animal abuse companies and individuals out of business. It is a non-violent campaign, activists
taking precautions not to harm any person or animal. Because ALF actions are
against the law activists work anonymously, either in groups or individually, and
do not have a central contact address or any centralised organization or co-
ordination.

```
*******************************************************************************
*                                                                             *
* WHEN YOU'RE FINISHED READING THIS NEWSLETTER CONSIDER PASSING IT ALONG TO SOMEONE ELSE. *
*           IT COULD CHANGE THEIR LIVES AND THE ANIMALS LIVES!                 *
*                                                                             *
*******************************************************************************
```

SUN

VOL. 12, NO. 179   September daily paid circulation, Mon. to Fri.   84,329   50 CENTS   72 PAGES

ANIMAL RIGHTS GROUP VANDALISM PROBED

Cops investigate incidents claimed by militant Animal Liberation Front cell: Page 2

MILITANT ANIMAL RIGHTS CELL THREATENS MORE VANDALISM

ALF EDMONTON
NEWS RELEASE
ANIMAL LIBERATION FRONT

SOMETIME IN JANUARY A SMALL GROUP OF PEOPLE WHO HAVE BEEN ACTIVE IN ANIMAL LIBERATION HAVE JOINED TOGETHER AS AN A.L.F. CELL. WE CARRY OUT ACTIONS AGAINST MCDONALD'S, BURGER KING, WENDY'S, HARVEYS, KENTUCKY FRIED CHICKEN, AS WELL AS VARIOUS BUTCHERS, FURRIERS, AND SLAUGHTER HOUSES.

ACTS OF ECONOMIC SABOTAGE ARE USUALLY SPRAYPAINTING THE BUILDINGS AND PROPERTY, SMASHING WINDOWS, GLUING LOCKS, ETC. WE TRY TO GET TOGETHER ONCE A WEEK AND WE HAVE AVERAGED LATELY ANY WHERE FROM 2 TO 9 TARGETS IN ONE NIGHT, COMPARED TO ENGLANDS AVERAGE OF 40 ACTIONS PER WEEK. WE FEEL PRETTY GOOD ABOUT OUR EFFORTS. WE WILL TRY TO KEEP THE VARIOUS MEDIA UPDATED ON OUR ACTIONS. IN THE EARLY MORNING OF OCTOBER 24th WE ATTACKED A KENTUCKY FRIED CHICKEN, A FURRIER, AND A LEATHER SHOP. THE EARLY MORNING OF OCT, 22 WE ATTACKED 7 FURRIERS INCLUDING THE BAY, A LEATHER SHOP, AND QUEEN CITY MEAT'S.

WE DON'T PLAN TO STOP WITH THESE SMALL ACTIONS (OR WHAT SOME WOULD CONSIDER SMALL) BUT PLAN TO INCREASE AND BROADEN OUR RANGE OF BOTH TARGETS AND TACTICS. PATIENCE, TIME AND PRACTICE ARE ALL IT TAKES!

[ANOTHER] ALF EDMONTON CELL

This photocopied communique was received yesterday by The Edmonton Sun.

Animal zealots surface

By TIMOTHY LeRICHE and MINDELLE JACOBS
Staff Writers

Police are investigating a militant, violent animal rights group which claims responsibility for a series of vandalism sprees in Edmonton and threatens to broaden its assault.

A communique delivered to *The Edmonton Sun* yesterday claims an Animal Liberation Front (ALF) cell was formed in Edmonton in January and its small band of activists has vandalized several food outlets and fur businesses.

City police say the warning is being taken seriously, and say it is the first time they've had a group claim responsibility for the damage.

They are now investigating the vandalism as the work of an ALF cell, said police spokesman Sgt. Mike Tabler.

Alberta Fur Council spokesman Donna Dunsmore, who is familiar with the worldwide group, said: "These people are very dangerous."

Dunsmore said some local furriers have received personal threats and although the aggressors did not give an identity, it is believed they are with the clandestine front.

ALF's anonymous, one-page photocopied notice to *The Sun* claimed responsibility for the Oct. 24 vandalism of an Edmonton Kentucky Fried Chicken outlet, a furrier and a leather shop; and for the Oct. 22 vandalism of seven furriers, The Bay and Queen City Meats.

The note to *The Sun* said cell actions include smashing windows, gluing locks and spray-painting buildings.

". . . we have averaged lately anywhere from two to nine targets in one night, compared to England's average of 40 actions per week; we feel pretty good about our efforts," said the letter.

"We don't plan to stop with these small actions (or what some would consider small), but plan to increase and broaden our range of both targets and tactics."

The owner of Queen City Meats, who requested anonymity, said vandals used acid to etch 'AFL' and 'scum' on to three large window panes. They also spray-painted 'meat is murder' on the side of the building at 11104 182 Ave.

Linda Fossenier, owner of Paris Furs, 10448 82 Ave., said her shop has been vandalized several times.

The door locks have been glued twice, most recently on Oct. 22, she said.

Vandals spray-painted the word 'murderers' near the back door about a week ago and smeared a cement-like substance on the windows several times over the past few months.

"I think they're very ignorant. I don't know what they intend to accomplish by doing this," Fossenier said.

Last December ALF took credit for bombing four exclusive London, England department stores. No one was injured.

"This is an incredible form of cowardice," said Alison Beal of the Fur Council of Canada, who said the sect has been responsible for firebombings in Toronto and Vancouver.

Five ALF members were arrested in Toronto in 1987 for vandalism at fast food outlets.

Anthony Lee

FURRIER FURIOUS AFTER DAMAGE SPREE

Traps urged for vandals

By PAUL RODGI
Staff Writer

An Edmonton furrier says leg...
be placed on Jasper Ave. to catch
...mals" who vandalized her shop
stores early yesterday
The...

•B2   The Edmonton Journal

...enough eve...
group exists.
"We had to hit...

...aragini said.

Underground group lives by guidelines

Anti-fur trade vandalism is intolerable, Reimer says

Furriers...

ANIMAL RIGHTS

Vigilante furriers banding together to fight radicals

Vandalism blamed on anti-fur lobby

More attacks blamed on ALF

By TONY BLAIS
Staff Writer

An Edmonton police de-
tective has been assigned
full time to co-ordinate
the probe into a spree of
vandalism by a militant
animal rights organ-
ization.
And poli...

...sponsibility for vandalizin...
...onstable Tom Gon records particulars from manager Brigitte Jackson, manager of Laura Lee Fur Salon, outside her damaged store.

...and a leather shop,
...are investigat...

Fur stores hit with rocks, glue, profanities

For the second weekend, anti-fur vandals attack five Jasper Avenue furriers

FLORENCE LOYIE
Journal Staff Writer

Edmonton

...dows of every furrier on
Avenue and 103rd St...

...This...
said.

FUR-THER DAMAGE

...thrown through two...
Jackson said it amou...   ...similar to ...erday's vandal... ...with profanities
...anti-fur slogans"...

Animal rights vandals slammed

By MINDELLE JACOBS and ...

An a...

HITS EDMONTON

Besieged furriers want help

"What we are really talking about here is safeguarding the rights of the small business

DAVID HOWELL
Journal Staff Writer

An animal rights group vandalizing numerous city businesses is acting "worse than terrorists" says a local shopkeeper
whose store has been hit.
The Animal Liberation Front (ALF) in a communique released earlier this week to The ...nton Sun...

ANIMAL RIGHTS VANDALS 'MISDIRECTED'

The Sun. "They are brave enough to do it but not brave...
to come forward"
The taxidermist wishe...
doesn't want...

Taxidermist slams terrorists

...yesterday.

"If they're using acts of violence to get ...operty damage. In
terrorist group and this cause... ...another group released 100
animals from a Toronto lab.

ALF's appear...
...ments we're presenting as
...animal rights groups will lose public sympathy be-
...s action"

However, the assistant dir...

...uel Trapping Society said, in a press ...
...vandalism "does nothing to help animals."

...d to help arrest ALF memb...
...few days. An an...

The Edmon...

The ALF guidelines are to:
● Liberate animals from
places of abuse (labs and farms)
and place them in homes where
they can live out their natural
lives.
● Inflict economic damage to
people who profit from the misery and exploitation of animals.
● Reveal the horrors and
atrocities committed against animals behind closed doors by per-
forming non-violent, direct actions and liberations.

Furriers say they won't surrender to 'terrorists'

GERRY WARNER
Journal Staff Writer

Edmonton

Jasper Avenue furriers say they
will win the battle against anti-fur
activists who vandalized several
fur stores last weekend for the second weekend in a row.
Spokesmen for the anti-fur lobby also deplored the vandalism but
said they could sympathize with
the frustration that caused it.
Donna Dunsmore, president of

intimidating our customers, but
sooner or later they're going to she
up and then they will !
swer to the courts," she...
Brigitte Jackson, m
Laura Lee Fur Salon
windows were damaged
said "This time they wen
"I think anybody who
something like this has
sick... I hope they're
and put where they belo
nightmares all weekend !

of the street...

Animal rights group has furriers worried

EDMONTON (CP) — Some   ...sands of dollars in property dam-
...up in arms   age to their stores.

JAIL SUCKS · SO SEND THEM A NOTE

Prison isolates people from the outside world. Besides visiting writing is the most important thing you can do to help break down that isolation. If you can't think of much to write then just a card wishing them well is great. Remember that all letters to prisoners are opened and censored, so don't write anything that could jeopardise someones freedom. The old group Support Animal Rights Prisoners(SARP) has merged with the ALFSG (UK). For updated prisoner lists contact them at their address. ALFSG(UK), BCM 1160, London, WC1N 3XX, England.

Ronnie Lee

Fran Trutt, in the USA was sentenced to 10 years in prison, suspended after 32 months, and 3 years probation. Having already served time while awaiting conclusion of court proceedings, she will be eligible for release in March. Fran was accused of planting a bomb in Nov.'88 near the parking area of Leon Hirsch, chairman of US Surgical Corps. Fran was set up by USSC officials who had infiltrated the animal rights movement.FRAN TRUTT, 199 WEST MAIN STREET, NIANTIC CORRECTIONAL INSTITUTE, CONNECTICUT 06357, USA.

Ronnie Lee still serving a ten year prison sentence for conspiracy to commit arson, criminal damage and to incite others to commit criminal damage. Before his imprisonment Ronnie was press officer for the Animal Liberation Front. RONNIE LEE, V02682, LB2 CLYDE, HM PRISON, CHANNINGS WOOD, DENBURY, NEWTON ABBOT, DEVON, TQ12 6DW, ENGLAND.

ALFSG - Toronto

October 1990 (An update)

Since 1984, the ALF Support Group here in Toronto has been working hard bringing you the information and news of the Animal Liberation Front. It has been a challenging and inspirational task to inform and disseminate the news of the ALF.

All of us who have been involved with the ALFSG in Toronto continue to work in various areas of animal liberation and struggle, both non-human and human. Many of us find ourselves working in many different kinds of political movements and issues, and currently there is not much focus on animal liberation issues.

This lull in activity is reflected by a similar phenomena in not just the ALF, but in the entire spectrum of the animal rights and liberation movements across Canada in recent years. It is for a combination of these and other factors that we have made the decision to put the working functions of the ALFSG in Toronto on the "back burner" for now.

We want to give a big "thank you" to all of you who have contributed, and helped make our work and this group a reality. Undoubtably, without your letters, news, time, energy, and of course your financial help, the ALFSG couldn't have existed!

We also want to apologize to any of you who have donated money over this past year and may in some way feel "ripped off." The small excess of funds we had in September, when we agreed to disband, has been distributed to four groups: The Hunt Saboteurs in California, the newly formed ALF Support Group in Edmonton, Alberta, the ALFSG in England and the Wimmin Prisoner Survival Network in Toronto. We encourage you to write and support these groups.

By all accounts and information we've received, we know that the Animal Liberation Front (and sister groups like the Animal Rights Militia, among others) continue to be growing and are increasingly a more effective force worldwide. Actions against animal exploiters and killers continue to happen, with the west coast of Canada and Edmonton in particular, seeing a lot of activity over the past two years. As a direct result, an ALF Support Group has formed in Edmonton, and we encourage you to support their work. They are producing action reports, a newsletter, and an excellent new handbook -- An Animal Rights Primer. As well, we have sent our stock of ALF T-shirts to them, so if you would still like to order one, it's not too late!

Hunt Saboteurs
P.O. Box 3412
Santa Cruz, CA 95062

Wimmin Prisoner Survival Network
P.O. Box 770, Stn. P
Toronto, Ont.
M5S 2X1 Canada

PRISONER SUPPORT CONTINUED

Barry Horne, Gari Allen, Michael Shanahan have been remanded in custody charged with 'conspiracy to cause explosions'. All are currently at Bedford prison. Please write letters of support to them, but please write to the prisoners individually. In other words, don't send a letter addressed to all three of them!
BARRY HORNE, HD2665,
GARI ALLEN, HD2670,
MICHAEL SHANAHAN, HD2664,
HM PRISON, ST. LOYES, BEDFORD, BEDFORSHIRE, ENGLAND.

Neil Theobald, was arrested on Sept. 27/90 following police raids at several homes in south England. Neil is being tried on 2 charges of arson and 2 charges of criminal damage with intent to endanger life. One of the arson charges and one of the criminal damage charges relates to an incident when incendiary devices were planted in a couple of vans belonging to a butchers. One device set a van ablaze. The other 2 charges are in connection with a similar incident when a meat wholsale firm, was attacked and a van damaged by fire. Neil is pleading not guilty to all charges. Please send all letters of support to:
NEIL THEOBALD, XC1567, HM PRISON, ROMSEY ROAD, WINCHESTER, HANTS, SO22 5DF, ENGLAND.

ALF Spokesperson Arrested

Crescenzo Vellucci, a 42 year-old spokesperson for the ALF, has been accused of participating in a 1986 raid of a University of Oregon research lab and may face a stiff prison term from an over-zealous prosecution.

The raid, which Vellucci denies he was involved with, liberated over 150 animals, including 18 cats, 24 rabbits, 12 hamsters and 100 rats.

Although Vellucci intends to plead not guilty, he says he is looking forward to the trial as an opportunity to combat the authoritarian harrassment both he and other political activists have been subjected to over the issue of animal liberation.

The prosecution, in typical tight-lipped manner, has refused to state what case, if any, it has against Vellucci, and said only that Vellucci is a suspect because he has acted as an ALF spokesperson in the past.

One member of the raiding party, Roger Troen of Portland who drove the getaway car, was arrested and convicted in 1988.

In addition to Vellucci, the State has issued warrants for the arrest of "several" other suspects.

Vellucci has been subjected to undue harassment by the authorities. Although he voluntarily turned himself in to police, he is being treated as a "fugitive" and, despite the lack of any concrete evidence, the judicial system is treating him as "guilty until proven innocent."

A support fund has been set up for Vellucci. All donations should be sent to the National Foundation for Animal Law, 926 J St., Suite 813, Sacramento, California, 95814.

Supermarket Sabotage

Supermarkets are showcases for many products of pain: items containing dangerous chemicals, goods imported from right-wing regimes and commodities which result from the abuse or poor treatment of workers. Supermarkets, one might say, are also cemeteries for dead animals. Pigs, cows, chickens and fish are wrapped in tight-fitting plastic suits and placed in refrigerated coffins until someone plucks them up and prepares them for cremation in a kitchen oven. Supermarkets, then, are the last link in a long chain of human and animal exploitation. If we can intervene in this process and force shoppers and store owners to question the value — financial, political and ecological — of continuing to sell and consume certain products, such action may translate into less waste and suffering.

Identify Domination and Death

Use stickers to tell people the truth about products. "Hamburger" and "steak", for instance, disguise the fact that both are animal flesh, so apply an adhesive label to them which reads "Warning: This package contains DEAD ANIMALS" or "Animals suffered to make this product." (See *Lomakatsi* #1 for other suggestions and advice on how to make or obtain the stickers.) When applying stickers, you may want to target specific items. In this way you can call attention to products associated with great amounts of pain — veal and battery eggs for example — and work to eliminate the sale of these items. The assault on the supermarket will also appear to be more focused and it may be easier to convince the manager to remove particular commodities from the shelf.

Shuffle the Shopping Containers

Have fun filling hand baskets and shopping carts with meat and other products and then abandon them in different aisles of the store. Be sure to load up with fresh cuts of flesh because when it sits for a period of time without refrigeration, it spoils and has to be discarded. You can quicken this process by slitting the cellophane wrapper with your fingernail, exposing the fish or flesh to the air. Whenever possible, it's helpful to place stickers on at least a few of the items that you've sabotaged so that others will recognize the meaning of the action and not mistake it for a prank. If you use leaflets, make certain they don't contain the name of an individual or group who could be held responsible.

Engage in Olfactory Warfare

Selling corporate food, fake food and dead food for profit stinks. So why not let supermarkets know that. Engage the senses of shoppers by creating a real stench. This can be accomplished by hiding fresh meat and other perishable products on the back of shelves, behind paper towels, rolls of toilet paper, cat litter and similar large items. After a few days the goods will go bad and begin to smell. Customers will undoubtedly complain to managers or, better yet, stop shopping there. Again, it's helpful to put stickers on the packages and, whenever possible, to tear part of the wrapper to expedite spoilage. Canned items, like cat food and sardines, can be sabotaged by using a small can opener to puncture an air opening in the top of the containers.

Use Theatrics

As you're leaving, load up a cart full of meat, eggs, cheese and boycotted goods and get in a check-out line. When the cashier has totaled your "purchase", dig frantically in your pockets and then "suddenly" realize that you forgot to bring money. At this point, a friend or someone in your group could start telling everyone around about the problems associated with the products in your cart: the chemical contents, the health dangers of meat, the practices of large corporations, and so on. You can then show interest in and sympathy for these arguments and decide that you don't want these things anyway. Your action may encourage others who are listening and watching to do so as well, or at least make them think twice about what they are buying. This is just one possible scenario for action. Improvise and experiment.

Some Suggestions

- Look out for store mirrors above the meat coffins and keep an eye out for employees who wander about restocking shelves.
- Switch to different supermarkets temporarily if you suspect the ones that you have been targeting are on the alert.
- Enter and exit the store by yourself or in small groups and choose days (Fridays and weekends) and times (5–7 pm) when the store is crowded so as not to attract attention.
- Keep pressure on the store in as many ways as possible. Someone not taking part in the actions might meet with store managers in your area to discuss chosen products which they stock and to inform them that many people plan to boycott the store until it stops selling these items.

reprinted from Lomakatsi #3/Box 633/1377 K st., NW/Washington/DC 20005

THE ALF STRIKES

EVERY DAY OF THE YEAR, MEN AND WOMEN OF THE ANIMAL LIBERATION FRONT DIRECTLY INTERVENE TO STOP ANIMAL SUFFERING, AT THE RISK OF LOSING THEIR OWN FREEDOM. THEY OCCUR EVERYWHERE ACROSS THE WORLD FROM ITALY TO AUSTRIA TO JAPAN TO SPAIN TO AUSTRALIA. BELOW ARE SOME ACCOUNTS OF ACTIONS IN THE LAST YEAR:

BELGIUM

All 4 tires of a hunting jeep were burst and "FLA" was scratched on the bodywork while owners were beating for game.

CANADA

EDMONTON
Feb. 6/90 Bomb threat at the Biological Sciences building(University of Alberta) Bomb squad brought in, no bomb found.
Mar. 23/90 Laura Lee fur salon had it's locks glued and was spraypainted.
April 6/90 Windows painted of 5 furriers.
April 13/90 5 furriers had their locks glued, and were spraypainted. Laura Lee fur salon had it's windows smashed.
May 25/90 Buckskin Fur & Leather had it's windows smashed and locks glued. Laura Lee fur salon was spray painted, locks glued, and windows smashed.
June 90 Strathcona McDonalds had it's window smashed.
June 6/90 Ken Belcourt furs had their locks glued and windows smashed.
July 90 The Fur Shop had it's windows smashed and a butcher shop had it's windows smashed.
July 14/90 Abbotsfield Mall McDonalds spraypainted and broke windows. Ken Belcourt Furs was spraypainted and locks glued. A sausage house was spraypainted.
Aug. 29/90 University of Alberta vivisector had his house attacked, a large rock was thrown through the front window marked "courtesy of the ALF"
Oct. 1/90 Artz fur & leather had thier window smashed.
Jan 91 A Kentucky Fried Chicken and Artz fur & leather had their windows smashed.

TORONTO
Oct. 9/90 The Animal Rights Militia claimed responsibility for a thanksgiving action where they disabled five trucks of Royce Dupont Poultry Packers by slashing all tires as well as cutting cables and fluid lines.

CORSICA

Jan. 9/90 A slaughter house was blown-up in Bastia.

FRANCE

April 30/90 Thirty dogs and twenty-three rabbits were liberated from a vivisection lab in Marseille.
May 90 "meat is murder-FLA" painted on a butchers van.

ENGLAND

AVON
In March, in Midsomer Norton, a lump of stone was hurled through two large windows of 'Lakes' butchers. Damage was estimated at £1000.

CAMBRIDGESHIRE
Breeding pens at Interfauna in Huntingdon were raided in April. 82 beagles and 26 rabbits were rescued. The value of the animals was estimated at £29,000. Annually the Interfauna produces 2,800 dogs, 80,000 guinea pigs, 17,000 rabbits 300,000 rats and 600,000 mice for vivisection. They have established production centres in France, Germany and Spain

THE ALF STRIKES

DEVON
In May, two Scottich wildcats at the Paignton zoo were rescued, in co-ordination with a similar raid in Essex at the Colchester zoo.

HAMPSHIRE
McDonalds restaurants in Fareham and Portsmouth, and a Burger King in Southampton came under fire attack during April and May. Early May, a Fareham meat wholesaler came under attack with trucks and buildings being daubed with paint, graffiti and paintstripper and the trucks also had their gas tanks filled with gravel. In June, in Petersfield, £50,000 worth of damage was caused to a cattle truck at Rowlands cattle farm. Slogans were sprayed on the farm and a week later the owner was told to stop supplying cattle for research or retribution would follow. Incendiary devices were attached to two vans at the Russel Hume meat company in Southampton. In Portsmouth, a vehicle belonging to a firm which supplies machinery to the meat industry were set on fire.

LIVERPOOL
In a statement from the ALF, an arson attack was explained to be in retribution for the horses killed during the Grand National. A pony was also liberated in May. "Cancelled" stickers were pasted over posters advertising a circus in June.

LONDON
Many butchers and fishmongers had their windows sprayed with acid, locks superglued and slogans painted over the premises.

GREATER MANCHESTER
In March, many butchers' windows were smashed; in Bury, Heywood, Bolton, Prestwich, Farnworth and Rochdale. In response to seven horses dying at Aintree, windows and a sattellite dish belonging to Ladbrokes were smashed. Vans belonging to Entwhistle Bacon Co. were damaged. Arthur Openshaw, who broke a hunt saboteur's nose and attacked another in a racist frenzy had his car windows etched. In May, an angler and a butcher had slogans painted on their windows. In Manchester, in June, 3 butcher shops were attacked and a puppy was rescued. £15,000 worth of damage was caused to an abattoir in Royton, Oldham.

NORFOLK
12,000 snails were liberated in April in Colby before an estimated £70,000 damage was caused at Peter van Poortvliet's breeding farm. In May in Thetford, £200,000 worth of damage was caused when broiler sheds were burnt down. In June, seven reptiles were taken from "Pets Pantry" in Norwich.

SUSSEX
Gun shops in Heathfield and East Grinstead who were members of the British Field Sports Society, and pubs which allow hunts to meet, had windows etched. A controlled explosion was carried out at the meat counter at Safeway in Hastings; two toughened plate glass windows at McDonalds were smashed with bricks at Bexhill-on-Sea. Culverwells car dealers, who paid to have the company listed in blood sports publications, had tires slashed, 21 windows and cars covered in etching fluid, and slogans painted on walls.

POLAND

Activists rescued ten rats and a tortoise from a laboratory. In Gdansk in June the locks of some fur shops were destroyed. In Pita some anglers equipment was destroyed and fish were released back into water. In Bytom a butchers shop had its screen and lock broken and slogans daubed over the premises.

SOUTH AFRICA

Mannock Furs shop in Durban was damaged
in an arson attack. This followed an
earlier action when the same shop was
covered in red paint. The owner offered a
reward in return for information leading
to the arrest of the activists responsible.

SWEDEN

Three Djurensbefrielsefront (ALF) groups
have carried out a number of actions
including 'painting' foxes and mink at fur
farms with red henna to make the fur
useless for the fur trade and other
actions have included pulling down and
sawing up hunting platforms.

UNITED STATES

July 4/89 Five cats were rescued from
psychology experiments at the Texas Tech
University Health Sciences Center in Lub-
bock. The electronic equipment and stereo-
taxic restraint devices were destroyed.
The stored brains of dozens of other cats
were taken for burial. A Texas Tech spoke-
swomen said the raid caused $70,000 damage.

Jan. 6/90 Three dogs were rescued from the
Vetrans Administration Medical Center in
Tucson, Arizona. The VA is suspected of
doin research for the University of Arizona
Medical Center, to help the latter get
around humane laws.
Jan. 14/90 documents, videotapes, slides
and floppy disks were taken from the office
of Adrian Morrison, anatomy professor at
the University of Pennslyvania School of
Veterinary Medicine. "Cat Killer" and
"ALF" was written on a wall.
June 9/90 15 fur stores in New York City's
fur district had their locks glued the day
before a big fur sale.
In California a fur shop was closed after
substantial damage was caused to it in
arson attack.
Thirty three turkeys were rescued from
Swanson turkey factory farm, slogans were
sprayed and equipment was damaged.

A Letter from Ronnie Lee

Dear Friends

This letter is to thank all SG members for the great support they have given me during the time I've been in prison. The SG has been a tremendous help to me in terms of money needed to buy educational materials, stamps for my letters, batteries for my radio, etc. and also to assist many of my visitors with the high cost of coming to see me in prison. Of course, that money comes originally from SG members, many of whom have also sent me direct donations, and words cannot express how grateful I am for this financial assistance which has made my time in prison so much more productive and easier to withstand.

My gratitude also goes out to all those SG members who've sent me letters of support. During my prison sentence I've received letters from well over a thousand different people, most of whom have learned of my situation through the SG. This correspondence has helped tremendously to keep me in good spirits and I only wish I was able to write back promptly to everyone who has written. Unfortunately, there is a limit to the number of letters I can write, so many people have not yet received a reply. This letter is especially dedicated to them, as a measure of my appreciation, and also so they can know a little about my present situation.

Out of my ten year sentence I will have to serve six years and eight months unless I am granted parole. I have already spent over 4½ years in prison, which means, at the very most, I have only about two years left to do, which to me doesn't seem too great a length of time. If I am granted parole I could be out even earlier, but I prefer not to think too much about that possibility, so as to avoid dissappointment.

The first twenty months of my sentence were spent in prisons where the conditions were pretty awful, but since then my situation has been a lot better. In this prison, for instance, I have a reasonably comfortable cell of my own and I am able to spend time doing such things as watching TV or taking a walk in the very pleasant prison grounds.

After I was first sentenced, I was treated as a top security prisoner, but now I am allowed a considerable amount of freedom in "semi open" conditions. I am also allowed a weekend's "home leave" every six months, which I spend with my parents. I shall never forget my feelings of joy on my first home leave when I was able to make a fuss of their collie (the first time I had stroked a dog in over 3½ years). I'm able to have a visit here from family or friends every two weeks, which is also a great boost to the spirits, but unfortunately, the visits aren't frequent enough for me to see everyone I'd like.

At the begining of my sentence I decided that if the powers that be were going to steal several years of my life, I was going to get a few back by keeping myself really fit and healthy. Therefore, I've always made sure to get plenty of exercise and enjoy playing badminton and tennis as well as going for runs around the sports field. It also helps that the vegan diet here is one of the best I've ever had in prison. It must all be paying off as quite a few of my recent visitors have said they've never seen me looking so healthy, and I'm certainly far fitter now than I was on the outside.

I have never felt that serving a prison sentence was any reason not to carry on my work for animal liberation and so in everything I do I still have the protection of animals in mind. At the start of my sentence I began learning foreign languages, in order to be able to help the animal liberation movement in other countries after my release. I have also gained myself a place at a polytechnic in London to study for a language degree after I get out and am in contact with animal rights campaigners in many different countries, whom I frequently communicate with in their own language.

When I was outside I was always so busy that I never allowed myself time to sit down and seriously think about the operation of the animal protection movement as a whole, but being in prison has given me the chance to do that and I feel I have been able to identify certain aspects that are are wrong and certain areas that need to be imporved. For instance, the vicious in-fighting which so frequently takes place within the movement is a serious bar to its effectiveness and to the acheivement of animal liberation. Rational debate, coupled with a spirit of care and respect towards other animal rights campaigners, really does need to replace the downright nastiness which so often arises between animal protectionists who have some relatively small differences of opinion. It was with this in mind, and also to provide comprehensive information about the activities of the whole movement that I became involved in the creation of a new animal liberation magazine; Arkangel. It is pleasing to hear of the very favourable. reception this publication has had amongst animal rights campaigners and after my release I intend to help extend the whole project with an information service for local animal rights groups, a scheme for helping the movement in other countries, a publishing service for booklets on various aspects of animal protection etc. etc.

There is little doubt that the SG news-letter is also read by certain agents of the authorities, who, in their efforts to prosecute and imprison animal liberation campaigners, are also agenst of the animal abusers. This letter, therefore, is also meant for them. My case is yet another example of how the imprisonment of animal liberationists has failed to halt the progress of the animal liberation movement. I was imprisoned for allegedly inciting others to damage the property of animal abusers, but in reality it is the cruelty of the animal abusers themselves which incites people to take action against them, rather than anything I, or anybody else, may write or say. During the time I have been in prison, the ALF has caused far more damage to the industries of animal persecution than ever before and has gained its greatest triumph through the large part it has played in the decimation of the fur trade. The number of people turning vegetarian or vegan has continued to increase and the yearly figure for experiments on animals continued to go down. Almost everywhere there seems to be increased awareness of animal rights and the need to protect the environment. Far from being defeated by the prison sentence, I feel that the chance to study and reflect that these years have given me has made me a far more effective campaigner.

I was greatly saddened to see the name of the ALF attributed to the "car bomb" attacks earlier in the year. It could well be that the claims of responsibility were made by someone wishing to discredit the ALF and, sad to say, that could well have been somebody within the animal rights movement, given the irrational and almost psychotic hatred that exists towards the ALF in some quarters. It is sad to see that hatred arising yet again in the misguided campaign of certain members of the Animal Aid heirarchy to bar ALF sympathisers from the animal rights movement and discourage people from contributing to the ALFSG. If the campaign were to succeed it would seriously split the movement and impede the important work of the SG in providing for the welfare of those arrested and imprisoned for helping the animals. Recent reports indicate, however, that most local A/R groups and a large number of Animal Aid members are opposed to the campaign, which has failed to destroy support for the ALF or the SG. It has, sadly, caused harm to the image of Animal Aid and it is very painful to see that important society damaged by the irresponsible behaviour of certain of its officers.

On the subject of "car bombs", it is quite easy to understand how the vicious cruelty of vivisectors can cause caring people to wish to take terminal action against them, but it cannot be justifiable to seriously endanger passers-by in the process. I refuse to use such hysterical and innappropriate words as "terrorists" or "maniacs" to describe the people responsible, but I would appeal to them to take great care not to injure the innocent in future.

Finally, to return to the SG members reading this letter, I would like to thank them once again for their much-valued support and urge them never to give up the fight against animal persecution, no matter how hard the battle may seem at times. Despite the setbacks this is a time of great hope for animal liberation with many victories being won. If we can continue our efforts the day of our ultimate triumph may be at hand

Very Best Wishes
Ronnie Lee

A.L.F.S.G.

DISTRIBUTION LIST

LITERATURE

BOOKLETS

'Without a Trace: A Forensic Manual For You And Me' $2.00 ppd
'The Proper Way To Harvest Wheat? Direct Action For The 90's' $1.00 ppd
'An Animal Liberation Primer' a DIY guide $2.00 ppd
'A.L.F. On Trial: Capitalism Under Attack in the 1980's' $1.50 ppd

JOURNALS

ALFSG(TORONTO) NEWSLETTER #1,#2,#3	$1.00ppd	NEW U.K. NEWSLETTER NOV. 89	$1.00ppd
ALFSG(TORONTO) NEWSLETTER #4	$2.00ppd	NEW U.K. NEWSLETTER MAR. 90	$1.00ppd
ALFSG(EDMONTON) NEWSLETTER #1	$2.00ppd	NEW U.K. NEWSLETTER JUL. 90	$1.00ppd
THE LIBERATOR-USA SG NEWSLETTER	$2.00ppd	NEW U.K. NEWSLETTER OCT. 90	$1.00ppd
ENDLESS STRUGGLE #12	$2.00ppd	NEW U.K. NEWSLETTER DEC. 90	$1.00ppd
THE AGITATOR-AUSTRALIA SG NEWSLETTER #1	$2.00ppd	BUSINESS AS USUAL SPRING 89	$2.50ppd
OLD U.K. NEWSLETTER #17	$3.50ppd	INTERVIEWS WITH ALF ACTIVISTS	$3.50ppd
OLD U.K. NEWSLETTER #18	$3.50ppd	LOMAKATSI #2	$3.00ppd
OLD U.K. NEWSLETTER-INTERNATIONAL RESCUE	$3.50ppd	LOMAKATSI #3	$3.00ppd

---

BUTTONS

FUR IS FOR
BEASTS

each $1.00 ppd.

T-SHIRTS

$10.00 ppd.

NEW SG T-SHIRT
FEATURING LIBERATION
SCENE ON FRONT AND
'VIVISECTORS ARE
SCUM' ON BACK

AVAILABLE IN GREY,BLUE,WHITE,RED PLEASE STATE SECOND PREFERENCE OF COLOR AND SIZE.

PLEASE MAKE ALL
CHEQUES PAYABLE
TO:
C.O.A.L.

ANIMAL LIBERATION FRONT
SUPPORT GROUP
Box 42, 10024-82 Ave.
Edmonton, AB, T6E 1Z3

Animal Liberation Front Support Groups:

ACTION FOR ANIMALS
P.O. Box 152
Lutwyche
Queensland 4030
Australia

ALFSG (CANADA)
BOX 42
10024-82 ave.
Edmonton, Alberta
T6E 1Z3, Canada

ALFSG (FRANCE)
B.C.M. 1160
London WC1M 3XX
England

ALFSG (USA)
P.O. BOX 3623
San Bernardino
CA 92413

SUPPORTERS GROUP FOR
ANIMAL ACTIVISTS
P.O. BOX 519
Eltham, Victoria
3095, Australia

ALFSG (UK)
B.C.M. 1160
London WC1M 3XX
England

DBF (SWEDEN)
BOX 2051
S-265 02
ASTORP 2
SWEDEN

Vrienden van het DBF
Oude Gracht 36
3511 Ap Utrecht
THE NETHERLANDS

MAIL SECURITY

If you are a member of an active cell, send any clippings, or your own report, with date, time, place, and a few details about the action. Send your reports on plain paper, using block capital letters, or a public typewriter that many people have access to. Wear gloves at all times so your fingerprints are not on the paper, envelope, or stamp. Do not give your address, and don't lick the stamp or envelope - wet it with a sponge. Remember you should expect that all of our mail and any other support groups mail is opened and read by the authorities.

An Animal
LIBERATION
Primer

EDITED AND COMPILED BY: @nu

NOW AVAILABLE FROM THE Animal Liberation Front Support Group is "An Animal Liberation Primer," a work descibed by its authors as "a tool to empower the average person to make a difference in this world." The pamphlet is an excellent production. It includes a discussion of the history and theory of the ALF. But most important, the pamphlet is a discussion of direct action tactics: how to stake out an action site, tips for breaking into buildings, how to react to police interrogation, et cetera.

The pamphlet, in short, provides an excellent synthesis of the ethical considerations of direct action and the means of effecting "economic sabotage." All animal rights activists are highly encouraged to get a copy of "An Animal Liberation Primer." Indeed, the topics discussed in the work are relevant to all persons active in the revolutionary anarchist milieu. To combat repression and oppression—of both animals and humans—we often need to go beyond mere protest and carry out direct actions.

$2.00
post paid
**ALF Support Group
Box 42, 10024-82 Ave.
Edmonton, AB, T6E 1Z3 CANADA**

THANKS
A very special thanks to all those people and publications that have helped us out
in tons of ways, sorry to anybody that we missed. Anarchist Youth Federation,COAL,
Love & Rage, Profane Existence, The Honkin Dog, Endless Struggle, Anarchy, ArkiAngel,
ALFSG(UK), Blue Leaf Book Shop, FARM, Greenpeace(London), Open Road,Effigy, HSA,SARP,
Spartacus Books, Squak Mountain, CIVIS/CIVITAS.
And a very special NO THANKS to some other people: CCAC, Life Force-Peter Hamilton,
People Against Cruel Trapping-Dick Faragini, McDonalds, CIA, FBI, RCMP-Integrated
Intelligence Unit, CSIS, Alberta Fur Council.

GREAT MOMENTS IN CHICKEN HISTORY

THREE GIANT CHICKENS CATCH COLONEL SANDERS IN A DARK ATLANTA ALLEYWAY AND PROCEED TO "SOUTHERN FRY" HIM PIECE BY PIECE, STARTING WITH THE BALLS.

Three new arrests in ALF crackdown.

In addition to Crescenzo Vellucci, two other animal rights activists have been indicted on felony charges of burglary, conspiracy, theft and criminal mischief for the October 26, 1986 raid of a University of Portland research lab that caused over $58,000 in damage.

Jonathan Paul, an organizer of the anti-blood sport group, the Hunt Sabateurs, and Bill Keogh, director of the Good Shepherd Foundation, as well as Vellucci, have pleaded not guilty to the charges and are awaiting pretrial. Both Keogh and Paul voluntarily turned themselves in to the authorities shortly after learning of police plans to arrest them.

Each of the four charges carries a maximum sentence of four years and a $10,000 fine.

Also being persecuted for alleged involvement with the Animal Liberation Front is Henry Hutto who was jailed on October 31 for refusing to testify before a California Grand Jury investigating the 1987 arson at the University of California at Davis. The fire, which burned down a veterinary medical building still under construction at the time, caused over $5 million damage. Hutto is presently being held in solitary confinement in a six by ten foot cell and is denied a vegan diet.

More information on the plight of these four men can be received from the National Foundation for Animal Law, 926 J Street, Suite 813, Sacramento, California, 95814 (1-916-441-7232). Any donations to help defray their legal costs should be sent to the NFAL as well. Letters are Henry Hutto's only contact with the outside world. All correspondence can be mailed to: Sacramento County Jail, Henry Hutto, X2235256, Floor 3E, Pod 3, Cell 18, 651 I Street, Sacramento, California, 95814.

Activists protest the treatment of Henry Hutto outside of the Sacramento Coiunty Jail.

The Bay quits the fur trade.

After 320 years, the Hudson's Bay Company has given up the fur trade. Barry Agnew, vice president of sales and promotion, announced January 30th that the Bay would no longer be selling fur garments in its department stores because their furs were "unprofitable" and only accounted for $10 million of their annual $2.2 billion revenue. Pressure from animal rights organizations was also mentioned as having "taken a toll" on the Bay's fur sales.

Naturally, the decision has brought criticism from members and supporters of animal abuse industries. The Fur Council of Canada claims the Hudson's Bay Company is "betraying its Canadian heritage" and has petulantly called for the government to revoke the Bay's Royal Charter.

Despite this near-hysterical reaction from the fur lobby, the Bay's decision represents only a tiny victory against the Canadian fur industry. The Bay's department stores only accounted for 2 per cent of all Canadian fur sales last year. Furthermore, even though fur will not be found on the Bay's clothing racks come April, the corporation's parent company, the North West Company Inc. is still heavily involved in fur trafficking. The North West Company, which bought Hudson's Bay Northern Stores four years ago, still operates as a major clearing house for the Canadian fur trade and will continue to sell their spoils to independent retailers as long as uncaring members of society provide a demand.

issue 2

combat

1992

NEWSLETTER OF THE ANIMAL LIBERATION FRONT SUPPORT GROUP CANADA

Bruce Edwards *The Journal*

Bryan Failwell, owner of Billingsgate Fish Company, and his wife Zlathy survey the fire damage to three of the company's trucks Sunday

BILLINGSGATE BURNS

In the early morning of Sunday, December 15/91, ALF activists descended on the premise's of Billingsgate Fish Market in Edmonton, Alberta. The team quickly went to work spraypainting the building and throwing paint bombs at it, slashing tires of the four trucks and spraypainting them. They then placed timed incendiary device's in each of the trucks. Some time later the devices ignighted engulfing three of the trucks in flames, destroying them completely ($100,000 damage). The last device in the fourth and largest truck failed to ignite.

In the ensuing blaze the fire on the outside of the building shorted out the building's electrical supply, cutting power to the building. According to the stores owner's, pumps supplying water to live lobster and crab tanks inside the store stopped, resulting in the deaths of 12 animals.

The deaths were told to reporters by the owners, the SG has not been able to verify their truth. They may be trying to just give the ALF a bad name? People may say, but they (the lobsters) were going to get boiled alive anyways, but thats not the point. People may say that doing $100,000 damage to the company, saved animals lives by costing them money. If it is indeed the truth, it is truly sad that an ALF action resulted in the pain of 12 animals.

We hope next time that more planning goes into the planning of any further actions of this kind, as this is not only unacceptable in any ALF action but is against Animal Liberation Front official policy to not harm any living being (animal or human animal).

Billingsgate Fish Market in Calgary has since spent money to hire a security gaurd for their store there. Billingsgate Fish Market in Edmonton rented three new trucks and was back in business the next morning.

Billingsgate Fish was visited again by activists on Jan. 9 when they had all three of their replacement delivery trucks spraypainted and tires slashed (18 tires).

ARM vs. The Canadian Cold Buster

It isn't listed on the wrapper, but one of the main ingredients in the Cold Buster Chocolate Bar is suffering.

Sixteen years of so-called "research" on animals by the University of Alberta's Dr. Larry Wang led to the developement of the Canadian Cold Buster Chocolate Bar, A candy snack that, supposedly, prevents hypothermia. One letter from the Animal Rights Militia nearly led to it's demise.

The poisoning hoax launched by the ARM against the Cold Buster bar would have come straight out the text book, if there were one.

On Jan. 2nd several major Albertan newspapers and TV stations received a communique from the ARM, claiming they had contaminated 87 Cold Buster bars with oven cleaning fluid and returned them to store shelves for public consumption. Included with the communiques were samples of the contaminated bars.

...continued on page 2

Although the RCMP reffered to the poisoning job as "amateur" and the contaminated bars were easily-identifiable, the manufacturers of the bar immediately recalled all of their product. Although the actual cost of the recall was not officialy released it was estimated by the media to be in the upwards of one million dollars.

Two weeks later, the ARM revealed the poisoning to be a hoax.

This attack by the ARM seems directly patterned after the Animal Liberation Front's Mars Bar hoax in 1984 (England). Because the Cold Buster bar represents 16 years of animal experimentation during which rats were starved, frozen and injected with drugs, including barbituates, it was and obvious target for the ARM. The inventor of the Cold Buster, Larry Wang. was also part-owner of the company which manufactured the bar. As a result, the economic damage caused by the ARM was inflicted directly to the researcher himself.

Although the Cold Buster was a relatively new product at the time of the scare and the company was on financially shaky ground, the hoax failed to put Wang and his colaborators out of business. Still the cost of the recall has caused significant damage to the Cold Buster, and rightfully so.

Wang may be a good business person, but he is not an honest one. During the hoax, Wang repeatedly lied to the media. He claimed that the experiments he performed on rats were " ...the same as those performed on humans." If this were truly the case, then why did wang experiment on animals at all? He offers no answer.

Wang also stated that none of the rats he used were killed. Despite the obvious falsity of this statement, the mass media was more than willing to believe them. In fact, a few weeks after he made that statement, the ARM sent a third communique out to media outlets and to the ALFSG refuting wang's lie. Included with communique were copies of an expermentation proposal, written by wang himself, which clearly states that rats were to be "sacrificed" after being starved, frozen and force fed drugs.

The major media ignored the bulk of all 3 of ARM's communique's. They, no doubt, preffer to believe Wang's reassuring lies and eat their candy without guilt, even if it means sacrificing the truth.

Maybe
in time
Beast and Bird shall
take back their
earth
    of which they
    kindly invited
    mankind
to live:
in trust
that
    all would be well.

Solid wild oak trees, with their twisting arms, seem to reach for space. Red manzanita bushes, stretching their limbs, full with delicious berries. Above lies a blazing fireball; 80, 90, 100 degrees easily. Below, a cracked, parched earth showing the signs of years of drought. There are rolling fields of yellow, dried grasses. Thick, scrawny chapparal bush everywhere, where a human cannot pass through. But the critters can! Salamanders and other lizards scamper through to safety. I hear but cannot see the snakes slithering by. I've seen deer, but no elk yet, though some folks have spotted a small herd in Benmore Canyon. Others have spotted two hunters at the mouth of Cache Creek, accompanied by the usual entourage of DFG and BLM cops. It's been a relatively quiet first weekend of this year's Tule elk hunt sab.

The most excitement so far has been the cat and mouse games with the DFG, who have been trying to i.d. us. Getting caught in the hunting fields is trespasing, as the area is officially closed for the 12 day slaughterfest, catering to the bloodlust of no more than six individuals. There were only six kill tags issued this year, all for females, which means that road kills and poaching numbers must be up.

The winds have stopped today. Two days ago they began, coming from the north and east. Though they weren't cold, they were strong and fierce. Unceasing, relentless winds easlily 50, 60, 70, miles per hour. They came and spoke through the trees and the grasses. Sleep was hard to find during those nights. It's also been hard to sleep with the blazing light of the near to full moon above. This is the Samhain moon, a celebration of the dead. Strange we should be attempting to stop such a celebration in hunters world. But obviously it's not the same thing. A celebration of people and animal lives for who they were is much different than a celebration of an act of ritualistic murder upon defenceless creatures.

Our numbers are down today, from 25 over the weekend to about 9 mid-week. That's okay since it's been quiet. Too quiet in fact. (Our first sighting of hunters will turn out to be our last. The DFG have confirmed one kill that weekend, and we believe that will be the total this year. For unexplained reasons most of the six hunters did not show up this year.)

Yesterday was a beautiful day, I went hiking through Stemple Canyon with three others on another fruitless search for hunters. We hiked to the creek and spent most of the day swimming. The cold water was perfect to cool our bodies from the heat of the midday sun, and to clean them from the dust and dirt of the thirsty earth. It's great to lounge without the confines of clothes, to soak in the sun and to view and admire human bodies; to feel the cold and the wet of the water, and the wind, and the heat of the sun. I could almost fall asleep, were it not for the flies that delighted in probing my flesh.

Water is such a finite resource here. I need at least two quarts on a day hike . There is none on the land we are camping on. Cache Creek is laced with mercury and other toxins. And the entire area is a tinderbox. Over two thousand acres are burning nearby. By day we can see the huge colmuns of smoke and by night the red glow of the inferno. Little effort is being made to contain it because most firefighters are down in Oakland and Berkely Hills where a huge fire has already torched 600 homes so far. (The Geyser fire out here eventually consumed more than 5000 acres, and the East Bay fire ate up over 3000 properties belonging mostly to rich people.)

Newspapers are crying about property loss, making little if any mention of human or animal death. The CDF fire marshals declare

...continued on pg. 7

Everyone out there who takes the fight for animal liberation out onto the street and into the night sometimes feels as if they are waging the war all alone. Everyone who supports the actions of the ALF sometmes feels that the front has withered away, because they have heard of no new action in the mass media.

Because the ALF is an organization that must survive underground, communication between active cells, and between activists and supporters, is almost impossible. The Animal Liberation Front Support Group has been designed to report on the activities of the ALF and to act as a source of information on what the ALF does and why.

It's not as difficult or dangerous running the support group as being a part of an active cell, but the SG does demand a lot of effort and money from it's organizer's.

When the ALFSG in Toronto folded, the task of communicating with the SG's 1500+ members was handed to the ALFSG in Edmonton, unfortunately, despite the fact that the entire workload was handed to Edmonton, It was accompanied by only a fraction of the old SG's bank account. The money that didn't make it to Edmonton SG was donated to other organizations dedicated to working towards overcoming human/animal and enviromental exploitation, But the resulting finacial squeeze has forced Edmonton SG to downscale it's activity. You have probably noticed this decrease already. Combat cannot be published on a quarterly basis and the SG is frequently unable to fill merchandise orders. The cost of postage alone to perform these tasks is crippling.

Until the SG's finacial situation gets better, we will be unable to put out a regular newsletter or send out a mailout to the entire membership. We feel that what the SG does is important, and apollogize for not being able to do a thorough job. We hope, however, that you can understand our situation and accept our apology.

- Animal Liberation Front
  Support Group Canada

Hunt   Sabbing   in   North   America

(Editors- Sorry this article is in such small type, it's the only way we could make it fit in this issue. grab your magnifying glass!)

The Hunt Saboteurs are a growing direct action force in the U.S. Since our inception in 1986 when a small handfull of us went out to the Mojave desert to try to stop the Bighorn Sheep trophy hunt, we've grown in numbers and in the range of hunts we try to interfere with. The past few years have seen Hunt Sab action at Cache Creek in Central California and at Grizzly Island near the San Fransisco Bay area for the Tule Elk, at deer hunts, for "youth" in California and general hunts in southern Oregon, at a Prarie Dog shoot-off in Colorado, at West Yellowstone Park in Montana where the Bison are under the gun, at Big-horn Sheep hunts in the desert in California and most recently at the KOFA Wildlife Refuge (sick joke) in Arizona.

Our tactics for sabotaging hunts are much different than those used by our counterparts in Britain for fox hunts, and they change depending on conditions and situations. We must always be flexible and adaptable. Our typical method for elk, deer and sheep hunts is this: We track the hunters, watch for the target animals, and when spotted, give a blast of our Wasco coastgaurd airhorns which will hopefully scare the animals away. Our method for bison is much different, as bison don't give much notice to loud noise's (them being used to obnoxious snowmobilers). Instead, we physically position ourseleves between the hunter and the hunted. A more precarious situation indeed!

Bighorn Sheep Hunt Sab, Mojave Desert, Dec.1-15, 1990
The main feature of the Hunt Sab action in the desert this year was the increase of harassment against us by the California Dept. of Fish and Game (Squish and Maim) and the U.S. Bureau of Land (Mis) Management. Hunter "harassment" is a crime in most states now including Calif., and is the basis for saboteur harassment. Our arival in the desert was greeted with a DFG plane sitting in the middle of the road at the point where we turn off to our campsite. We had to swerve onto the gravel shoulder to avoid a collision, and we were then cornered in by BLM and DFG vehicles. Everyone was photo- graphed, and our first "crime" had been committed - "posses- sion of illegal feathers". I was given a ticket for having feathers of a non-game birds strewn a cross my dashboard. (The intention of the law is to curtail the illegal trade of animal parts by ruthless humans, but no matter if the "illegal" feathers were from a roadkill found by an animal protecter. The law is the law, afterall, right?)

The stopping of vehicles, vehicle serches, identification and photos of activists taken were the most common feature of harass- ment, and two more sabbers were given similar feather tickets at a later date. But we didn't let their pettiness stop us from trying to do our job.

Each day we would wake up between four and five a.m. and prepare to be dropped off at various points in the Old Dad Mountain range. Fully camoflauged, we would hike up to strategic points to sit and wait for the hunters.

sheep, and BLM and DFG cops, who were trying to find us. When a hunter spots a sheep and prepares to fire, the sabber sounds the airhorn. After one unfortunately f ailed sab attempt where the sheep was killed despite the horn, the DFG and BLM cops took the drastic step of closing off the entire hunting area as a "crime scene". (Closed only to sabbers, that is) The guilty people made their way back to camp on foot avoiding the numerous vehicle searches. No one has yet been charged in California under the hunter harassment law, though we look forward to the day when someone is, so we can challenge it in the courts as a freedom of expression issue.

This year (1990) we held off most of the kills for the first of the two weeks of hunting, but eventually all seven kills were made. (The number of hunting tags issued each year varies) What is of particular intrest is that a mountain lion has been in the area and has killed, according to wildlife officials, seven sheep in this year. There is a natural balance that can be restored, and this is what should be strived for. A full reintroduction of natural predators is what we demand. The hunt, described as "conservation", is nothing but a sick blood lust by humans to put the head of a beautiful animal on the wall of their suburban home.

Bison Hunt Sab, West Yellowstone Park, Jan. 1991
In the eyes of the U.S. governmant and Montana State, it seems there is little difference between Native Americans and the bison. Both have been forced onto reserves, and both face extinction. The Native Americans are allowed off their reserves, but only to face assimilation and perhaps extinction through white man's greed. The bison are not allowed off of their reserve however. If they step over the line, they are shot and killed.

The bisons reserve is Yellowstone National Park in Montana. Their land used to be the entire plains. These are a free roaming animal, and imaginary and arbitrary boundaries , along with puny fences and "private property" do not stop them from foraging for food in the winter months.

The threat to their existence (as well as numerous species including the Elk and Bighor n Sheep) comes from the ranching indutry, who have forced the Park Service and State officials to do their dirty work of mass murder. The reason, these humans claim, that the bison need to be killed, is that aprox. half the herd of 2000 carry a disease called brucellocis (so the officials say), Brucellocis causes female cows to abort their fetuses. It also causes increased expenses for ranchers in the way of more inspections of dead cows headed to the butcher. Never mind that there is no more than 15 cow ranching intrests around Yellowstone calling the shots. Never mind that cow ranching is one of, if not the main factor in the destruction of wilder ness areas and is the cause of the slaughter and disappearance of many species. Never mind that there has never been one single documented case of transmission of brucellocis from bison to cow in the wild!

For this action, the Hunt Saboteurs teamed up with Earth First! to try to stop the slaughter. From our base in a cozy cabin near the park, we skied daily to

...continued on pg. 7

A CALL OF THE WILD

This comminque was mailed to the SG we feel it goes a long way to explaining the feelings of ALF members. It is printed verbatim:

A CALL OF THE WILD

Written on the eve of the raid on Oregon State University's Experimental Fur Farm

Let it be recognized that the Earth, and all life upon it, is under massive attack by human forces that would destroy all of nature for the sake of economic, and personal gain. We are at the most critical stage of ecological destruction in human history, with every form of indigeneous non-human life threatened with continues explotation, and biological extinction.

If the animal nations, and the land they live in is to survive, then we must act now.

Hundreds are murdered every minute, thousands every hour, and millions of animals are slaughtered everyday. All for meat we eat, the leather and fur we wear, and the countless other by-products fed to our society by the earth-destroying industries involved in animal abuse. The reasons behind predator control, and over-grazing, are to protect the intrest of the livestock industry. We know the facts, and even who is doing it, now is the time when direct action speaks louder than words.

Over the last fifteen years, the Animal Liberation Front has maintained an active role in covertly chanllenging the instituions of animal abuse, and also enviromental destruction. The Animal Liberation Front has rescued thousands of animals from vivisection laboratories and suppliers, factory farms, fur-farms, and other places where they were being imprisoned, and tortured. The Animal Liberation Front has also caused tens of millions of dollars of damage to property being used to destroy life, by continuing an effective campaign of "economic sabotage". But this is not enough.

In order to topple the infrastructure of animal exploatation it is neccesary to launch a full-scale guerilla war against animal, and earth abuse industries. Unlike any other war, the war fought by the Animal Liberation Front in the last fifteen years, has been one where life is the highest value, not real estate, or political power. It is a struggle where we restrain a moral high ground above our political power. It is a struggle where we retain a moral high ground above our enemies because we attack only machines and property of destruction, and not those that opearate them. To justify the destruction of life, is to forfeit our call for respect of all life. The defense of nature and animals can be attained without more killing. The full benefits of economic sabotage have not yet to be tapped by the animal, and enviromental movements.

It is time to continue the re-evolutionary process that will spare natural diversity, and non-human beings from the remorseless path of modern society. It is time to be acknowledged as a part of the solution, not a part of the problem. There is no more middle of the road, or fence to sit on any longer. It is time to abandon out biological prejudice, and speciecism that prevents us from risking our own freedom to obtain that of an imprisoned sister or brother. If we truly believe in an inifnity with all life on Earth, then let us now defend it by all means neccesary.

There can be no freedom as long as one of our non-human family members is imprisoned by the power of human-kind. The destiny of the Earth is in our own hands. We can choose to spend our precious time and energy on mild reforms, and temporary victories, or we can strive for total liberation of the animal nations by refusing to accept the ineffective avenues of change that governments offer us.

We must never expect the power-structure to release it's strangle-hold on nature and animal-kind voluntarily. Nor can we expect to liberate the animal nations through the sanctioned methods of the very institutions that oppress them.

It has been one-hundred and twenty years since human tribes aggresively challenged the United States Government to defend animal life. Unfortunately for Western North America, and all that lived upon her, that battle was lost. But the struggle has just begun again. In the spirit of the buffalo, prairie wolf, and laboratory rat, we must organize an effective undeground movement that can maintain a relentless campaign of economic sabotage against the anti-life corporations that mutilate animals, and ravage their homelands. We must continue our attacks, and strike repeatedly until the anti-nature forces are beaten down from their dominating platform of oppression.

For too long we have tried to reach the hearts of the heartless, while our sisters, and brothers have continued to fall. We have appealed for peace on every level governments have offered us. Always with the same dissapointing results. We can no longer compromise the lives of those we have no right to repesent at the bargaining table of anthropocentric society. There is no more time to wrestle with philosophies that place animal life below that of property. To disregard the sanctity of life is a moral crime, as well as a breaking from the laws of nature. There is no longer a use for passive resistance, such tactics are only effective against an opposition that respects life. There is only time for aggressive self-defense of the innocent victims of human greed, and patriarchy.

The genocidal war being waged against the Earth, and all that live upon her, is unjustifiable , and unnaceptable to human beings that still embrace compassion, and freedom as highter values than material wealth, and power. It is very important to recognize in our struggle, that the forces that exploit the Earth, and animals, have amassed too much power, and authority, in order to fight them overtly. We must not offer our own lives as fodder for the police. They have all the guns, the money, but we have the spirit of nature on our side, and sabotage must be the Earth's revenge.

This is only one human voice from the front-lines of the war to protect annimals, and defend the Earth. There are few of us, and many of them. We are tired, and grow weary. We desperatley need others to fight the struggle, or the Animal Liberation Front will exist only as a memory, like the native riders of the Great Plains.

As in the case with many other members of the Animal Liberation Front, I am ready to die for the defense of our mother Earth. We will not escape the clutches of the government forever. For this reason, we must recruit new members is we are to turn the tide of animal exploitation. This is a call to those who can no more turn away from the cries for freedom emitting from every research laboratory, factory farm, fur-farm, circus, and wilderness. A call to individuals who can no longer tolerate the screams of pain from our non-human sisters, and brothers. You are the Animal Liberation Front, and the animal nations need you.

Do not send money to ease your conscience, do not attend more police monitered demonstarions, do not write letters to political waste-paper baskets.

Instead organize, strategize, and act now. Locate friends that you

continued next page...

trust that feel the same way you do, then keep your mouth shut. Remember, one individual can make a difference, and a group of people can change the world. Do not look for romantic adventure, or self-gratification in this struggle. In autonomy is the birth of true personal liberation. There will be rewards, and they will be beyond your wildest imaginations. They will come as you fight for freedom with others in the night. They will come everytime a fur shop you strike goes out of business, everytime and animal you liberate runs free, and everytime an animal concentration camp you torch burns to the ground.

There will come a time when we ourselves begin to fall, when we are the imprisoned animal behind bars. It will not be the first time someone is imprisioned because of their adherence to the laws of nature.

Then is when we must remember that whatever happens to us in a jail cell, is little compared to the torture inflicted upon animals by industry, and government. With good security, and common sense, we can deny the opposition a victory over us, and the Earth. We can remain free. It has been seven years since my first Animal Liberation Front action. Governments cannot imprison ideas, and spirit, neither can they quash the voice for freedom, and the struggle for justice for all. To Government, nothing is more dangerous than a people that rise above their control, and empower themselves with the self-confidence to act against state-sponsored terrorism.

We must also discover that liberation is a process that begins with ourselves. It must be your first animal liberation action. It will come as you question, and reject the guidelines and laws of our society forced on us since birth. Values and beliefs that have only served to breed apathy, and insensitivity to the crimes being commited daily around us. Rules of society that have allowed so much death and destruction to continue against the Earth, animals, and ultimately, ourselves. We must instead strive to live with one another in a non-oppressive, life-respecting way that allows for us to rediscover all that the

Earth offers us if we only choose to listen. listen to the language that others have forgotten, and what others have attempted to destroy. I do not speak for myself only, but try to also speak on behalf of those without a voice. Through the years I have seen their eyes behind the wire, and have witnessed their agony in death. It is a very real tragedy, what we do to our fellow beings on Earth. Rather than hate ourselves because of what our species has done, we must show the animal nations that all of human-kind is not evil. We must make our lives an example of how peacefull co-existence can become a reality. It all starts with you. The strength of a small group of people is limit-less when we start to break free.

As we raid Oregon State University's Experimental Fur Farms tonight we will see hundreds of animals in cramped cages that will be killed this November. We will try to save some of them. For the rest, I will beg of you to throw down your petitions, and pick up your pry-bars. Membership in the Animal Liberation Front begins with your first "illegal" direct action on behalf of animals.

Animal liberation is literally only a stone's throw away, it must spread to your local butcher shop, fur salon, and chicken farm. May the flames of animal liberation engulf every structure representing animal and earth abuse. The Animal Liberation Front must never die, for if it does, the hopes of freedom for billions of animals will be forever drowned in the business as usual attitude af the animal abuse industries.

For the women, and the men of the Animal Liberation Front, I call on you to join us as warriors of a new society, one that will onclude all species in our global community. A place where the cry of the coyote, and the song of the whale mean as much as the voice of any human. May we rescue natural diversity and all animals that belong in it, from ecologial genocide at the hands of patriarchal domination. Be driven not by anger, or frustration, but by love and the desire to be free in a world where all are equal.

Western Wildlife Cell Member
ANIMAL LIBERATION FRONT

It is sad to read constant condemnation of the ALF, from so many called animal rights people. The core of the matter as I see it, depends on which side of the fence you are sitting on. If you are an animal screaming for help in a blood drenched slaughter house, or in terminal bondage of stereo-taxic restraining chairs, would you be so critical of your savers?

The ALF are unpaid soldiers, risking their freedom to save others. Does it matter what kind of life they save? Soldiers at war are getting medals for doing the same thing! The ALF has never harmed anyone. At this very moment people are blowing each other apart, and we call them brave !!!

Wake up to yourselves and leave the ALF to do the job they must do. The ALF are the heroes of tommorow and without them we would be in the dark as to what goes in behind closed doors. To all of you unknown people wherever you are, my heart goes out. You are the real angels.

In closing I would like to quote Martin Luther King Jr.:
"Cowardice asks the question, Is it safe?
Expediency asks the qeustion, is it politic?
Vanity asks the question, Is it popular?
But conscience asks the question, Is it right?
And there comes a time when one must take a position that is neither safe, nor politic, nor popular, but he must take it because his conscience tells him that it is right......" reprinted from ArkAngel #5

Of My Gods

As their
spirits weep for their
brothers,
So shall Mother
Earth.
The skies grow
sad when
man
walks within the
forests, and
leaves
a trail of crimson
when he
leaves.

DIARY OF ACTIONS

EVERY DAY OF THE YEAR, WOMEN AND MEN OF THE ANIMAL LIBERATION FRONT DIRECTLY INTERVENE TO STOP ANIMAL SUFFERING, AT THE RISK OF LOSING THEIR OWN FREEDOM. ACTIONS OCCUR ACROSS THE WORLD FROM ITALY TO AUSTRIA TO CANADA TO SWEDEN. BELOW ARE SOME ACCOUNTS OF RECENT ACTIONS:

CANADA

1991

Mar. -Edmonton AB; J. Rose a store that sells furs has their mural and wall painted, locks glued and windows smashed.
-Edmonton AB; Darek's Furs had their windows smashed.

Feb. - Edmonton AB; The ALF paid a visit to the house of a vivisector from the University of Alberta who has been killing dogs for over 11 years. They painted his house and two cars, slashed all the tires, and smashed two front windows of his house.

June -Edmonton AB; Derose Bros. Meats had their shop painted with slogans and two trucks were spray painted, daubed with paint stripper, and had their windsheilds sprayed with etching fluid $2000 damage.

Aug.20 -Edmonton AB; Two trucks belonging to DeRose Bros. Meats were spray painted and one set on fire. $17,000 damage.

Sept. -Edmonton AB; Paris Furs had SCUM daubed on their front window with etching fluid. They have since installed a video security camera monitering their front window.

Nov. -Edmonton AB; Queen City Meats spraypainted with slogans, a Kentucky Fried Chicken had their locks glued.
-Edmonton AB; Hurtig Furs shop in Edmonton Centre shopping mall had 4 windows daubed with etching fluid.
-Darek's Furs had windows daubed with etching fluid.

Dec. -Edmonton AB; Three Fur Council of Canada billboards, were paint bombed.

Dec.14 -Edmonton AB; Three delivery trucks of Billingsgate Fish Company were spraypainted, had their tires slashed and set ablaze . The building was also painted with slogans and a sign damaged with paint bombs. A fourth device failed to ignite in another truck. $100,000 damage

Dec.30 -Edmonton AB; Activists set ablaze a truck belonging to Hook Advertising and spraypainted others with slogans, $10,000 damage. Hook signs carried ads from the Fur Council of Canada earlier this month.

1992

Jan.1 -Edmonton AB; Ouellette Packing Plant was spraypainted and had paint bombs thrown at it. Their van was spraypainted, tires slashed, and set ablaze.

Jan.3 -AB; Animal Rights Militia claims to have poisoned 87 Canadian Cold Buster Chocolate bars in Calgary and Edmonton because of the University of Alberta vivisector Larry Wang's 16 years of animal experiments that led to the invention of the bar.

Jan.4-7 -Calgary AB;Saks Furs had windows smashed, Rupps Meats had windows smashed and spraypainted, 3 Kentucky Fried Chicken shops spraypainted, 1 fur shop on 17th ave. had windows etched, 1 fur shop on 4th st. had windows etched, one fish shop had windows etched and spraypainted, 1 fur shop had windows smashed, and a butcher on McLeod Trail spraypainted.

Jan.8 -Edmonton AB; A delivery truck of Ouellette Packers had it's tires slashed.

Jan.9 -Edmonton AB; Billingsgate Fish had all three of their replacement delivery trucks spraypainted and tires slashed (18 tires).

Feb. 7 -Calgary AB; Fur stores were damaged

ENGLAND

1991

Jan. -West Yorkshire; Sky Commercial Rabbit Farm received a visit from the ALF, liberating 80 rabbits, the entire contents of one shed. Afterwords the group set fire to the shed, burning it totally to the ground, thereby ensuring it will never again be used to exploit animals.

Jan. 10 -Lanashire; activists broke into Lancashire Polytechnic and liberated 106 mice, 43 doves, 11 rats, two rabbits, and a guinea pig. Documents were also taken in the raid. The liberators entered through a skylight in the roof and then had to saw through bars in the ceiling.

-actions occur so often in England we don't have enough room in this whole newsletter for all of them, the above is a sample-

ITALY

1992

Jan. 12 -Milan: ALF activists injected blue chemicals into milk cartons in supermarkets.

SWEDEN

1991

Apr. 27 -Ljungby; A slaughterhouse got its walls and windows spraypainted with slogans "Meat is Murder", Let the Animals Live" and "Long Live DBF"

May 3 -Activists paid a visit to a dogbreeding unit, The owner was supposed to have died a short time earlier and that the dogbreeding facility was closed. In order to prevent relatives to tak e over, they destroyed the kennels, fence, and much else.

May 14 -Helsingborg; Four fur shops had their locks glued, painted with red paint and anti-fur posters.

June 6 -Four more fur shops had their locks glued, painted, and anti-fur posters.

July 26 -Lund; 26 rabbits liberated from a vivisection breeder.

Oct. 4 -Stockholm; 18 fur shops got the usual "visite".

UNITED STATE$

1991

Jan. 1 -Chicago IL; Cook County Hospital's Hektoen Laboratory was raided. Liberating 11 rabbits and 10 guinea pigs. They also gave 20 baboons dried fruit and banana's.

June 10 -Corvallis OR; Oregon State University's Experimental Fur Farm was broken into, where activists destroyed equipment and data base, and set fire to a storage shed. $62,000 damage.

June 15 -Edmonds WA; the ALF planted incendiary devices in Northwest Fur Foods Cooperative. The cooperative is a major supplier of foods for Northwestern fur farms including OSU Expermintal Fur Farm. The resulting fire caused $800,000 damage.

Aug. 13 -WA; Seven coyotes released, 6 mink and 10 mice liberated and $50,000 in damage done to two laboratories. (no more details available at press time)

Dec.21 -Yamhill OR; An incendiary device was set that destroyed the processing plant at the Malecky Mink Ranch.

ANIMAL LIBERATION FRONT
GUIDELINES:

The Animal Liberation Front carries out direct action against animal abuse in the form of rescuing animals and causing financial loss to animal exploiter's, usually through the damage and destruction of property. Their short term aim is to save as many animals as possible and directly disrupt the practice of animal abuse. Their long term aim is to end all animal suffering by forcing animal abuse companies and individuals out of buisiness. It is a non-violent campaign, activists taking precautions not to harm any animal(human or otherwise). Because ALF actions are against the law activists work anonymously, either in small groups or individually, and do not have a central contact address or any centralised organization or coordination.

the herd to see how they were doing, to see how close they were getting to the bouday.

The original planned scenario was this: When and if the bison left the park, the Montana officials would call up hunters who had paid $200 each and were put on a waiting list. They would be personally escorted to the bison , and then from a close range, shoot them. It's sort of like going to the mall with your dad to buy a sofa, except you put a couple slugs into it instead.

Directly due to our presence in the area, Montana Fish, Wildlife and Game decided they were not going to use hunters due to the perceived "danger". Hell, they're the ones with the guns! Instead, they said, they would do the job themselves. Our job would have been to physically position ourselves between the hunters and the hunted. Short of trying to corral the bison back into the park (which is only a short-term solution that may save them from immediate death), there is not much else we can do. During the month of January, we did not have to take any action because the bison remained inside the park.

Latest news: 150 bison have been killed in 1992. State and Park officials are responding to complaints from private landowners, many of which are coming from Claire Prophet's Church of the Universal Triumphant.

From Conflict to Community

The Hunt Saboteurs in the western U.S. are a unique group of individuals. Over the past years, we have grown to know each other better, and are in fact building a community. We are attempting to effectively mix political action with our lifestyles, and are growing to know, love, and support each other in many ways. During Hunt Sab actions, our dinners are vegan and communal. For the most part, we share an ideology of saving all things wild, mixed with a deep respect for the balnce of life on this planet, of ecosystems unmolested by humans. Combined with our anti-authoritian direct action a proach to most things in life, we strengthen our commitments and our bonds to each other when ever we sab together, or travel together or whatever.

We ar e a nomadic community in many ways, with strong connection to the Earth. We share a lot of experinces, and in so doing, share joy and sadness, but with support maintainjoy and humor and comraderie. Without doing so we face much frustration, depression, and burnout. We need each other for physical, spiratual, and emotional support.

It may s eem at times to others that we are so tight a group that our closeness may tend to exclude others from getting involved, but this is not the case. Our community grows larger each year. We hope that many more people get involved in hunt sabbing, with us here in California and also in your own local area. Write to us to get more information on doinf that. We can offer advice, knowledge, tips, but also encouragement and perhaps contacts in your area as well. We also need the usual green stuff, if you've got any to spare! Just remeber:

SAB THE BASTARDS!   -By Freebird

Hunt Saboteurs: P.O. Box 67121, Scotts Valley, CA 95067 (408)438-8631 and soon to be in British Columbia! Get in Touch: c/o Terra Prima! P.O. Box 6491, Depot 1, Victoria, BC, V8P 5M4

TULE ELK HUNT SAB '91 continued...

that the fires can continue to burn out here because there are no humans or their property nearby, in this so-called "rattlesnake infested" area, Meanwhile, we continue to walk on this fragile land treading lightly, trying to save a delicately-balanced species of elk. Amid the chaos of wind and heat and fire, and the tragedy of hunters, BLM and DFG, we perserve in our mission.

Some things are just more important than property, fenced off or burning down.

-Freebird '91

THANKS, A very special thanks to everybody that has helped out in any way, sorry to anybody that we missed: AKdistribution :3 Balmoral Place, Sterling Scotland, FK8 2RD / Anarchist Youth Federation: PO Box 8585, Minneapolis, MN 55408, USA/ Anarchy: c/o CAL, POB 1446, Columbia, MO 65205-1446, USA / Ark Angel : BCM 9240, London, WC1N 3XX, England / Autonome Forum: PO Box 366 Williamstown, MA 01267, USA/ **Bound Together:** 1369 Haight Street, San Francisco, CA 94117/ **CIVITAS:** Box 26, Swian, NY 14884 / FARM: 10101 Ashburton Lane, Bethseda, MD 20817/ **Fact Sheet Five:** 6 Arizona ave., Rensselaer, NY 12144-4502 / Greenpeace(London): 5 Caledonian road, London, N1, England / Hippycore: PO Box 195, Mesa, AZ, 85211, USA/ **Hunt Saboteurs :** P.O. Box 647121, Scotts Valley, CA 950647, USA /Hunt Saboteurs International: PO Box 148, Belfast Bt1 2FF, Northern Ireland/**Karma Badges:** 18 Richmond road, Oxford, Ox1 2JL/ **Left Bank Books:** 92 Pike street, Seattle, WA 98101, USA/ Love & Rage Box 3 Prince St. Station, New York, NY 10013, USA/ **Mad World Survival Guide**, P.O. Box 791377, New Orleans, LA 70179-1377 / **Ned Ludd Books,** P.O. Box 5141, Tucson AZ 85703 / **PETA:** PO Box 42516, Washington, DC, 20015, USA / **Profane Existence:** PO Box 8722, Minneapolis, MN 55408, USA / Resistance: c/o Freinds of Durruti, PO Box 790, STN. A, Vancouver, BC, V6C 2N6, CANADA/ **Spartacus Books:** 311 West Hastings, Vancouver, BC, V6B 1H6, CANADA/Still Angry Dist: 283 Roncesvalles Ave., Toronto, ONT, M6R 2M3, CANADA/The Shadow:PO Box 20298, New York, NY, 10009, USA/Wind Chill Factor P.O. Box 81961, Chicago, IL 60681———

S.G. DISTRIBUTION

JOURNALS

combat #1 ALFSG(CANADA)   -$2.00
S.A.R.P. (Support Animal Rights Prisoners) newsletter   -$2.00

BOOKLETS

An Animal Liberation Primer - A DIY booklet of direct action tactics : how to stake out an action site, tips for breaking into buildings, how to react to police interrogation, et cetera.   "...an excellent production."   -   Love and Rage Now in it's second edition! $2.00 post paid anywhere

Into the 1990's with the A.L.F. - an up to date, how to book - from England on new ALF tactics. Short but good - $2.00

Interviews with Animal Liberation Front Activists - Compiled in England from interviews with many different ALF cells. Covers most aspects of the ALF. Recommended - $5.00

Without A Trace a forensics manual for you and me - An excellent lay-persons guide on forensics (finger-prints, clothing etc)and how not to leave them lying around. A lot of good tips about security (yours) and how not to get caught. - $2.00

A.L.F. On Trial : Capitalism Under Attack in the1980's - an excellent account of the UK government attempt to break the back of the A.L.F. - $1.00

The Proper Way to Harvest Wheat ? Direct Action for the 90's - an interesting look at direct action, some thoughts for the future of direct action. - $1.00

WHOLESALE PRICES AVAILABLE UPON REQUEST
All prices are postpaid in North America.
Overseas orders please add 20% postage charge
Send cheques, money order, or well concealed cash to:
ALFSG Box 42, 10024 - 82 ave., Edmonton,
AB, T6E 1Z3, Canada

Mail SECURITY

If you are a member of an active ALF group/cell, send any news clippings, or your own report, with: time, date, place(city & country), and a few details about the action.

- DO send your reports on plain paper.
- DO use square block capital letters (ie. LIKE THIS.   ),   or   a   public typewriter that many people have access to (library, university, etc.) .
- DO wear gloves at ALL times so your finger-prints are not on the paper, envelope, or stamp.

- DO NOT give the return address (yours) anywhere.
- DO NOT lick the stamp or envelope - wet it with a sponge.
- DO NOT tell us about upcoming actions.

Remember you should expect that all of our mail and any other support groups mail is opened by the authorities. These steps are essential and should NEVER be left out. These practices will help ensure your safety, and allow you to keep on with actions to stop the suffering now.

ADDRESS LIST:

S.A.R.P.
(Support Animal Rights Prisoners)
P.O. Box 96
Northhampton
NN5 5JT
England

ALFSG - ENGLAND
BCM 1160
London
WC1N 3XX
England

HUNT SABOTEURS
P.O. Box 647121
Scotts Valley
CA 95067
USA

Sea Shepherd
P.O. Box 484446
Vancouver
BC
V7X 1A2
Canada

EARTH FIRST!
WESTERN CANADA
P.O. Box 6491 Depot 1
Victoria
BC V8P 5M4
Canada

EARTH FIRST! JOURNAL
P.O. Box 5176
Missoula
MT 59806
USA

Djurens Befrielse Front
(Swedish A.L.F.
Support Group)
Box 2051
S-265 02
Astorp 2
Sweden

ANIMAL LIBERATION FRONT SUPPORT GROUP CANADA
Box 42, Edmonton, Alberta, T6E 1Z3, Canada

FURTHER READING

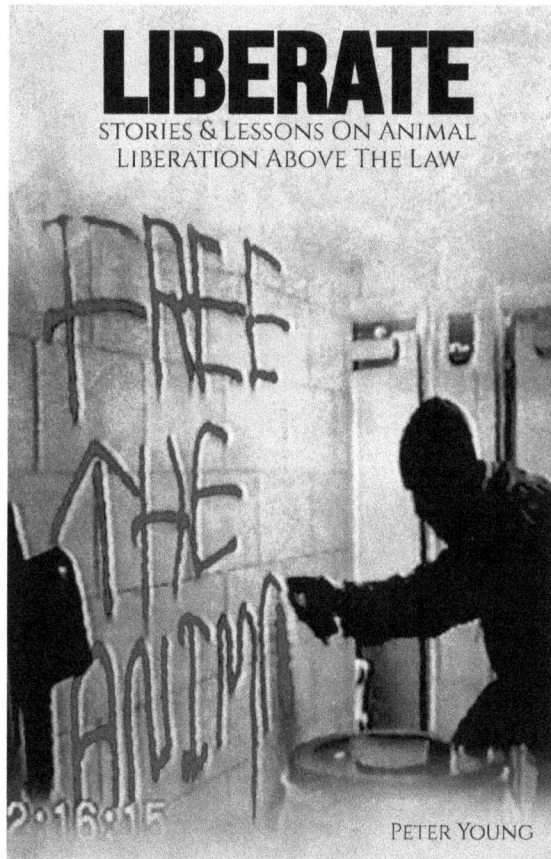

LIBERATE
STORIES & LESSONS ON ANIMAL
LIBERATION ABOVE THE LAW

PETER YOUNG

From Dusk 'til Dawn
An insider's view of the growth of the Animal Liberation Movement

Keith Mann
with an endorsement from Morrissey
and a foreword by Benjamin Zephaniah

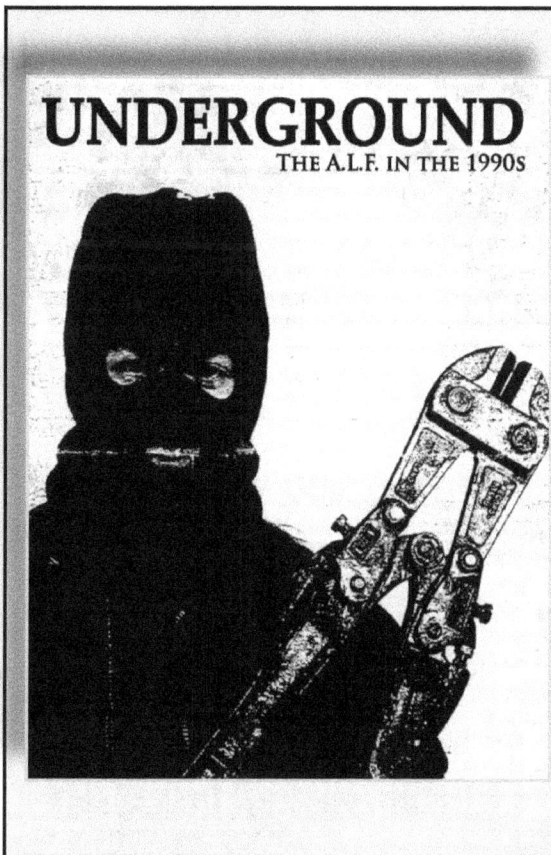

UNDERGROUND
THE A.L.F. IN THE 1990s

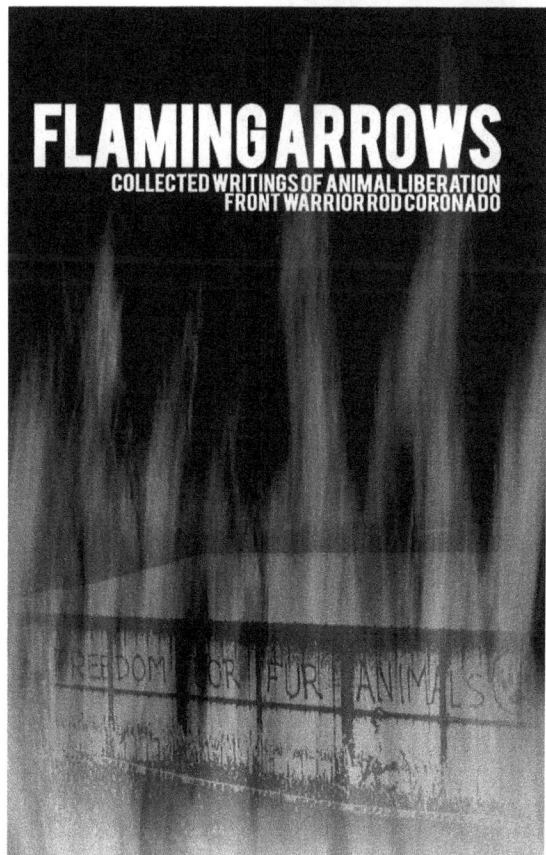

FLAMING ARROWS
COLLECTED WRITINGS OF ANIMAL LIBERATION
FRONT WARRIOR ROD CORONADO

FURTHER READING

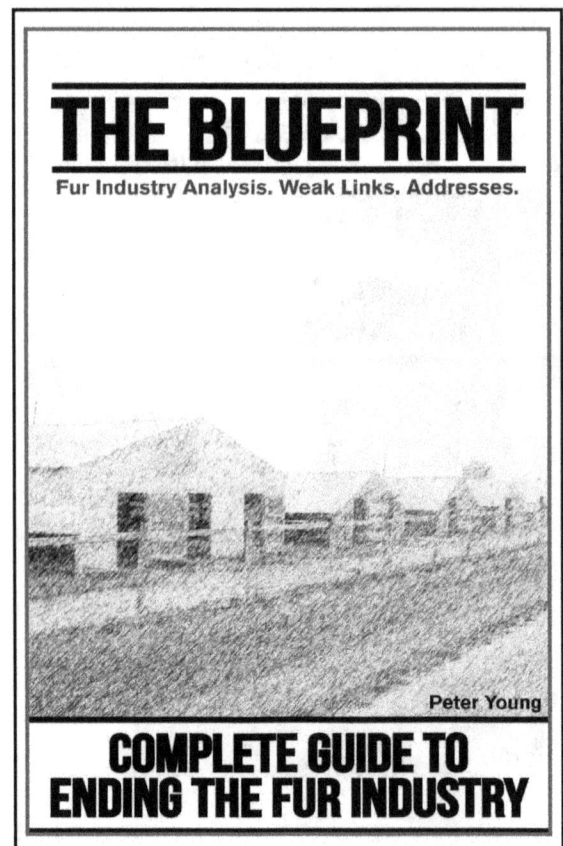

THE A.L.F. STRIKES AGAIN
COLLECTED WRITINGS
OF THE NORTH AMERICAN
ANIMAL LIBERATION FRONT

Edited by Peter Young

ANIMAL LIBERATION FRONT
COMPLETE DIARY OF ACTIONS

Peter Young, Editor

LAST WORDS, FOR WAR

STATEMENTS OF THE
SYMBIONESE LIBERATION ARMY

THE BLUEPRINT
Fur Industry Analysis. Weak Links. Addresses.

Peter Young

**COMPLETE GUIDE TO
ENDING THE FUR INDUSTRY**

www.ingramcontent.com/pod-product-compliance
Lightning Source LLC
Chambersburg PA
CBHW081649270326
41933CB00018B/3408

"Fighting in the front lines for Animal Liberation"

Vivisection labs covered with graffiti. wildlife habitat wa

Farm Freedom Fighters
The following press release was sent photographs and a

ACTION REPORTS

— 6 —

U of T Dentistry Raid

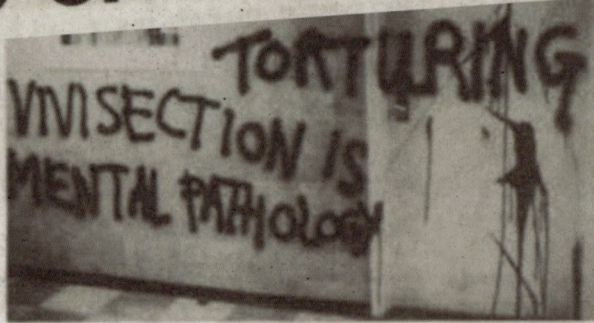

TORTURING

VIVISECTION IS MENTAL PATHOLOGY

...er Brown hadn't learned from ...st visit, one liberator took ...s to safety while the others ... the barn. The barn was empty, ...s torched.
..., 'Farmer Brown'.

— April, 1986

longing to Victory Furs had ...res slashed. was spraypainted ...he words, 'SCUM', 'MURDERERS' ...LF'. Windscreen wipers were ...l the windscreen was smashed.

— April 19, 1986

A collection of rare Canadian Animal Liberation Front (ALF) zines from the 80s and 90s, reprinted in book form for the first time.

This collection brings together all issues of *Frontline News* and *Combat*, two animal liberation zines published by the Animal Liberation Front (ALF) Supporter's Group from 1986 to 1992.

These zines covered the work of the Animal Liberation Front ("the radical fringe of the animal rights movement"), an underground movement of animal rights activists who break the law to rescue animals and inflict property damage on animal abusers.

Included in this book:

- Animal Liberation Front action reports
- ALF prisoner updates
- Animal Liberation Front court case reports
- Newspaper article reprints on ALF actions
- ALF prisoner addresses
- Interview with Animal Liberation Front activists
- Animal Liberation Front communiques
- Essays and editorials on animal rights and veganism
- How to carry out sabotage actions against animal abusers
- Animal Liberation Front analysis
- Letters from Animal Liberation Front prisoners

...and much more.

This is a rare look at the underground animal liberation and animal rights movement in the Canada in the 80s and 90s.

WARCRY COMMUNICATIONS
Publishers of actionable media

ISBN 978-1-957452-05-0
90000
9 781957 452050